This book is to be returned on or before
the last date stamped below.

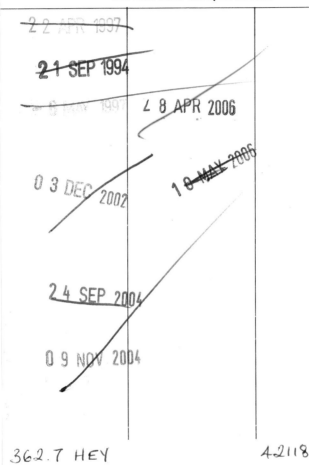

**LIVERPOOL POLYTECHNIC
LIBRARY SERVICE**

LIBREX

CHILDREN IN CARE

INTERNATIONAL LIBRARY OF SOCIOLOGY

Founded by Karl Mannheim
Editor: John Rex
University of Warwick

A catalogue of the books available in the INTERNATIONAL LIBRARY OF SOCIOLOGY and other series of Social Science books published by Routledge & Kegan Paul will be found at the end of this volume.

CHILDREN IN CARE

The development of the service
for the deprived child

by

JEAN S. HEYWOOD

ROUTLEDGE & KEGAN PAUL
LONDON, HENLEY AND BOSTON

First published in 1959
by Routledge and Kegan Paul Ltd.
39 Store Street,
London WC1E 7DD,
Broadway House,
Newtown Road,
Henley-on-Thames,
Oxon RG9 1EN and
9 Park Street,
Boston, Mass. 02108 U.S.A.

Second edition (revised) 1965
Reprinted 1966, 1970

Third edition (revised) 1978

Printed in Great Britain by
Lowe & Brydone Printers Ltd.
Thetford, Norfolk

British Library Cataloguing in Publication Data

Heywood, Jean Schofield
Children in care. – 3rd ed. –
(International library of sociology).
1. Child welfare – Great Britain – History
I. Title   II. Series
362.7'32'0941   HV751.A6   77–30370
ISBN 0 7100 8733 0

To

My Mother and Father

CONTENTS

Contents

PREFACE

THIS book was written primarily to help my students to explore the changing social patterns and ideas which lie behind the history of attention and care given to the deprived child. But it tells also a story of human struggle, endurance and inspiration which seems to me to belong not only to the professional social worker but to the people and the community at large, and to them I offer it in the hope that it will interest them.

I should like to express my gratitude to those who have so generously helped me to refer to the wealth of material bearing on this subject, almost every aspect of which, I am well aware, could be the study of a lifetime. In particular I should like to mention Lady Allen of Hurtwood ; Commander C. R. Burgess, R.N., Secretary of the Marine Society ; Mr. John W. Cox of the Department of History, University of Leeds ; Miss Joan M. Dorrell ; the Very Rev. Canon C. B. Flood of the Crusade of Rescue ; Mr. F. W. Esbester, Assistant Secretary of the Church of England Children's Society ; Mr. A. C. Greg ; Mr. S. H. Henshall of the Quarry Bank Mill, Styal ; the Rev. Walter C. Lazenby ; the Rev. John W. Waterhouse, Principal of the National Children's Home ; the Feoffees of Chetham's Hospital ; the Secretary of the Thomas Coram Foundation for Children ; the Home Office Inspectorate ; the National Trust ; and the Librarians of the City Reference Libraries of Leeds and Manchester, of the Brotherton Library, University of Leeds, and of the Municipal Library, Middleton, Lancashire, who, courteously and unfailingly, met all my many demands upon them. I thank also Mrs. Lilley and Miss Margaret Field for their patient work with the drafts.

To my friends and colleagues Mrs. Barbara N. Rodgers of the University of Manchester and Miss Alice Eden of

Homerton College, Cambridge, Miss Marion Jones and Mr. A. C. McBryan, Children's Officers of Burnley and Bury respectively, who read through my typescript and made many corrections and constructive suggestions and criticisms I am very grateful, and also to Mr. Kenneth Brill, Secretary of the Children's Officers' Association, and to my brother, John B. Heywood, who read through the proofs and gave me throughout the work much sound and invaluable advice and help.

My thanks are due to the writers and publishers who have given me permission to quote from their books. Acknowledgement of them will be found in the footnotes and in the bibliography.

I would finally like to express my gratitude to Professor E. Grebenik and Miss Ida E. Brown of the Department of Social Studies, the University of Leeds, whose continual challenge, stimulation and encouragement enabled me to write this book, and to whose teaching I owe a debt which I can never adequately discharge.

JEAN S. HEYWOOD.

September, 1958.

PREFACE TO THE SECOND EDITION

SINCE the first edition of this book was published the major changes of the Children Act of 1948 have led to new developments both in policy and in methods of care which culminated in the Children and Young Persons Act of 1963. This new edition brings the legislative changes and current trends up to date, and has enabled me to make a number of minor corrections in the main body of the text and to include some important additions to the bibliography. I have also added, as Appendix VII, a reprint of my article published in *Case Conference* (Vol. 6, No. 6) *Boarding-Out and the Wordsworths*, which describes one of the earliest fully documented accounts of the fostering of deprived children.

I am grateful to my former colleague, J. W. Freeman, Children's Officer for Sheffield, for reading through the final chapter and for the very valuable suggestions and emendations which he made, and also to Mrs. Isabel Makin for her indispensable help.

JEAN S. HEYWOOD.

December, 1964.

PREFACE TO THE THIRD EDITION

Since the second edition of this book there have been great changes in the social services brought about by the cultural changes of the 1960s, the growth of greater understanding of our psychological needs and development, and the loss of responsibility which tends to come from the breaking down of old-established communities and patterns of living and the search for new identities. New legislation has absorbed the old children's departments into a reorganized Social Service concerned not only with children but also with the physically or mentally handicapped and with the elderly. The small, very personalized children's departments have gone, but, hopefully, have contributed an ethos which will again be formative when the upheaval of reorganization is over. The history of child care will then be seen to have been crucial in setting standards for the whole of social work in local authorities.

The last chapter of this third edition has been rewritten to take account of the legislative changes of 1969 and subsequently.

JEAN S. HEYWOOD

May, 1977.

CHAPTER ONE

THE CHILD IN THE EARLY COMMUNITY

THERE is little positive evidence for the care of the deprived child in English history before the Reformation. Most of it has to be pieced together from casual references, the absence of information about the deprived child at this time being just as significant as would have been copious references to him. The manorial group of medieval society was self-sufficient and room could be found for the homeless child within the community, in the cottage of the childless villein or to replace those sons of villeins who had gained permission from the lord to leave the manor to become clerks or monks. Such children were mostly orphans who could not be cared for by relatives, or were illegitimate. The illegitimate child was completely without rights, the property of the mother's master, if she were a servant[1], and the Church, in upholding the sanctity of marriage, condemned his very existence, forbidding him to inherit or to be ordained. Yet while he was nobody's child, he was also the child of the people,[2] and some community obligation was implied towards him. Then, as now, the natural families absorbed him and the motherly and childless, whose poverty was not too great, were glad to care for him. Sometimes a distant relative would take him in, particularly if his mother was an erring daughter of the Church, who, like Langland's nun, had borne a child in cherry time, to the scandal of the parish.[3]

[1] 'A servant woman if she conceive a child it is thralle or it be borne, and it is taken from the mother's womb to servage.' Trevisan, *Bartholomew*, Lib. vi, chaps. 12 and 15, quoted in G. G. Coulton, *Social Life in Britain, from the Conquest to the Reformation*. Cambridge University Press, 199, p. 339.
[2] *Nullius filius. Cui pater est populus; pater est sibi nullus et omnis.* Coke, Commentary on Littleton, Institutes, Vol. 1, sect. 188.
[3] Eileen Power in *Medieval English Nunneries* quotes the story of the scandalous nun Nicholaa whose sister took her illegitimate child, p. 669.

In practice the distinction between the legitimate and the illegitimate appears to have been a largely artificial one, however, and bastards were acknowledged by fathers and provided for in wills equally with the legitimately born,[1] while special dispensations to enable illegitimate sons to be ordained or hold ecclesiastical office were frequent.[2] Among the wealthy it was not difficult to find a wet nurse and afterwards to send the child, along with lawful children, to a monastery or nunnery for boarding education, or to the house of some other member of the nobility. Trevisan, an Italian who in 1496 accompanied an ambassador from Venice to the English court, describes this as the usual practice for all children among the well-to-do after they reached the age of seven or nine. He ascribes it to 'the want of affection in the English . . . because they like to enjoy all their comforts themselves, and think they are better served by the children of strangers than they would be by their own children.'[3] This form of deprivation existed in the middle ages as a commonplace among the prosperous families. Many children of the nobility spent the greater part of their childhood away from home, in ecclesiastical houses or homes of the wealthy, while their parents, for example, were holding office abroad; and when child and parent were incompatible such arrangements seemed sometimes a convenient and easy solution to an exasperated and weary mother. For this we have the testimony of Margaret Paston writing to her son in 1469:—'Also I would ye should purvey for your sister to be with my lady Oxford or with my lady of Bedford, or in some other worshipful place whereas ye think best, for we are either of us weary of each other.'

The procuring of wet nurses and the fostering of young motherless children must also have been a common practice among those with means. In the fourteenth century *Legends of Holy Women*, translated by the English Augustinian, Osborn Bokenham, there is a story told which puts into words the people's feelings about the hazards of child life of long ago. It tells of a prince and princess who set sail on a visit to Rome.

---

[1] See Eileen Power, *Medieval English Nunneries*, Cambridge University Press, 1922, p. 451.

[2] F. A. Gasquet, *Eve of the Reformation*. Bell, 1927.

[3] Trevisan, *A Relation of the Island of England*. Camden Society, 1847, p. 24.

During a storm at sea the princess gave birth to a son and died. The prince persuaded the crew to take his wife's body ashore to an island where it was left, together with the living child, whom he committed in prayer to the care of Saint Mary Magdalene,

'For he nowt hath wyth fostryd to be.'

Two years after, returning on his way home, the prince visited the island and found his son alive and well, miraculously preserved and fostered by the Saint.

The Church in the middle ages had an important part to play in providing help for the deprived child. From the time of Constantine it had been officially concerned on behalf of the state to secure care for the poor and fatherless along with other people needing help. Special houses or hospitals were used for the care of the sick, the old, the beggar and the new born child, and the monasteries and convents from the time of St. Benedict had attempted to carry on this work of the early Church. At the end of the middle ages, however, there is little evidence that the religious houses at this period gave habitual care to the deprived child as such. Their care of children seems to have been confined to giving expensive boarding education for the children of the wealthy as a means of providing revenue. Eileen Power in her study of medieval English nunneries has examined the records of nunnery accounts which show that the schoolgirls boarded in the convents were invariably of aristocratic families. We have Chaucer's evidence, too, that this is the usual background of convent educated girls. In the Reeve's Tale, the Miller's wife, daughter of the parson of the town, is described as 'y-comen of noble kin' and 'was y-fostered in a nunnery'. The only indication of any care being given by nuns in their convents to poor country girls is found in a letter from Cranmer to the Abbess of Godstow. 'Stephen Whyte hath told me that you lately gathered round you a number of wild peasant maids and did make them a most goodly discourse on the health of their souls, and you showeth them how goodly a thing it be for them to go often times to confession. I am mightily glad of your discourse.'[1] The contact appears slight. On the other hand monastic houses frequently maintained schools for poor children

[1] Eileen Power, op. cit., p. 261 ff.

3

and may have lodged the boys within the monastery, including fatherless children.

The deprived child as we know him, while very young, seems more likely to have been found in the medieval hospital, though his stay was probably brief. These hospitals were staffed by a master or warden with two or three priests and religious, or sometimes lay, brothers or sisters, and were the community's expression of man's duty towards his neighbour.[1] A statute of 1414 describes their purposes as being 'to sustain old men and women, lazars, men and women out of their senses and memories, poor women with child, and other poor persons.' There is mercifully no specific mention of children being cared for as permanent inmates in these places of compassion, but some who were born in the lying-in hospitals and became deprived by the death of a mother in childbirth, and abandoned children, for whom a home could not be found, were cared for in them.[2] If the babies were to survive it must have been imperative to find a wet nurse for them, either within the hospital, or, more likely, in a family outside. The clergy and nuns of the hospital may have taken on responsibility for placing the children in foster homes within the parish, as in the early days of Christianity they had been enjoined to do. But widespread poverty must have made this difficult while the child was dependent, and many must have died.

Because of the poverty of the middle ages the child had to become economically useful to the feudal group as soon as possible and his period of childhood and protection was short. He worked from an early age. The parish, however, had from earliest times regarded itself as a community with funds to help the poor and the distressed. Such funds, gathered in tithe, as well as being used for the leper and the lame and others

[1] See R. M. Clay. *The Medieval Hospitals of England*, Methuen & Co., 1909. Their funds came not only from endowments of the wealthy and privileged but from free-will offerings, alms of pilgrims, legacies and soliciting of alms after Mass.

[2] R. M. Clay, op. cit. In London the two hospitals of St. Mary without Bishopsgate and St. Bartholomew undertook the care of women during childbirth, and, if the mother died brought up the child until the age of seven. Holy Trinity, Salisbury, provided for fatherless children and widows. St. Katharine's-by-the-Tower, London, was a permanent home for women, and the daughter house was a home for deprived children—'certain orphans placed in danger through the negligence of their friends, and deserted, and brought into the hospital of St. Sepulchre, guarded and educated there.'

in need, may also have been used for the orphaned and the deprived child, frequently to apprentice a boy or dower a girl. If he could not be absorbed within the community the contemporary evidence at the end of the middle ages points to the conclusion that the deprived child found his livelihood as a beggar. Indeed there is some evidence that begging was an accepted pattern of his life only rarely relieved by monastic shelter. There is the story of the twelfth century St Bernard of Tiron in Picardy, for example, who tried to put into practice in his monastery the spirit of divine charity preached by St. Benedict. 'For he sent no man away who ever came to him, neither blind nor lame, nor halt nor crooked nor maimed, but all alike were fostered in the wide bosom of his mercy. He shrank not from receiving men with their womenkind bearing sucklings on their backs; none was driven away however mean or contemptible or poor. Wherefore pupils or orphans hearing this—*such as beg their livelihood from door to door or tend other men's flocks in the fields*, hearing this they would comfort each other, saying, "let us also go to that haven where all are received." '[1]

Boccaccio, in telling the story of the exiled Count of Antwerp, describes how he stood with his two motherless children begging for alms outside a London church door, and how 'a certain great lady, the wife of one of the King's marshals of Oxford', being struck by the little girl offered a home for her. 'Having thus disposed of his daughter' the Count then went into Wales where another of the King's marshals took his little boy.[2]

The care of the deprived child was haphazard and quite unorganised but the agricultural nature of medieval society, its hierarchy and its lack of unemployment, particularly after the scarcity of labour produced by the Black Death, did not make it difficult to absorb someone of working capacity and in good health, while the moral values on which contemporary

[1] Quoted in G. G. Coulton, Vol. 4 of his *Life in the Middle Ages*, Cambridge University Press, 1929–30. St. Bernard of Tiron's example did not survive him. Although this story refers to France it is unlikely that the accepted practice or nonpractice of monastic charity varied very much in medieval Europe. Medieval English wills contain many bequests to children who should come begging to the town on the day of the testator's funeral.
[2] Boccaccio, *The Decameron*. The eighth story told on the second day.

life was based also made it less likely that the child was home-less for very long. The Church taught with powerful sanctions the duty of the seven corporal works of mercy[1] and in the giving of alms and the feeding, clothing and sheltering of the homeless the humblest citizen could secure for himself treasure, not of earth, but, more important as he believed, in heaven.

Yet it would be unrealistic and untrue to suppose that such children were not exploited, and that the charity disbursed to them was not sometimes given more for the good of the giver's soul than the welfare of the recipient. Boccaccio's story hints at the tensions in those families which fostered a beggar's child and at the distinction made in standards of living and conduct between natural and foster children. Such children were used too, as they have been in recent times, to assist the travelling tinker or professional beggar,[2] for which purpose child-stealing was not unknown. We have the record of one Alice de Salisbury who in 1373 stole Margaret Roper, the little daughter of a London grocer, carrying her away and stripping her of her clothes so that she might not be recognised by her family. Alice intended the child should go begging with her, but the theft was fortunately discovered, Margaret was claimed, and Alice did penance one hour a day in the stocks.[3]

Wardship of the orphan child with means was a profitable business in medieval society. They were 'bought and sold as beasts,' and we have business accounts of merchants, guardians of orphans, which show how they were able to invest at interest the money left for the child, and, while providing for him, make handsome profit of which they would claim half.[4] This practice, widely found, was an obvious field of profit and exploitation. In most of the large towns the Chamberlain was made the special guardian of orphans mainly in order to safe-guard their property; in London, for example, there was a

---

[1] Based on the teaching in Matthew xxv, 34 ff. 'For I was an hungered and ye gave me meat, I was thirsty and ye gave me drink, I was a stranger and ye took me in, naked and ye clothed me, I was sick and ye visited me, I was in prison and ye came unto me. . . . Verily I say unto you, Inasmuch as ye have done it unto one of the least of these my brethren, ye have done it unto me.'

[2] See, in our own day, Emma Smith, *A Cornish Waif's Story*. Odhams, 1954.

[3] Quoted in G. G. Coulton, *Social Life in Britain*, p. 325.

[4] G. G. Coulton, op. cit., p. 94.

regular court of orphans.[1] Clearly there had been considerable abuse of a vulnerable group on whose behalf the state had to intervene.

The state intervened, too, to regulate the parishioners' charity to the poor ; an early statute of 1388[2] gave responsibility to every neighbourhood for the support of its own poor. In the fifteenth century local administration of voluntary poor relief through the community of the parish became firmly established.

The pattern changes as the economic pattern of the middle ages changes with the Reformation and the Tudors. The destruction of the feudal system destroyed also one great field of employment of earlier society, service in the army or the houses of great nobles; the growth of commerce and manufactures, while in a transitional stage, brought unemployment to the craftsmen who became dependent on trade crises and foreign policies; England became the great wool-producing country of the world and farming land was turned over to sheep with consequent unemployment among the agricultural labourers. These factors gravely increased the poverty and distress in the early years of the sixteenth century.

So the position of the deprived child in society underwent a change. In pre-Reformation England the orphaned or illegitimate had a place in a feudal and employed community, though opportunities were open and found for human nature to exploit him. His safeguard, if it existed, lay in the communal nature of the society and its ethical canons, expressed—

[1] E. M. Leonard, *The early history of English poor relief* Cambridge University Press, 1900, p. 9. Earlier urban custom towards children needing protection is shown in a report of a case in the King's Bench under Edward I (Hilary, 1285). 'And when the Mayor of the aforesaid town of Bristol had noticed the aforesaid children wandering about without protection, the same mayor, who has charge of orphans and all other things pertaining to the aforesaid town (on behalf of the) community of the town of Bristol, took the aforesaid Cecily, daughter of the aforesaid Christian, and (delivered her to Henry) as uncle of the aforesaid child wandering about in this way, because the aforesaid child is better looked after by reason of this affinity.' Selden Society, Vol. LV (1936) case 90, p. 135.

[2] The statute of Cambridge ordered local authorities to look after their impotent poor or required that they should go to other places locally which could look after them, or that they should return to the place where they were born. Forty days seems to have been the time limit for this shuffling of responsibility.

though not always observed—in the teaching against usury, on the duty of almsgiving, on the efficacy of the corporal works of mercy. In the fact that life was centred round the community rather than the family there lay the possibility of opportunity and protection for the unwanted child. In the community obligations of medieval society a way could be found to provide for him and the family setting was less vital to him than it is to us to-day.[1] The medieval Church had exalted not the private family but rather the greater one, Christian society, endowing chastity, asceticism and celibacy with greater virtue than the sacrament of marriage. It was at the Reformation period when economic as well as religious changes were taking place, that men turned from the Church's teaching on celibacy, and as they found the social order crumbling away they discovered that in family life there could also be an opportunity to witness to the glory of God.[2]

The ideal of the small home and personal family life could hardly be achieved until a middle class came into existence. The sixteenth century Tudor households of yeomen farmers, of small merchants and tradesmen provided the setting in which real family life became possible, and in a growing urban society, which was neither stable economically, nor ruled any longer by a philosophy based on the good of a united community, the family became of major significance. Without it the individual was unsupported in society and became without identity.

The spread of destitution which followed the social and economic changes of the sixteenth century was the cause of the increasing legislation dealing with poor relief in the Tudor era. Vagrancy increased with unemployment, and everywhere the old order was breaking down and a new and as yet unstable society being formed.

The discharging of servants and apprentices increased the numbers of deprived children while the growth of poverty,

---

[1] Compare to-day the report of the Saudi Arabian Government for the United Nations study of deprived children published in 1952, ' As long as the care of the children in the home is not in contradiction with the Koran, there is practically no government interference with their upbringing,' *Children deprived of a Normal Home Life*. E /CN.5 /271.

[2] This is clearly seen in the household of Sir Thomas More. See H. Maynard Smith, *Pre-Reformation England*. Macmillan 1938.

vagrancy and unemployment made it more difficult for them to find a home or to be fitted in to the pattern of village life. Collections made for the poor in the parish churches were unable to meet the demand for alms. The dissolved houses of the monks and nuns were no longer able to provide out-relief, and the hospitals were falling into decay.[1] In consequence laws were passed to make each parish responsible for providing a place where the sick, the old and the 'succourless poor child' could receive shelter and care. At this time, too, the right of destitute children to beg was recognised and they were given a licence. In London sermons were preached by the bishop in public places exhorting the people to charity, and appeals for funds were made by the Lord Mayor, Aldermen and other prominent citizens in the parish churches in order to repair the old hospitals or build new ones. In this way was founded Christ's Hospital in 1552 and the Bluecoat School for fatherless boys, an enlightened attempt to cure vagrancy by education, when the child could profit by it. Earlier still, in 1530, authority was first given for the compulsory apprenticing of vagrant children between the ages of five and fourteen, though sixteen years afterwards further legislation had to reduce the severity of apprenticeship regulations and give justices power to liberate children badly treated by master and mistress.

The crowds of vagrants and unemployed at this time (which included the child "unapt to learning") were seen not only as a chronic nuisance but a serious danger to society, as social failures for whom the community was now legally and financially responsible. Nor can the frustration and lack of stability which the vagrant and unemployed experienced in a time of upheaval have made him an easy person with whom to deal. So many of the composite hospitals which were established at this time, at first by persuasive and finally by compulsory taxation, for the relief of the poor became also houses of correction and punishment for the idle, as well as technical schools for the young. The deprived child, in need of training, and old and sick people in need of care were accommodated

---

[1] See. E. M. Leonard, op. cit., p. 26 ff. She quotes a list of fifteen hospitals existing in London in 1536 of which eight were in immediate danger of dissolution by the King.

together with vagrants sent for punishment.[1] The degradation of the pauper had begun.

It was the Elizabethan statute, the poor Relief Act of 1601, which set the pattern for our system of relief to the poor until 1948. Those responsible for the care of deprived children, the churchwardens and the parish overseers, were to take such measures as were necessary for setting them to work or binding them as apprentices.[2] These bald embodiments of a constructive principle of care remained unaltered in our legislation for three hundred and forty-seven years, until the shadow of a grim farm-house fell across them, and darkened them for ever.

The Tudor and early Stuart statesmen thought of poverty as a social phenomenon caused by the economic disruption of the times; they tackled pauperism in a constructive way by providing work and a trade for paupers, children and adults alike. By the reign of Charles I all children, whether homeless, destitute or well cared for had to be trained to work or taught a trade. Very frequently the children, including the younger sons of gentry, were apprenticed, the fees being paid by the parents or the parish as the case may be, and throughout the seventeenth century there are many records of private bequests for the binding of poor children as apprentices.[3] This custom gave a home and family, as well as a craft, to the deprived child. And as it was usual for family children to be apprenticed and to board with their master there was nothing extraordinary in the position of the parish apprentice in the seventeenth century. Both kinds of apprentice were bound in the same way, and it is not likely that any distinction was made between them. The weakness of the pauper child was in his complete dependence on the parish overseer or charity trustee to find

[1] Such was Christ's hospital established in Ipswich in 1569. For details of the constructive training given to the destitute child in the sixteenth century see the articles 'The State and Child in the Sixteenth Century' by I. Pinchbeck, in the *British Journal of Sociology*, vol. VII, No. 4 (December, 1956), and Vol. VIII, No. 1 (March, 1957). This emphasis on education as a preventive of future pauperism is characteristic of Elizabethan poor law policy and does not appear again until the late nineteenth century.

[2] With regard to poor children the purpose of the Act was ' for setting to work the Children of all such whose Parents shall not by the said Churchwardens and Overseers, or the greater Part of them, be thought able to keep and maintain their children ' and 'also for the putting out of such Children to be Apprentices, to be gathered out of the same Parish, according to the Ability of the same Parish.'

[3] See E. M. Leonard op. cit., p. 215 ff.

him a good master. Abuses and lack of care must have existed, but we have no evidence that the evils of pauper apprenticeship were very great or very widespread in the early part of the seventeenth century. Before the century ended, however, a fatal step was taken when, in order to provide a home and trade for a child, even reluctant masters became compelled by law to take the apprentices bound to them by the overseers.[1] Ill treatment and cruelty by private masters was made almost inevitable by this system which was not abolished till 1844.

In the seventeenth century can also be seen an attempt to bring together in the state private charity and public assistance. Simultaneously with the passing of the Poor relief Act the Statute of Charitable Use had encouraged the individual to make public gifts, by protecting his bequest from abuse. It is in this period, a time of crisis and change, that the state rallied both statutory and voluntary help in efforts to build a sound society in which both rich and poor contributed as they were able. So while the parishes provided houses of correction with special departments for destitute children where they could be trained for trades and kept from begging on the streets, private individuals and groups in the early years of the century founded schools and orphanages and perpetuated for the public good the care and charity so conspicuous in the medieval wills.[2]

Yet by the middle of the century among the established gentry charity was failing and the administration of poor relief was becoming much less efficient. The unsettled conditions of civil war, the casualties and destruction of homes and the deaths from plague must have greatly increased the number of deprived children, while the poverty and chaos reduced the ability of the administrator to deal with them. The wars

---

[1] 8 and 9 William III c. 30, sec. 5.

[2] In the rising manufacturing towns of the north private charity could step in where the need was great. Humphrey Chetham, a Manchester merchant who had acquired wealth by trade and banking interests, established in 1649 a boarding school for the sons of poor, honest men. After his death in 1653 the school was endowed by the terms of his will and became known as Chetham's Hospital. Children of wandering beggars or idle rogues and the illegitimate were expressly excluded ; but a high proportion of the children admitted were boys with one parent or none at all. Children found after admission to be illegitimate were expelled—see minute book of the feoffees of Chetham's Hospital, the entry for 7.5.1685.

reduced the income of many rich landed people and they could no longer give.[1] In the country there are several records of poor children being boarded out and then forgotten, and people complained to the justices that they had kept parish children but could get no pay from the town for them. Before the Derbyshire justices of the Easter sessions of 1648 one citizen complained he had kept the lame child of a Royalist soldier since 1646 when his father took up arms, and though promised 8d. a week in payment by the parish overseer he had received it for only nine weeks.[2] The breakdown of administration was widespread over country and town.

The state of the London streets in 1655 was a cause for great alarm. Beggars hung on coaches and shouted for alms at the doors of churches and private houses, pilfering and stealing in the streets by day and breaking into shops and houses by night. Some evidence of the neglect of the poor in these troubled times is seen in a tract of the period (1653), addressed to Parliament and described as the Poor Outcast Children's Song and Cry :

> 'Grave Senators that sit on high
> Let not poor English children die
> And droop on dunghills with lamenting notes :
> An Act for Poor's Relief they say
> Is coming forth; why's this delay?
> O let not Dutch, Danes, Devils stop these votes.'[3]

The legislation, when it came, surrounded with obstacles the right of the poor to relief and confirmed the existing practice of treating unemployment as a deliberate attempt of the poor to avoid work.[4] A new philosophy based upon economic interest had begun to appear.

This new philosophy was an inevitable consequence of the

[1] Many of the charitable institutions could hardly be kept up. Christ's Hospital (London) was maintained by charitable gifts and rents from land. The tenants, whose land had been despoiled by fighting and billeting, could not pay the rents and the number of children so maintained in the hospital fell from 900 in 1641 to 597 in 1647. See E. M. Leonard, op. cit. p. 268.

[2] See Margaret James, *Social Policy during the Puritan Revolution*. Routledge. 1930, p. 249.

[3] Thomasons Tracts 1653, quoted in E. M. Leonard, op. cit.

[4] Act for the suppression of vagrants and idle persons 1657. Act of settlement 1662.

individualism which followed the commonwealth. While the spiritual independence of the Puritan made an immeasurable contribution to the democratic and religious freedom of society, in his pre-occupation with the light, his emphasis on individual responsibility and conscience, he allowed the shadows to fall upon the more catholic concept of a community where grace may be revealed through failure as well as through achievement.[1] The qualities of enterprise, thrift, and hard work, so much admired, and so fruitful in this generation, became equated with goodness, and the conception that poverty was due, not to economic dislocation, but to the moral failings of the poor, broke upon the country when the old agricultural pattern began to give place to one in which the effectiveness of the very soil to support the people depended upon a combination of initiative, organisation, hard work and wealth.

[1] See R. H. Tawney, *Religion and the Rise of Capitalism*, Pelican Books 1938, and Margaret James, op. cit.

CHAPTER TWO

INDUSTRIAL SOCIETY AND THE CHILD

THE two largest classes in the agricultural England of the end of the seventeenth century were 'cottagers and paupers' and 'labouring people and outservants'. The former, who outnumbered the latter,[1] picked up their livelihood from the common land, the others were wage earners. Almost all families at this time had small rights in land, from which they could obtain their wood for fuel, graze their geese for profit and their cow or pig for dairy produce or bacon. In this way the village labourer had a status and independence which came from his ability to produce his family's food as well as to work for it. All this changed with the enclosures of the eighteenth century agricultural revolution by which alone the productivity of the soil could be made to keep pace with the growing urban population.

The enclosure of common land meant that the family was no longer an economic unit but dependent upon the breadwinner whose wage was unrelated to his family's size. And while the labourer's economic independence was destroyed by the enclosures, the status of the family was destroyed by the consequences which followed them, unemployment and pauperism.[2] The State in 1722 gave parishes permissive powers, singly or in combination, to provide workhouses 'for the lodging, keeping and maintaining, and employing' of poor persons, and 'to take the benefit of their work, labour and service'[3].

Before this assistance was given to the poor a workhouse test was to be applied, 'no poor who refused to be lodged and kept

---

[1] 1,300,000 compared with 1,275,000—see the figures of Gregory King quoted in Sir Frederick Morton Eden's *State of the Poor*, Vol. I, p. 228 (1797).

[2] See J. L. and Barbara Hammond, *The Village Labourer* Guild Books, 1948.

[3] 9. Geo. I, c.7.

in such houses should be entitled to parochial relief'. The test was evidently applied to the fatherless child too,[1] and it is clear that the economic value of each individual in society was assuming major importance at the expense of his uniqueness and his need. The statutory poor law made no pretence of setting itself up as a humanitarian measure to meet individual need in a time of distress, this was the part of private charity and philanthropy which had flourished so abundantly in the reign of Queen Anne. Meanwhile in the countryside pauperism increased and illegitimacy, too,[2] and with it the problem of deprivation.

It is not difficult to account for the rise in illegitimacy during the eighteenth century. The familiar pattern of community life was torn across, the old life of the agricultural pattern changed; in the new towns the social and moral controls of the small intimate parish were absent ; in the villages it was not so easy for irregular sexual relationships to be followed by marriage. Eden, in his contemporary account of the state of the poor, held that the Settlement Act of 1662 actually promoted illegitimacy, since parish officers often attempted to remove to their last place of settlement young men about to marry, on the ground that their family might become chargeable to the parish. The eighteenth century was a cockpit of social evolution at home and wars abroad, and in such a time of unrest, when many people were implicated in political risings, when gaoling and transportations were common punishments and troops moved about the country to keep the peace or defend the coast, many girls lost touch with the fathers before the child was born. It was, too, an atmosphere in which many of the poor felt that the present had more reality and value than any future they could foresee.

As homeless and illegitimate children increased, the problem of providing for them increased too. The illegitimate child

[1] For example the Leeds Workhouse Committee Order book contains the following entry for 10.9.1726: 'It is agreed that Samuel Boll be taken out of the workhouse and returned to his mother; he being an idiot and incapable of doing anything towards his maintenance'.

[2] Mary Hopkirk in *Nobody Wanted Sam*, John Murray, 1949 quotes the parish registers of Letheringham, Suffolk, as typical of the illegitimacy rise all over the country. From 1588 to 1600 there were no extra-matrimonial births recorded. From 1600 to 1650 there was one in every 144 registered births. From 1650 to 1700 there was one in 74 ; from 1700 to 1750 one in 33; and from 1750 to 1800 one in 21.

could no longer be accepted, if only for the sake of his potential working capacity, into the family, for the old agricultural communities which could have found a place for him were finally breaking down. The unmarried mother could not provide for him herself and so he, and frequently his mother too, became the liability of the parish.

Where wealth is exalted and its acquisition possible it is natural to resent anything which increases the economic pressure upon individual income. Illegitimacy had always been an offence against the laws of morality; because of the cost which was laid upon the parishes it now became an offence against society. This combination of moral deviance with lack of financial responsibility became a sin from which a largely secularised society now recoiled, with a conspicuous absence of compassion for the needs and conditions which had occasioned it. Some expression of this is seen in the social attitude to the un-married mothers at this time both in the parish workhouse and in the penitentiaries opened for them by religious charities. Eden's contemporary account of the workhouses shows that they were sometimes deliberately given less food than the legally married women during the lying in period,[1] and, if they were chargeable a second time on account of bastardy, they had to wear distinguishing gowns as a mark of their disgrace.[2] Many women were forcibly returned home in an advanced state of pregnancy under the settlement laws, there to face the ignominy of being discovered by their relatives and friends. In the penitentiaries they were expected to expiate their guilt by a life of humiliation and sacrifice, and the happiness of caring for their baby was not allowed them. It is small wonder that in an attempt to escape the consequences, illegitimate babies were abandoned by their mothers on waste land, dung-hills and doorsteps or given or sold indiscriminately to any one willing to take them, while many, a measure of the mothers' desperation, were found murdered in rivers and ditches.[3]

It was in this setting that Thomas Coram, a retired sea captain travelling daily from Rotherhithe to London, and

[1] At St. Martin in the Fields.
[2] At Newport, Isle of Wight.
[3] Mary Hopkirk, op. cit., c.VI.

moved by the numbers of abandoned children he saw on his journeys, determined by personal efforts to try to prevent some of the tragedies which the attitude of society had helped to create. By faith, sincerity and sheer hard work lasting nearly twenty years he procured in 1739 a Royal Charter for the setting up of a foundling hospital where desperate mothers could leave their children, without condemnation, in the knowledge that they would be cared for.[1] After opening in temporary hired premises[2] the famous Foundling Hospital was built in Lamb's Conduit Fields in 1747, on land which still bears Coram's name and now serves the children's needs as they have changed with changing society.

But in providing for immediate care where need was desperate Coram did not forget the child's future too and the pull of his natural affections. It was the custom for the mother to leave some small distinguishing token with the baby which could be kept and catalogued should she later return and want to make a home for him.[3] Meanwhile boarding out in the country was developed extensively and a proud tradition of fostering was built up among families, a tradition which has persisted through many generations and still exists to-day. This practice undoubtedly saved the lives of many young children needing individual nursing attention, and the humanity and enlightened administration of the Hospital had an important influence on public opinion.[4]

In the crowded workhouses the death rate among young children was enormous. Eden[5] quotes Dr. Price, an eighteenth

---

[1] 'The person bringing it shall come in at the outward door, and ring the bell at the inward door, and not go away until the child be returned or notice given of its reception; but no questions whatsoever shall be asked of any person bringing a child, nor shall any servant of the Hospital presume to discover who such person is on pain of being dismissed'.

[2] See Appendix I, p. 209.

[3] These still remain in the Museum of the Foundling Hospital. They were also used to vindicate the mother should she be accused of having murdered her missing child.

[4] For a full account of administration, etc., see R. H. Nichols and F. A. Wray, *The History of the Foundling Hospital*, Oxford University Press, 1935. The difficulties of trying to deal with the whole problem are shown in the Government response to the need—an annual Parliamentary grant was made to the Hospital from 1756 on condition that all children brought there should be admitted. Such indiscriminate admissions encouraged traffic in unwanted babies and the death rate in the Hospital rose steeply. In 1770 the grant, with its conditions, was withdrawn.

[5] Eden, op. cit., Vol. I, p. 338.

century demographer, as saying that before the passing of Hanway's Act in 1767 almost all parish infants in the metropolis died in their first six years. This piece of legislation, providing for the compulsory removal to the country of London workhouse children, was inspired by the merchant philanthropist Jonas Hanway, a Governor of the Foundling Hospital on whose practice it was based. It reduced the mortality of pauper children, but created other problems which had not been foreseen. The chief one was how to provide care for their increased numbers. The Act obliged parishes to send all pauper children under six years of age, within a fortnight after they were born in, or received into, the workhouses, to a distance of not less than three miles from any part of the cities of London and Westminster. The children were to be nursed there till they were six, and maintained afterwards until they were either put out as apprentices or returned to the workhouse. Not less than two shillings and sixpence weekly was paid to the foster parent for each child up to the age of six, and afterwards not less than two shillings till he was taken away.[1] Five 'noblemen or gentlemen' were to be appointed guardians of the parish poor children, with powers to visit and see the children, and were to meet and report every six weeks. To induce the foster mothers to take good care of their charges a sum of not less than ten shillings was paid to each foster mother who had nursed a child satisfactorily for a year. The parish officers had to provide proper clothing for each child sent into the country, pay his travelling expenses to get there and the cost of his medicines or burial. Doubtless some children, by the good offices of their foster parents, were apprenticed nearby, but many were separated from them and returned to the workhouse at the age of six or seven where their numbers were now an embarrassment and their apprenticeship a matter of urgency.

Among the poor the care of dependent children was a heavy financial liability. Many children of destitute parents and of widows, as well as motherless children, found their way with the

---

[1] Eden, op. cit., Vol. I, p. 450 says this made it understandable for a mother to abandon her child to the parish officer who could provide for him better than she could. By 1797 the weekly allowance had risen to 3s. or 3s. 6d. 'What poor woman could expend such a sum in the maintenance of her child?'

illegitimate into the workhouse.[1] There, if they were not apprenticed they are described as 'reared in crowds'.[2] Great numbers of boys and girls were thronged together at the spinning wheels or looms or at other forms of mechanical employment often in dirty and insanitary conditions. The sickness and depression so caused must have meant that the children were hardly profitable producers, and the overseers began to look around for avenues through which they could be apprenticed elsewhere.

The poet Crabbe, writing at the very beginning of the nineteenth century, described with calm realism in his long poem 'The Borough' the everyday conditions of the life of the poor, and the fate of the London parish boy bound apprentice by unscrupulous overseers to far away tradesmen who, for one reason or another, were unable to find a local apprentice. So on the Suffolk coast the drunken fisherman Peter Grimes looked in vain for an 'obedient boy to trouble and control'. To meet the needs of country masters and of parish overseers there arose workhouse-clearing men who undertook with the overseers to bind pauper children apprentice at trifling expense :—

> Peter had heard there were in London then—
> Still have they being!—workhouse clearing men.
> Who, undisturbed by feelings just or kind,
> Would parish-boys to needy tradesmen bind ;
> They in their want a trifling sum would take,
> And toiling slaves of piteous orphans make.[3]

The miseries of the workhouse child so apprenticed were very great. They were horribly ill used, as the reports of the Old Bailey trials show. Many were the victims of murder, manslaughter, assault and rape, and although legislation had been passed in 1793 providing for the punishment of masters who ill treated apprentices few children knew of this or had courage or opportunity to invoke it.[4] Most ran away and

---

[1] The Report of the Committee on Parish Apprentices of 1815 said that in London relief was 'seldom bestowed without the parish claiming the exclusive right of disposing, at their pleasure, of all the children of the person receiving relief.'

[2] Eden, op cit., Vol. I, p. 420.

[3] George Crabbe, '*The Borough*, Peter Grimes', 1810.

[4] For the evils of the private apprenticeship of parish children see Dorothy George, *London Life in the Eighteenth Century.* Kegan Paul Trench, Trubner and Co. Ltd., 1925 c.V.

swelled the crowds of vagrants, beggars, and pickpockets in the towns.

But now the field of apprenticeship widened with the development of the machine factories in the north of England and their need for labour. Arkwright's invention of machinery came before the discovery of steam power and the new factories were dependent on water power and were built by fast flowing streams and waterfalls, many of them in the lonely Pennine valleys. In these situations there was insufficient local labour to man them even if the independent countryman had not seen in them an unwelcome similarity to the crowded workrooms of the houses of correction and workhouses, and turned aside. From London and the south, overburdened by the cost of rates maintaining the unskilled and the unemployed, the overseers sent pauper families to supply the much needed labour, and in such factories they 'apprenticed' their growing numbers of homeless and pauper children.

The parish children were apprenticed to employers at the age of seven or upwards and the apprenticeship lasted till they reached the age of twenty-one or, in the case of girls, was terminated by marriage.[1] The system was most conspicuous during the period 1775 to 1816, after which the change from water power to steam power made it possible to build factories in towns and to employ local children instead of apprentices imported from elsewhere.[2] The picture of neglect, degradation and promiscuity of these young apprentices revealed in the contemporary accounts is a disturbing chapter of our social history. Child life was cheap in a country where the fall in mortality generally was leading to concern about the rapid increase of population,[3] and the general standard of living

[1] The Elizabethan statute of 1601 fixed the duration of apprenticeship to twenty-four in the case of boys, twenty-one for girls. The age was reduced after 1768.

[2] J. L. and Barbara Hammond, *The Town Labourer* Guild Books, 1949. See also Mary Hopkirk, op. cit.

[3] The number of people in England and Wales is estimated at about five and a half millions in 1700 and six and a half millions in 1750. The first census in 1801 revealed a population of nine millions and by 1831 this had increased to fourteen millions. Malthus, in his *Essay on Population* (1798, revised 1830) held that populations would increase beyond the means by which they could subsist unless vice, misery and moral restraint held them in check. This theory, though not wholly accepted by his contemporaries, powerfully influenced the social policies of the nineteenth century. See *Introduction to Malthus*, edited by D. V. Glass, Watts & Co., 1953.

among the people was such that, while the excesses are condemned, it would be unrealistic to judge them by the immeasurably higher standards which prevail to-day. Before Hanway's Act the annual death rate of parish infants had been between sixty and seventy per cent. Those who now lived to become apprenticed had to take their place in a world where the smallest child could be utilised to increase the labour of his parents, at first in his own home, while the clothing industry was still in the domestic stage,[1] and later in the factories. The later inventions of Hargreaves and Crompton enabled factories to be built in the towns, powered by steam, and, as handloom weaving decayed, the paid labour of children in factories became important to their own family, and they became breadwinners. Parish relief was often refused to a father if he had children he could send to the mill and the working conditions of these children were often worse than those of the apprentices, for they were younger and bound to the work by ties of family affection. Small children of only three and four years of age were employed to pick up cotton waste creeping under unguarded machines, where bigger people could not go. The older children worked for fifteen hours a day, and on night work too under conditions which were often enforced by fear and brutality. If this was the setting of the family child it is small wonder that the unprotected deprived child fared so tragically.

Under the early factory system the employment of large numbers of children was essential to the industry and the parish overseers made use of the opportunity. The numerous

[1] Dr. Aikin's *Description of the County from 30 to 40 miles around Manchester*, published in 1795, p. 154, quotes a description of the towns of Manchester and Salford annexed to a plan of the towns taken about 1650 which says that the trade in Manchester consists chiefly of woollen frizes, fustians, sock cloths, mingled stuffs, caps, inkles (linen tapes), tapes, points, ' whereby not only the better sort of men are employed but also the very children by their own labour can maintain themselves.' Defoe, travelling England during the years 1724–7 thus describes the homes of the Yorkshire clothiers. 'Within we saw the houses full of lusty fellows, some at the dye-vat, some at the loom, others dressing the cloths, the women and children carding and spinning, all employed from the youngest to the oldest, scarce anything above four years old, but its hands were sufficient for its own support.' D. Defoe, *A Tour Through Great Britain*. Vol. III, pp. 144–146. Ed. 1769. The well conducted mill could be very advantageous to the family in that it removed these unhealthy and crowded conditions from the home—see Ivy Pinchbeck, *Women Workers in the Industrial Revolution 1650-1850*. Routledge. 1930.

destitute, the orphaned, the illegitimate parish children of London and of the sea-port towns, particularly the children too difficult to apprentice with private masters, were sent with their indentures to the factories of the north. There they worked the twelve or fifteen hour day, including night shifts, and lived in Apprentice Houses attached to the factories. In the worst mills, confined and crowded about the machinery lit by tallow lights in poorly ventilated rooms, the children worked each day from 5 a.m. till 8 p.m. with two half-hour breaks, one for breakfast at 7 a.m., and one for dinner at 12 noon. They were allowed to eat something while working in the afternoon, but there were no places to relax, no seats in the mill, and at the end of the day the child crawled exhausted to his bed as it was vacated by another apprentice for the night shift. On Sundays they cleaned the machinery from 6 a.m. till 12 noon.[1] To some of the mill owners they seem to have been regarded as extensions of the machinery rather than human children needing love, physical care and companionship. The very nature of the friendships which the children made with one another must have been conditioned by the inhuman way in which they were regarded. They were known to have been put up for sale and publicly advertised as part of the property in a bankrupt's effects; and one Lancashire millowner contracted with a London parish to take one idiot child with every twenty sound children.[2] Some masters, in need of money, were not above murdering them in order to get a fresh premium with a fresh apprentice.[3]

In such appalling conditions the apprentice children from London and the growing towns were left. No one came from their parish settlements to see how they were getting on. No outside person, not even parent or magistrate, came to see their conditions, for none had the right to enter either a mill or an apprentice house.

Crowded with overworked and dirty and neglected children

---

[1] Blackbarrow—in the parish of Cartmel, Lancashire.

[2] See Hansard, 6.6.1815. Col. 626.

[3] Romilly, a member of a Committee taking evidence on the conditions of factory apprentices and reporting in 1815 ,drew attention to the fact that 'instances (and not very few) have occurred in our tribunals, of wretches who have murdered their parish apprentices, that they might get fresh premiums with new apprentices.' Quoted in J. L. and Barbara Hammond *The Town Labourer*.

the cotton mills were breeding grounds for fever. An epidemic of fever broke out in one of the cotton mills in Radcliffe in 1784 and succeeded in drawing the attention of the public to the condition of the apprentices. Influenced by a local practitioner, Dr. Percival, the Manchester magistrates passed a resolution refusing to sanction indentures for parish apprentices to cotton mills where they would be worked at night or more than ten hours by day. Other northern magistrates passed similar resolutions but children still continued to be sent from other areas, for example from the south, Liverpool and the Midlands.

In 1802 was passed the first Sir Robert Peel's Act 'for the Preservation of the Health and Morals of Apprentices and others employed in cotton and other mills.' The Act contained clauses to improve working and living conditions for parish apprentices. Girls and boys were to have separate dormitories in the Apprentice Houses and not more than two children were to share a bed. Hours of work were not to exceed twelve a day, excluding meals, and provision was to be made for the religious instruction of the children. Factory Visitors[1] were to be annually appointed within counties, with the right to enter any factory at any time. Unfortunately these provisions for inspection were not strongly enforced, and the regulations governing the labour of children were evaded in many of the worst mills.

Worse even than the lives of the apprentice children in the factories were the lives of those apprenticed to chimney sweeps or in the mines. The majority of these children were sent to the Staffordshire mines, and the workhouses there were said to be empty of boys, but many were also found in Lancashire and the West Riding where girls were also employed. The facts about the conditions of their employment are found in the First Report of the Commission on the Employment of Children and Young Persons in Mines presented to Parliament in 1842. The report describes the children as being wholly in the power of their butties[2], employed down the mines for twelve hours a day, as trappers, opening and shutting the doors to guide the

[1] Justices at their Midsummer sessions each year were to appoint two Visitors, not interested or connected in any way with the Mills and Factories, to visit and report on the conditions of the factories and the apprentices. One Visitor had to be a Justice of the Peace and the other a Clergyman of the established Church.
He generally kept a tommy or truck shop, and paid the wages of his labourers in goods.

draught of air through the mine, filling skips and carriages with the coal, pushing or drawing trucks along from the miners to the foot of the shaft. The children who suffered most were the apprentices from the workhouses, 'these lads are made to go where other men will not let their own children go. If they will not do it, they take them to the magistrates who commit them to prison.'[1] An eight year old girl, Sarah Gooder, in the West Riding so described her day, 'I'm a trapper in the Gauber Pit, I have to trap without a light, and I'm scared. I go at four and sometimes half past three in the morning and come out at five and half past. I never go to sleep. Sometimes I sing when I've light, but not in the dark: I dare not sing then.'[2] Girls in the West Riding mines who drew the trucks along were described by the Commissioners—'Chained, belted, harnessed like dogs in a go-cart, black, saturated with wet, and more than half-naked—crawling upon their hands and feet, dragging their heavy loads behind them, they present an appearance indescribably disgusting and unnatural.'[3] The fearful life to which the parish child was apprenticed is perhaps most vividly and most poignantly drawn in the remarks of one of the sub-commissioners, 'I can never forget the first unfortunate creature that I met with: it was a boy about eight years old, who looked at me as I passed through with an expression of countenance the most abject and idiotic—like a thing, a creeping thing, peculiar to the place. On approaching and speaking to him, he slunk trembling and frightened into a corner, under an impression that I was about to do him some bodily injury, and from which neither coaxing nor temptations would draw him out.'[4]

The demand for chimney sweep apprentices arose at the end of the eighteenth century when architecture began to express the more elegant standard of living and chimneys were contracted in order to avoid smoke pouring into the rooms from the older wider chimney flues. At the beginning of the nineteenth century it has been estimated that there were about four hundred master sweeps and about one thousand boys in England.[5] The boys were almost invariably unwanted children.

[1] First Report, Children's Employment Commission. Mines. 1842, p. 41.
[2] Op. cit., Appendix, Part I, p. 252.
[3] Op. cit., Appendix, Part II, p. 75.
[4] Op. cit., p. 77.
[5] J. L. and Barbara Hammond, *The Town Labourer*, c. IX.

The smaller the child the more suitable he was thought to be for the work[1] and so the under-fed and the undersized work-house children were much in demand, while the neglected children of parents who did not want them could be disposed of and sold for two or three guineas. Some children were apprenticed as young as four or five years of age, but most were aged between six and eight. In the thick, choking darkness of the narrow passages, which often turned at right angles, the little sweeps climbed to the top of the chimney and then descended, brushing the soot down on their way. Many a frightened child would seem to lose his way and panic, and could suffocate himself in the pile of soot which collected at the angles. To induce the boy to climb up some masters no doubt coaxed by kindness, but most had to use fear or cruelty to drive the boys into the terrifying work, setting fire to straw beneath them or sticking pins into their feet. Once in the long chimney flues the boy supported himself in climbing by his elbows and knees which gradually became covered with sooty, cartilaginous growths. Many of those children who survived the accidents of fire and suffocation by soot, remaining unwashed for years on end, died from a painful cancer of the scrotum.[2] Others became deformed by the difficult positions they had been forced to take up in the chimneys over long periods, or by carrying heavy loads of soot before their bodies were fully developed.

The history of the legislation to improve the conditions of working children in the chimneys, mines and factories, is long and humiliating in its exposure of the motives lying behind human conduct. Legislation to improve the conditions and eventually to prohibit the employment of children as chimney sweeps was debated in Parliament for over eighty years,[3] one speaker using as an argument against reform the fact that 'the boys generally employed in this profession were not the children of poor persons, but the children of rich men begotten in an improper manner.'[4]

---

[1] The master sweeps used to advertise 'Little boys for small flues'. See Sydney Smith's essay on 'Chimney Sweepers' in the *Edinburgh Review*, 1819.

[2] See Charles Turner Thackrah, *The Effect of Arts, Trades and Professions on Health and Longevity*. 1832. Reprinted. with an introductiory essay by A. Meiklejohn, by E. & S. Livingstone Ltd., 1957.

[3] 1788 to 1875.

[4] See *Hansard*, 22.2.1819. Col. 550.

The immortal name of the great Lord Shaftesbury will be for ever associated with the fight, against bitter opposition, to reduce the hours of work in factories and mines and to prohibit the employment of children underground and in the work of chimney sweeping, but there were other men too who prepared the public mind[1] and stormed Parliamentary opposition to bring the right to live, rather than the right to be exploited, to their poorer contemporaries. In 1788 Daniel Porter, a good master chimney sweep of London, petitioned Parliament for legislation which reached the statute book, but remained a dead letter till 1834. Lord Althorp's Factory Act of 1833 limited the working hours of children and young persons in textile mills and appointed factory inspectors with right of entry. The factory child was to attend school for two hours a day. This, with Shaftesbury's factory legislation of 1844–7 provided the soil from which all our modern factory legislation has grown, and in 1875 the legislation finally brought to an end the employment of little boys as chimney sweeps. In 1842 Lord Shaftesbury's Mines Act prohibited the underground employment of women and of children under ten and paved the way for the Mines Inspectorate of 1850 and gradual intervention by the State in securing the safety and better conditions of mines. When introducing the 1842 Bill in the House of Commons on the 7th June, Lord Shaftesbury in his moving speech quoted from the Report of the Commissioners the story of a little Rochdale pauper apprentice, Edmund Kershaw, employed by a Bagslate collier in a mine on Rooley moor. Edmund was examined by a surgeon, Mr. Milner, who ' found on his body from twenty-four to twenty-six wounds. His back and loins were beaten to a jelly ; his head, which was almost cleared of hair on the scalp, had the marks of many old wounds. One of the bones in one arm was broken below the elbow, and seemed to have been so for some time. The boy, on being brought before the magistrate, was unable either to sit or stand, and was placed on the floor of the office. It appeared that the boy's arm had been broken by a blow with an iron rail, and the fracture had never been set, and that he had been

---

[1] Crabbe, *Peter Grimes*, 1810; Kingsley, *The Water Babies*, 1863; Chas. Dickens, *Oliver Twist*, 1838. Of this G. K. Chesterton has said 'by making Bumble live, he created something by which it will always be possible to kill bureaucracies.'

kept at work for several weeks with his arm in that condition. It was admitted by the master that he had been in the habit of beating the boy with a flat piece of wood, in which a nail was driven, and projected about half an inch. . . . The blows had been inflicted with such violence that they had penetrated the skin, and caused the wounds described by Mr. Milner. The boy had been starved for want of food, and his body presented all the marks of emaciation. This brutal master had kept him at work as a waggoner until he was no longer of any use, and then sent him home in a cart to his mother, who was a poor widow, residing in Church Lane, Rochdale.'[1]

Yet the picture of the pauper child in the eighteenth century is not entirely black, and there are in the contemporary records pages of compassion, of paternalistic care, even of charm, which illuminate the darkness in the workhouses and factories. In the workhouse at Leeds Eden specifically mentions the goodness and kindness of the master there,[2] and some workhouse masters with their wives and families could do a great deal to make the children's lives happier. Samuel Bamford, a veteran of Peterloo and a nineteenth century radical, spent part of his childhood in the staff quarters of the Manchester workhouse where his father was appointed master in 1794. He describes the work as 'a theatre for the active habits and kindly feelings' of his family. The whole of the Bamford family interested themselves in the work and 'a new life, a confiding spirit, was infused into the poor inmates.' The orphans, 'as well as ourselves, had now a kind father, mother and uncle.' Samuel developed small-pox, and it is obvious from his account of the reaction of the workhouse children to him when he was well enough to play with them again, how much they gained from this contact with a good family life.[3]

And some of the factories to which apprentices were bound were centres of a community life which could be both a rich-

---

[1] See *Hansard*, 7.6.1842, col. 1,346. The description is quoted from the First Report of the Children's Employment Commission (Mines), Appendix, Part II, pp. 182, 183.

[2] Eden, op. cit., vol. III, p. 858.

[3] Samuel Bamford, *Passages in the Life of a Radical and Early Days*, Vol. I : In spite of his political acumen Bamford was something of a sentimentalist with a touch of vanity and the passage needs interpreting in that light.

ness and an opportunity to them.[1] One such early factory community was the Quarry Bank Mill, built by Samuel Greg in 1784 in the soft Cheshire countryside by the confluence of the river Bollin and the river Dean. Greg was the son of a Belfast ship-owner, adopted by his uncle, a Manchester manufacturer, and received part of his education at Harrow. In order to obtain labour he built cottages and bought farms to supply food, milk, butter and dairy produce for his work-people, and later built a non-sectarian chapel and school. When the factory was first opened the adult labour was provided by the parish overseers, and the apprentices were of two types, those taken from the workhouses and those engaged on a contract for a small wage made direct with their parents.[2] Some of the children had homes too far away for a daily journey and so all the apprentices lived together in the Apprentice House provided for them beside a large orchard on raised land above the level of the river. In 1790 there were eighty apprentices there under the care of a master and mistress, the boys and girls in separate sides of the house in airy, whitewashed rooms. The services of a doctor were engaged to care for the children and a retaining fee paid to him. The records show that the children were brought from far afield, from Newcastle-under-Lyme, Liverpool and London, as well as from Cheshire workhouses. The whole Greg family took special pride in caring for them. Several rose to the best positions in the factory, becoming overlookers or mechanics, and one became book-keeper in the firm. At least two of the managers started their career as parish apprentices, one rising to a position of confidence in the Greg family, and publishing a treatise on the slide rule.[3]

The manuscripts still at the Quarry Bank Mill give a good idea of a well conducted apprenticeship system of care at this time. The children worked twelve hours a day and overtime

[1] See the article by Frances Collier, 'An Early factory community' in *Economic History* for January, 1930, and her monograph 'Samuel Greg and Styal Mill' of February, 1941 from Vol. 85 of *Memoirs and Proceedings of The Manchester Literary and Philosophical Society*, Session 1941–43.

[2] See Appendix II. The earliest extant indenture at Styal, p. 203.

[3] James Henshall: 'Practical Treatise on the Slide Rule, with an appendix containing instruction for the improved double slide rule.' Printed by Thomas Woolley, 1835, June, Styal. *Quarry Bank MSS.*

was common, but they were well fed and clothed and educated and their individual tastes were catered for. The purchase of a sliding rule or a flute occurs several times in the ledgers, as well as the more necessary purchases of boots and new clothes.[1] From time to time children ran away. Two runaway boys, discovered and brought before the magistrates in 1806, were closely questioned in court about the conditions of their life there, but said they had no complaints about it. They had run away to London because they wanted to see their mothers.[2]

In twenty-eight years there is a record of twenty-three children running away, and in the early days the account books record '100 advertisements for lads eloped'. Occasionally a poor law child was allowed to leave the service before completing the apprenticeship if there were special circumstances. Such a child was Catharine Sullivan, aged 11 years, who had been bound by the Liverpool workhouse in 1828 for seven years. A note found among the indentures at Quarry Bank explains the position :—

'Catharine Sullivan eloped from her parents at Bradford and wandered to Liverpool where she was taken up and put in the workhouse and from there she was taken as an apprentice to Messrs. Greg & Co. and after serving 5 years and three months she was found out by her parents who came to claim her, and Mr. Greg allowed them to take her away on Saturday, January 21st, 1832.'

Small gifts and concessions were sometimes made to the children on binding as apprentice. Sometimes 'paid 6d. on hiring' is written on the indentures or promises of small gifts at festival times are made. Thomas Harding, for example, a boy apprenticed by the Stoke Poor Law authorities in 1785 has written on his indenture 'to get 6d. at Whitsuntide'. Two children from Pownall in 1819 and two from Woodford in 1827 are each to receive a yearly Christmas present. 'Shall and will pay and allow unto the said apprentice the sum of one shilling at or upon every Xmas day during the said term.'[3] Some clauses give the child right to an annual holiday away from the factory. It seems likely that these were the children

[1] See Memoranda and Apprentices Stoppage Book in *Quarry Bank MSS.*
[2] Memoranda, *Quarry Bank MSS.*
[3] *Quarry Bank MSS.*

of poor widows or destitute parents whose children were compulsorily apprenticed by the Poor Law, and who managed to secure these small concessions when the indentures were signed.[1]

Nowhere is the care of the children so evident, or the contrast with the evils of the factory apprenticeship so marked, as in the records of attention to the sick child in the Quarry Bank Mill. Many children came with deficiency diseases from the workhouses, many were thin and starved from want of care. The doctor's prescriptions give evidence of a high standard of medicine for the period[2] and careful understanding and attention for the individual child.

'Let him stay in bed. Let him have his skin washed twice a day with water nearly cold and care should be taken to wipe the skin very dry afterwards. He may drink toast water, apple tea, whey and buttermilk. His linen should be changed at least every other day and when taken off should be immediately put into a bucket of cold water.' (John Steele, Dec. 13th, 1804.)

' Let her sit up to the middle in a tub of water of new milk warmth, for ten minutes, immediately before going to bed. Let this be repeated each night for four nights; and let her be afterwards well rubbed with a warm cloth, and have her limbs wrapped in a little warm flannel.'
(Betty Knight, March 1st, 1806.)

'Let her have off all animal food and live upon eggs, milk, mashed potatoes, buttermilk, puddings. Let her take a small teaspoon of salts each morning.'
(Sarah Dunkerley, Nov. 4th, 1827.)

' Let her bathe in the river every other day.'
(Anne Henshall, May 18th, 1828.)

'Let her take a raw egg twice or thrice a day, with a little warm milk and water, whenever the pain in the stomach is severe.'
(Mary Gibbon. May 31st, 1830.)[3]

The pauper child in the industrial revolution was the victim of the circumstances of social and economic change. The raising of the standard of care for the very young workhouse

[1] See Walter Lazenby, 'The Social and Economic History of Styal,' unpublished. M.A. thesis for Manchester University.
[2] The same doctor was also private physician to the Countess of Stanley at Alderley.
[3] Prescription Book, *Quarry Bank MSS.*

child created administrative poor law problems in feeding, clothing and employing the increased numbers of those who thus survived. From the industrial point of view they were a godsend to the factories, but the opportunity to use them, and so often to exploit them, came before the public conscience was aware of the nature of the problem or able to take steps to see that the conditions under which they lived and worked were brought to an endurable standard. This was a failure of administration which left each individual child dependent upon the overseer who set about apprenticing him, and upon the magistrates who signed his indentures to the individual mine or factory owner. Many of these owners, not without blame, were ignorant of the conditions existing in their properties, which were accentuated by brutal managers or foremen, who dare not, or by their natures could not, allow themselves to feel compassion ; the chain of human responsibility broke at its weakest link.

Administration must wait upon the public conscience, therefore in the absence of national standards enforced by the State, expressing the will and conscience of the people, the improvements could come in only two ways, through the example of the paternalistic system seen most clearly in the work of such employers as the Gregs, the Arkwrights, Samuel Oldknow of Mellor[1] and Robert Owen of New Lanark, and through the fire of the philanthropists whom the Government, by fear of revolution at home, was constrained to hear. It was the widespread exploitation of the children in the worst factories which drew attention to the helplessness of the parish child, and roused, for the first time, public feeling and action. Until minimum standards were laid down the parish apprentice was, indeed, a child of chance whose life was written at the age of seven or eight upon the seals of his indenture. The nature of this chance is seen in the great gulf which divides the wild-eyed child, the creeping thing in the black tunnels of the mine, from the frail apprentice girl, who, on a May morning, bathed from the fresh and flowery banks in the waters of the river Bollin.

---

[1] It was evidently the practice of the Foundling Hospital to apprentice their difficult girls with Mr. Oldknow, in whose factory they usually did very well. See Nicholls and Wray, op. cit. pp. 151, 195, 197, 200.

CHAPTER THREE

THE CHILD AND THE INEFFECTIVE FAMILY

OUR own experience during and immediately following the second world war has proved that children are profoundly affected by changes in the stability and values of society and this was as true in the eighteenth century as it is in our own time, and was correspondingly expressed in the problem of young offenders who lacked moral standards and needed guidance and understanding. But no authority in the eighteenth century had the duty of providing care and protection for the children in moral danger who stood so urgently in need of it, and those who begged, roamed the streets in a neglected condition and eventually appeared before the magistrates for offences even at the age of eight and nine were sentenced to death, imprisoned with felons or transported across the great seas to the penal settlements of Canada and Australia. Law-breaking children were thought to be a dangerous infection to be removed from society, but already some people were beginning to wonder if society itself did not contain the germs of contamination and to think of measures which might be taken to prevent the spread and development of delinquency and to reform the delinquent once discovered. In 1754, for example, the blind Sir John Fielding, chief magistrate at Bow Street and brother of the novelist, after sending five boys to prison for stealing, wrote these words, 'It is indeed a melancholy truth, which I have learned from experience, that there are at this time in town some hundreds of this kind of boys. They might be made useful to society if they were collected together before they commence thieves, and . . . placed either in men of war or the Merchants' Service.' The unrelieved discipline and restraint of such a life may have been hardly what the neglected delinquent child most badly needed but the suggestion appeared attractive, providing a disciplined training and at the same time rescuing the child from the hideous conditions in which he lived. 'In the latter end of the year 1755,' wrote Fielding, 'it appeared that there were a vast number of wretched boys, ragged as colts, abandoned, strangers to beds, and who lay about under bulks, and in ruinous empty houses, in Westminster and its environs'[1]. In January 1756 the commanding officer of H.M.S. *Barfleur* wrote to Fielding, asking him to send thirty boys for employment in his ship as officers' servants. Fielding complied, and on their way to Portsmouth the boys were seen by a Mr. Fowler Walker of Lincoln's Inn. Impressed by the novel and constructive aspect of Fielding's plan he set about raising subscriptions to fit out an even larger number of poor boys to go to sea in this way and so avoid the opportunities and temptations to crime in the city. Soon the Marine Society was founded in July, 1756 'for the redemption and reformation of young criminals', and undertook to clothe the boys for whom applications had been received from the captains of many English ships. In 1786 a training ship was started for the boys, a shelter which was also a source of recruits for the navy. Sir John Fielding, now one of the Society's administrators and a member of its committee, in February 1758 had also drawn attention to the number of homeless young girls in London, some of whom had become prostitutes at the age of twelve.[2] As a result of his interest and support the Female Orphan Asylum and the Magdalen Hospital were both founded before the end of the year as measures of prevention and reform.

Even more definitely preventive measures were taken in 1788 when the Philanthropic Society was founded 'for the protection of poor children and the offspring of convicted felons, and the reformation of children who have themselves been engaged in criminal practices, that they might learn the happiness and benefit of a home'. The society placed the children in groups of twelve in three small, rough cottages at Hackney, but four years later this family system of care was discontinued and the Society moved its quarters. In 1800 it was incorporated by Act of Parliament and re-organized, later consisting of three departments, a prison school for young convicts, a workshop for the employment of destitute boys, and a training school for pauper girls. The care of the destitute and

[1] R. Leslie Melville, *The Life and Work of Sir John Fielding*, c. VIII.

[2] Sir John Fielding, *A Plan of the Asylum or House of Refuge for Orphans and other Deserted Girls of the Poor of the Metropolis*. London. 1758.

the reformation of those in moral danger were brought together first by the voluntary societies—as part of one whole problem which the poor law administration was not solving.

In fact the poor law now was a relief agency, taking, where necessary, palliative measures for the relief of poverty, and unable any longer to organise within the small parish system constructive measures to prevent destitution or to deal with the many other social problems which stem from poverty. The inadequate and sometimes inhuman methods, which the poor law administrators used in order to fulfil their statutory obligations to the homeless and orphaned children were responsible for the development of alternative forms of care pioneered by humanitarians and philanthropists. Various voluntary homes were opened in the early nineteenth century by which some attempt was made to group children according to their social background. For example, the London Orphan Asylum founded in 1813, required the marriage lines of a child's parents to be produced before the child could be admitted. In 1836 Muller's Orphan Homes were founded in Bristol for legitimate children, and other orphanages were provided for fatherless legitimate children from homes where relatives were unable to support them.[1] Some of these Homes required part payment by relatives or the securing of votes or subscribers letters in an attempt to ensure the genuine eligibility of the child who was admitted. These efforts to provide alternative care for children of an acceptable social background were the community answer of the middle class to the harsh methods of poor law care, but they left the more difficult problems of social failure, the neglected, abandoned and deserted as well as destitute children, to the responsibility of the poor law, whose attitude to failure had become punitive rather than positive. There were not lacking humanitarians who saw the need for a wider and more constructive approach than the parishes were adopting to the deprived child, and in 1830,

---

[1] See *Annual Register and Digest of Charities*, 'Homes for Boys and Girls: The Royal Alexandra School was founded as an orphanage in 1758 ; as a rule no child was admitted whose parents had received parish relief. The Royal Infant Orphanage, Wanstead, was founded in 1827 for middle class orphan children. The Royal United Service Orphan Home for Girls was founded in 1839 for the daughters of sailors, soldiers (and now airmen) to train them to earn their own living. Homes for specialized groups increased throughout the nineteenth century.

another retired sea captain, Edward Pelham Brenton, founded the Children's Friend Society for the Prevention of Juvenile Vagrancy and opened in West Ham a reception home for destitute children from which they were taught trades and later emigrated to the colonies under supervision.

There was, too, a good deal of self-help among the poor in caring for the orphaned or homeless children in the neighbourhood; Miss Mitford, for example, tells the delightful story of the eccentric village molecatcher, who, while the parish Bumble was hesitating about the expediency of boarding out a five year old orphan in preference to putting him in the workhouse, took the child into his own home.[1] This practice, indiscriminate and unsupervised, had obvious dangers and abuses accentuated by the social conditions of the time, but at its best is perhaps most beautifully and movingly expressed in the life story of Kitty Wilkinson, herself a poor working woman, and once a factory apprentice, who during the great cholera epidemic in Liverpool in 1832 opened her home to many of the children who ran neglected and wild about the tenement streets while their parents lay dead or dying.[2]

By this time, in the second quarter of the nineteenth century, the administration of the poor law had reached a crisis. The effect of the Speenhamland policy in granting out-relief in supplementation of wages had become acute. Under this system wages had been kept low, and the distinction between the employed workman, the genuinely unemployed and the wilfully idle disappeared in a universal pauperisation which was ruinous to the ratepayers. The Poor Law Commissioners appointed in 1832 to review the whole administration made recommendations which resulted in a new Poor Law Amendment Act of 1834 and coloured for the next hundred years the whole attitude of the people towards relief. Unable themselves to raise the standards of employment or minimum wages the Commissioners aimed at reducing pauperism by a method of deterring people from poor relief. This policy was put into

[1] Mary Russell Mitford, *Our Village*. The Molecatcher. See also my article *Boarding-out and the Wordsworths*, published in *Case Conference*, Vol. 6, No 6, November, 1959, and reprinted in Appendix VII.

[2] See Appendix III: *Memoir of Kitty Wilkinson of Liverpool*, p. 205, and Appendix VII *Boarding-out and the Wordsworths*, p. 232.

effect by withholding out-relief from the able-bodied unemployed, who could now only be given help by leaving home and
going into the workhouse where life was to be less attractive
than the most unpleasant means of earning a living outside.[1]
Within the workhouses men and their wives were separated to
prevent childbearing, but in spite of express recommendations
of the Commissioners that the different handicapped groups
should be segregated, the old, the disabled, the senile, the sick,
the prostitute, the lunatic and the destitute child continued to
be maintained together in the deterrent atmosphere of discipline and punishment.[2] Yet in the pattern of the new administration was woven the possibility of its own reform ; in the
compulsory union of parishes into a larger unit which might
permit segregation and specialisation, and in the formation of
the more widely elected Boards of Guardians to administer the
Act we see an attempt to work towards a national system and a
common standard higher than could ever be achieved by the
small local parish autonomies; its weakness lay in the fact that
the fate of the poor law was in the hands of its administrators
and was limited by their limitations of vision and insight, that
the work-people themselves were disenfranchised and their
opinions unrepresented on a matter which touched them at
every turn.

It is true that in rural areas the new poor law after 1834
benefited the community as a whole. The refusal to give out-
relief in supplementation of wages brought about in the country
a general rise in income from earnings, but in the industrial
areas the picture was very different. The old poor law had
relieved the unemployment caused by fluctuations of trade or
introduction of new machinery, and the removal of out-relief
and separation of families by the workhouse test, which now
fell heavily upon the unemployed, caused a universal revulsion
and hatred of the poor law whose echoes are not silenced even
to-day, and which bred among the poor the conviction that
they were being punished for their poverty. With pride and

[1] A policy referred to as 'the principle of less eligibility.'
[2] Commentators in 1852 stated they had 'seen nothing in the prisons and
lunatic asylums of Europe to equal conditions in the English workhouse where
children, lunatics, incorrigible, innocent, old, disabled were all mixed together'.
Quoted in S. Webb, *English Poor Law Policy* (1910), p. 38. This in spite of the
attack on mixed workhouses made by Gilbert's Act in 1782.

independence they turned away from it, preferring to beg or to endure among themselves rather than to receive help in the disciplinary and deterrent conditions of the workhouse. The poor law administration became justly stigmatized because it was a service based on the prevention of poverty by deterrence with no concept of constructive individual help. Outside the pages of the great Victorian novelists some idea of the life of the poor, following the failure of the poor law to meet their needs, is found in Henry Mayhew's descriptions of the answers given in their own words of the lives of the men, women and children he personally questioned in their homes, on the streets and in the workhouses of London.[1] The failure of the poor law even to fulfil its duty to relieve destitution among children is seen in the character of the little eight year old girl, a street seller and breadwinner in a poor family, whose life began and ended with the watercresses she sold and the prices they fetched,[2] or again in the character of the fifteen year old pickpocket with hands 'of singular delicacy and beauty.' Mayhew asked him what he thought was the cause of so many boys become vagrant pickpockets. His answer is interesting as it must reflect the opinion of the time, ' Why, sir, if boys runs away, and has to shelter in low lodging houses[3]—and many runs away from cruel treatment at home—they meet there with boys such as me, or as bad, and the devil soon lays hand on them. If there weren't so many lodging houses there wouldn't be so many bad boys—there couldn't. Lately a boy came down to Billingsgate and said he wouldn't stay at home to be knocked about any longer. He said it to some boys like me; and he was asked if he could get anything from his mother, and he said, "Yes, he could." So he went back, and brought a brooch and some other things with him to a place fixed on, and then he and some of the boys set off for the country; and that's the way boys is trapped. I think the fathers of such boys either ill-treat them or neglect

---

[1] Henry Mayhew, *London Labour and the London Poor*. Published by Charles Griffin and Co. (1851). A selection of the descriptions of the characters has been prepared and edited by Peter Quennel, and published, under the title *Mayhew's Characters*, by Griffin and Co., 1951.

[2] See 'The Watercress Seller.' *Mayhew's Characters*, op. cit.

[3] The conditions of these are frequently described in the memoirs of Dr. Barnardo, the public did not become concerned about them until the notorious murders of Jack the Ripper in 1887.

them, and so they run away. My father used to beat me shocking; so I hated home. I stood hard licking well and was called "the plucked one." ' This boy first stole flowers, currants and gooseberries out of the clergyman's garden more by way of bravado, and to ensure the approbation of his comrades, than for anything else.

'He answered readily to my inquiry as to what he thought would become of him?—"Transportation. If a boy has great luck he may carry on for eight years. Three or four years is the common run, but transportation is what he's sure to come to in the end." This lad picked my pocket at my request, and so dexterously did he do his "work" that though I was alive to what he was trying to do, it was impossible for me to detect the least movement of my coat. To see him pick the pockets, as he did, of some of the gentlemen who were present on the occasion, was a curious sight. He crept behind them much like a cat with his claws out, and while in the act held his breath with suspense; but immediately the handkerchief was safe in his hand, the change in the expression of his countenance was most marked. He then seemed almost to be convulsed with delight at the success of his perilous adventure, and, turning his back held up the handkerchief to discover the value of his prize with intense glee evident in every feature.'[1]

The description of the three boys aged thirteen, sixteen and seventeen who were inmates of the workhouse casual wards is equally telling and illustrative of common opinion of the time. 'The last statement I took was of a boy of thirteen. I can hardly say that he was clothed at all. He had no shirt, and no waistcoat; all his neck and a great part of his chest being bare. A ragged cloth jacket hung about him, and was tied, so as to keep it together, with bits of tape. What he had wrapped round for trousers did not cover one of his legs, while one of his thighs was bare. He wore two old shoes; one tied to his foot with an old ribbon, the other a woman's old boot. He had an old cloth cap. His features were distorted somewhat, through being swollen with the cold.' The mother of this boy had died at Hadley a year ago. He tells his story with a practised art. ' "I didn't know how she was buried. She was ill a long time, and I was out begging; for she sent me out to beg for myself a

[1] The Young Pickpocket. *Mayhew's Characters*, op. cit. p. 118.

good while before that, and when I got back to the lodging house they told me she was dead. I had sixpence in my pocket, but I couldn't help crying to think I'd lost my mother. I cry about it still. I didn't wait to see her buried, but started on my own account. . . . I came to London to beg, thinking I could get more there than anywhere else, hearing that London was such a good place. I begged; but sometimes wouldn't get a farthing in a day; often walking about the streets all night. I have been begging about all the time till now. I am very weak —starving to death. I never stole anything. I always kept my hands to myself. A boy wanted me to go with him to pick a gentleman's pocket. We was mates for two days, and then he asked me to go picking pockets; but I wouldn't. I know it's wrong though I can neither read or write. The boy asked me to do it to get into prison, as that would be better than the streets. He picked pockets to get into prison. He was starving about the streets like me. I never slept in a bed since I've been in London: I am sure I haven't: I generally slept under the dry arches in West Street, where they're building houses—I mean the arches for the cellars. I begged chiefly from the Jews about Petticoat Lane, for they all give away bread that their children leave—pieces of crust and such-like. I would do anything to be out of this misery." ¹

It was in this setting that the Ragged Schools were opened as a rescue movement for the destitute and neglected children of the streets, growing mainly from the example of John Pounds² the crippled Portsmouth cobbler who, at the age of fifty-two, in the early years of the nineteenth century, gathered together the ragged children about him, teaching them reading, writing and arithmetic and the rudiments of a trade, simple cookery for the girls, and shoe-making for the boys. The Ragged School movement spread rapidly in the middle of the century and attracted among both the humble and the well-to-do some of the most noble and charitable men and women of the time.³

¹ Boy Inmates of the Casual Wards. *Mayhew's Characters*, op. cit.

² Born 1766, died 1839.

³ The majority of the great nineteenth century reformers in child care received their introduction to the work through the Ragged Schools, and many undistinguished people, through this voluntary service, became conscious of the hardships and needs of the neglected children of the cities, which would otherwise have remained hidden from them.

Among them was Mary Carpenter, the talented and cultured daughter of Dr. Lant Carpenter, a Unitarian minister, who believed that the effectiveness of the Ragged School could be extended as an even greater instrument of reform by the professional use of paid teachers chosen for their capability and skill. In 1846, at the age of thirty-nine, Miss Carpenter superintended the opening of a Ragged School near her home at Lewin's Mead in Bristol which led directly to her work for the care of delinquents and neglected children by which reformatories and industrial schools were substituted for the sentence of prison.

It is worth while to look in some detail at the work of Mary Carpenter and the background of the children in the service of whom she spent her life. The nineteenth century had no unified administrative arrangements for providing assistance both to the destitute and to the neglected child. It was the duty of the poor law authorities to care for the child who was destitute, orphaned or deserted, or who came with his family into the care of the parish, his parents being too poor to look after him. Children who lived in their own homes and with their families, however much they were neglected and exposed to moral danger, and those who were homeless but somehow maintained themselves, were the responsibility of no one until they became delinquent, when they found their way into the punitive and contaminating atmosphere of the nineteenth century gaols.[1] There was no duty upon the poor law to seek out homeless children and provide for them. The schools founded for these ragged children were a preventive measure, an attempt to provide on Sundays and in the evenings a place for companionship and moral teaching which would modify the wild delinquent pattern of behaviour of the streets. Some idea of this work is found in a letter written by Mary Carpenter's mother on August 7th, 1846, in which she describes the opening of the new Ragged School.

'At home we are beginning to be busy as usual. We had it in contemplation to begin a "Ragged School", which waited for Mary's return. She returned on Thursday night; the master,

[1] The select committee of the House of Lords appointed to inquire into the conditions of juvenile offenders in 1847 had reported on the uselessness of prison for young offenders.

Mr. Phelps, came on Friday, and on the following Sunday nearly twenty boys were assembled. The seven which Mr. Phelps had collected brought a dozen more in the afternoon, which showed that they liked it; but, beginning to be tired in the afternoon, one of them said, "Now let us fight", and in an instant they were all fighting. Peace was, however, soon restored, and they have gone on with increasing numbers and more order than could have been expected; and to Mary's astonishment, she did not meet with one group of boys gambling or fighting on Lewin's Mead yesterday. It is literally a "Ragged School"; none have shoes or stockings, some have no shirt, and no home, sleeping in cases on the quay or on steps, and living, I suppose, by petty depredations; but all appear better fed than the children of the decent poor are. I have furnished the women of the house with towels and soap, and some sort of approach to cleanliness is insisted upon.'[1]

What a tough proposition such schools were to those without the necessary skill is shown by the following account in the diary of a master of a Ragged School in London:—

'To compose the children, if possible, I proposed that we should have a little music, and sang very sweetly the first verse of the Evening Hymn. We then invited the children to follow us, and we got through the first line or two very well,— but a blackguard youth thought proper to set up on his own account, and he led off a song in this strain.   I need scarcely add that every boy followed this leadership, ay, girls and all, and I could not check them. After some time, I spoke to them very gently and sadly, and having gained attention to some degree, I ventured to close the School with a very short prayer. I did do. Fearful to relate, in the midst of the Lord's Prayer, several shrill cries of "Cat's meat" and "Mew, mew" added another fact to the history of the school. So by the help of God we must both work harder. It is a post of honour. It is a forlorn hope'[2]

It is evident from the extract that neither an ardent heart nor hard work was the remedy.

[1] Letter of Mrs. Carpenter to Mrs. Timothy Smith, quoted in *The Life and Work of Mary Carpenter*, by J. Estlin Carpenter. Macmillan 1881, p. 82.
[2] Quoted in Mary Carpenter, *Reformatory Schools for the children of the Perishing and dangerous classes and for juvenile offenders.*

As she worked among the vagrant and the delinquent children in the ragged school, growing to love and to understand them as she guided and helped them, Mary Carpenter became convinced of two things, firstly that ragged schools were not sufficient to meet the real needs of these children, and secondly, because many of the boys were young thieves who had been convicted and served sentences, she became aware that imprisonment in the ordinary gaol system of the time produced in children a lasting injury. She felt the need for a place where the young criminal could be kept under detention, and trained by a mingled discipline of firmness and love to better ways.[1]

In her thinking she had been greatly influenced by the continental experiments with young delinquents, particularly the Rauhe Haus at Hamburg, and La Colonie Agricole, at Mettrai.[2] In November 1833 Emmanuel Wichern and his mother took possession of a small cottage with about an acre of land in a village about three miles from Hamburg. In the course of a few weeks he brought there to the 'Rauhe Haus' fourteen delinquent street boys, aged between 5 and 18, all regarded as outcasts by society, one twelve year old had been convicted by the police of 93 thefts. In the cottage they were able to make a break with their past life and find a real home of their own. Not only did the land and buildings belong to them, but the man responsible for the scheme was in the place of a father to them, his mother was their mother, too. Working as part of one family they set about together improving their

[1] Mary Carpenter, op. cit., p. 114.

[2] La Colonie Agricole at Mettrai, near Tours, founded in January 1840 under the influence of M. Demetz was based on earlier experiments of the Rauhe Haus at Hamburg. The objects at Mettrai were, in Mary Carpenter's words, 'to restore to society, as honest and useful members of it, those young persons who have subjected themselves to punishment and to do this by substituting the discipline of a school and a family rather than that of a prison.' Here four hundred boys were grouped into "families" of 40 with a master and two assistant masters and had their own separate houses. The master lived with the boys and gave them as much individual and personal care as possible. All the boys were given in turn some share in the government of the establishment. Vocational training was given, and education at an elementary level, with opportunities for more advanced work. All the boys were taught music. Only a very small percentage of the boys had criminal records after leaving. Work with farmers and tradesmen was found for each boy as he left and a 'patron' found who reported every six months on his progress and conduct. A full account of the continental experiments is found in Mary Carpenter's book *Reformatory Schools*, c. VI.

farm, and 'the faith that they could do something, be something and own something grew daily with them.' As their numbers increased they built a new cottage to which other boys were sent, and so there grew up 'a cottage village of boy-families, with workshops and dwelling-houses, a little chapel, a wash and drying house, a printing-office, bake-house.' Gradually the scheme was extended to include girls and there were altogether 4 boy families of 70 boys and 2 girl families of 25 girls. In this way, with government support and approval, a home and industrial school was substituted for prison for convicted juveniles.

These experiments Mary Carpenter referred to in a letter written to the Rev. John Clay, chaplain of the Preston Gaol, in November 1850.

'Since the prison system, even as best conducted, is proved ineffectual as a preventive and reformatory measure for children and such institutions at Mettrai have exceeded their expectations, they should be tried. . . . It is not the spirit of fear, but of power and of love, and of a sound mind, which can be powerful enough to subdue these hard hearts; and without touching the inner spirit no external measure will be of much avail.'[1]

But in our own country, too, there were private experiments of voluntary organisations to provide a setting, a home, a school, a place of reformation for delinquent boys. The Philanthropic Society[2] in 1849 opened a farm school at Red Hill, Surrey, for boys who 'had entered on a criminal career'. They came as volunteers after completing their imprisonment, or at the desire of their parents, or as a condition of their discharge, having received a conditional pardon. In the green and wooded Warwickshire countryside at Stretton-on-Dunsmore twelve to twenty boys from the Warwick and Birmingham gaols lived in a pleasant three storey house under 'the advantages and comfort of a well ordered family', hired out as labourers while they completed their sentences.[3] Although the experiment at Stretton-on-Dunsmore was said to have proved after thirty years of experience that it was cheaper to the country to reform boys than to punish them, both these

---

[1] J. Estlin Carpenter, op. cit, p. 115.
[2] See page 33, ante
[3] See Mary Carpenter, op. cit., c. VI.

experiments were severely handicapped by lack of money and that at Red Hill, by the lack of any power to detain a pupil either against his inclination or that of his parents.

Seeing in these experiments a more effective answer to the prevention of juvenile crime Mary Carpenter set about stimulating public interest and enlisting public support for the work. In the winter of 1851 she published her remarkable book *Reformatory Schools for the Children of the Perishing and Dangerous Classes and for Juvenile Offenders* in which she advocated special forms of treatment to meet the particular needs of the neglected children of the time. In the cities there were many destitute children who were refused admission to the existing National and British schools because of their bad family background and for these she urged the setting up of good Free day schools, as an extension of the Ragged Schools, but with qualified and well paid teachers chosen for their special aptitude for the work with difficult children.[1] This group is described as children of the perishing classes. For the children who wandered about the streets, begging, refusing to attend any sort of school and developing dishonest patterns of behaviour she recommended the provision of Feeding Industrial schools such as had been opened ten years earlier by Sheriff Watson in Aberdeen for 'the children of the poorest classes, and chiefly those who are found to infest the streets, begging and stealing.' Here the children were fed and given some training of personal help to them—sewing and laundry for the girls, shoemaking and tailoring for the boys—returning to their families at night. Attendance of the children was to be enforced by magistrates and the cost recovered partly from the parents and partly from rates. Finally, to meet the needs of those children actually convicted by the Courts of offences against the law she pleaded for penal reformatory schools in place of prison sentences. These last two groups were 'the dangerous classes'. Influenced by the continental pioneers she asked that magistrates should have power to commit convicted children to these schools which should have power to detain them and be supported by government inspection and grants. Weekly payments for maintenance of the child should be made from the rates or by the parents. 'The parents being in reality the guilty parties,

[1] See Mary Carpenter, op. cit., c. III and IV.

rather than the children, since juvenile delinquency usually originates in parental neglect, every parent should be chargeable for the maintenance of a child thrown by crime on the care of the state, as much as if the child were at large, and should be held responsible for the maintenance of a child in a Reformatory School, or made in some way to suffer for the non-discharge of this duty.'[1] It is interesting to note here the transfer of punishment from the child to the parent, whose failure has only recently been seen as part of the whole problem, requiring constructive treatment too.[2] The nineteenth century reformers attacking the problem of the neglectful parent and breaking family used retributive methods and economic pressure, and in doing so, beat their wings in vain against walls of stone. This separation of the problem into punishment of the parents and treatment of the child, had far-reaching effects on social attitudes to neglected children and children in care, and on the administration of services provided for them.

Public support, following the publication of Mary Carpenter's book, led eventually to the appointment on 6th May, 1852, of a House of Commons Committee of Inquiry on Juvenile Delinquency before which she gave evidence. Her views on the treatment of the delinquent child were novel, difficult and startling then. 'A child will never behave well in prison from any moral sense. I have in point of fact found that those who behave best in prison are really more likely to do badly when they come out. Those who I have been most able to act upon have been somewhat rebellious in prison. *I would then enlist the will of the child in the work*, and without this I do not think that any true reformation can be effected.'[3]

The recommendations of the Committee, which supported Mary Carpenter's views, were not issued till the summer of 1853. In the meantime she was anxious to prove to doubters in this country the correctness of her views, and the opportunity came to her to set up a Reformatory school on her own lines. Near the village of Kingswood, about four miles from Bristol, were some vacant premises formerly occupied by a Wesleyan school; the house had been built by Wesley himself and twelve

[1] Mary Carpenter, op. cit., c. VI, p. 348.
[2] See *Post*, c. XI.
[3] J. Estlin Carpenter, op. cit., p. 133.

hundred children could be accommodated in the buildings which were surrounded by many acres of land. The lovely west country setting, with its opportunities for creative work on the land, and for contact with the simple but enduring values of country life and scenes, seemed to Mary Carpenter to be an ideal background for her work with the delinquent city children. The property was purchased for her by a Mr. Russell Scott of Bath who had visited the Rauhe Haus in Hamburg, and other friends helped with gifts of money and the cost of furniture and fittings. In September, 1852, Kingswood was opened as a mixed Reformatory School.

The principles of treatment on which she worked are expressed in a passage of her new book *Juvenile Delinquents, their conditions and treatment*, which appeared early in 1853.

' The child . . . must be placed where the prevailing principle will be, as far as practicable, carried out,—where he will be gradually restored to the true position of childhood. He must be brought to a sense of dependence by re-awakening in him new and healthy desires which he cannot by himself gratify, and by finding that there is a power far greater than his own to which he is indebted for the gratification of these desires. He must perceive by manifestations what he cannot mistake, that this power, whilst controlling him is guided by wisdom and love; he must have his affections called forth by the obvious personal interest felt in his own individual well-being by those around him; he must, in short, be placed in a *family*. Faith in those around him being once thoroughly established, he will soon yield his own will in ready submission to those who are working for his good; it will thus be gradually subdued and trained, and he will work with them in effecting his reformation, trusting, where he cannot perceive the reason of the measures they adopt to correct or eradicate the evil in him. This, it is apprehended, is the fundamental principle of all true reformatory action with the young, and in every case where striking success has followed such efforts, it will be traceable to the greater development of this principle, to a more true and powerful action on the soul of the child, by those who have assumed towards it the holy duties of a parent.'[1]

[1] Mary Carpenter, *Juvenile Delinquents, their Condition and Treatment*. 1853, c. IX, p. 298. The italics are in the original.

The testing out of the reformatory and preventive measures by private individuals such as Mary Carpenter, and voluntary organisations, such as the Philanthropic Society, led to the Reformatory Schools (Youthful Offenders) Act of 1854 and the Industrial Schools and the Reformatory Schools Acts of 1857. By these Acts the reformatories and industrial schools became subject to Government inspection by the Home Office, which was enabled to make grants to them. Courts, by these Acts, could order juveniles who had been convicted to be detained in reformatories, for periods between 2 and 5 years, and require parents to contribute to their maintenance there, and very young offenders, and children aged between 7 and 14 years charged with vagrancy, could be sent to industrial schools. Local authorities were empowered to make contributions towards the establishment of reformatories, and juveniles could be allowed out on licence from them when at least half their sentence had been completed. Public opposition towards the relaxing of the punitive attitude was still strong, however, and juveniles had still to spend fourteen days in prison before going to the reformatory school. In 1858 the Government inspector reported that in England and Scotland there were forty-five reformatories with 1,973 boys and 370 girls in them. Reporting for the first time on industrial schools in 1861 he found nineteen of these: both groups of schools increased rapidly during the next fifty years, the industrial schools increasing more rapidly and becoming residential in nature.[1] Reformatories were corrective of crime, the industrial schools aimed at preventing it by caring for the neglected before they could become delinquent. In 1856, therefore, the Reformatory and Refuge Union was created to co-ordinate the work of the voluntary bodies engaged in both curative and preventive work.

So we find that by this time the public care of children was itself becoming specialised both in its field of eligibility and in its administration. The orphan, homeless and destitute child was the responsibility of the poor law, but many voluntary organisations had developed to try to provide for such children alternative care more suited to their individual backgrounds.

[1] E. C. Wines, *The State of the Prisons and of Child Saving Institutions of the Civilised World.* Cambridge University Press. 1880, p. 223.

47

The industrial schools tried to reclaim or provide for the child where family responsibility had broken down and took in also destitute children who did not fit in to the more specialised voluntary orphanages;[1] the reformatories dealt with the corrective treatment and reformation of the more difficult delinquents.

The statutory poor law did not seek out the children for whom such care was needed. Its purpose was to relieve a need when required to do so. Rescue work among children, inspired by charitable motives and aiming to prevent the destruction of morality and character, became pre-eminently the field of the great voluntary societies in the last half of the nineteenth century.

[1] In 1878 their object is described as 'to bring up destitute or criminal children in habits of religion and virtue.' Local Govt. Board Education of Children (Poor) 1878.

CHAPTER FOUR

THE PHILANTHROPIC CARE OF CHILDREN

THE last half of the nineteenth century saw the final disintegration of the unique and individually stable way of life which characterized agricultural society. The food-producing England of rural life and scenes, so lovingly described by her painters and her poets, gave place to the rising prosperity of a great industrial and mechanised nation. While the decay of agriculture at home led to the development of emigration to the rich-yielding farmlands of Canada and the Antipodes, the overseas competition from the continent in industrial skills and techniques led to a more organised efficiency at home, seen perhaps most effectively in the new legislation dealing with education and with local government and the growth of the civil service. Democracy became more collective and more bureaucratic, and the social reformers now spent their energy on the one hand in attacking the distribution of wealth or on the other in fighting to ensure what they called a scientific organisation of benevolence in contrast to indiscriminate philanthrophy.

It was inevitable that these new philosophies should be reflected in the field of child care. But the principles of collectivism and mutual aid, by which men in a new society again attempted to accept responsibility for the welfare of each other, were difficult to apply for the help of the destitute and neglected child separated from his family and community. It is true the poor law care represented the collective responsibility of the community towards its inarticulate deprived children, but the poor law officers had no duty to go out into the streets and slums of the great cities and bring in those children exposed there to degradation and moral danger because of their loneliness and destitution. This rescue work became the province and expression of evangelical influence, and of the

Church's corporate life revived by the Oxford movement in the 1830's. Because of its urgent nature in the circumstances of the time it became separated from the more analytical charity which developed from the teaching of the organised schools of thought, aimed at preventing the causes of distress.[1] The terrible conditions to which thousands of children were exposed without protection, described for us so graphically by the Victorian writers, roused the philanthropists to action in a crusading spirit. The disease and mortality rates of the great cities, and the cholera epidemics which so tragically punctuated the nineteenth century, tended to solemnise men's minds and render them open to evangelical witness and moral influence. So the workers in this field saw their urgent duty not only as an opportunity to rescue children from neglect and cruelty and desertion in all its forms, but also to bring souls to the kingdom of heaven.

The bravest and most war-like of all the crusaders was the famous Dr. Thomas John Barnardo whose life and work is a clear illustration of the rescue principle.[2] Barnardo was converted from agnosticism at a Dublin revivalist meeting in 1862 when he was a youth of seventeen. Four years later he travelled to London, enrolling as a medical student at the London Hospital intending to qualify as a medical missionary and go out to China. But while still a student he and some of his friends opened a little Ragged School in a rough district of Stepney, where they taught the children in their spare time. Here, in the school, came the turning point in Barnardo's life, the meeting with the ragged, homeless boy, Jim Jarvis, who, after the class was done, begged his teacher to allow him to stay and shelter by the fire all night. When Barnardo learned from him of the hungry, half clad children, sleeping in makeshift shelters night after night in the London streets, he could not rest until he had verified for himself the unbelievable reality. He describes how, half an hour after midnight, the boy led him through a narrow court in Houndsditch into a long empty shed used by day as an old clothes market. Presently they came to a high wall up which Jim climbed, telling the doctor to follow.

[1] See Charity Organisation Society, *post*, p. 105.
[2] For fuller accounts of this man's great achievement the reader is referred to A. E. Williams, *Barnardo of Stepney* and Norman Wymer, *Father of Nobody's Children*.

'There on the open roof, lay a confused group of boys, all asleep. I counted eleven. They lay with their heads upon the higher part and their feet in the gutter, in as great variety of postures as one may have seen in dogs before a fire—some coiled up, some huddled two or three together, others more apart. The rags that most of them wore were mere apologies for clothes. One big fellow appeared to be about eighteen, but the ages of the remainder varied, I should say, from nine to fourteen.

'Just then a cloud passed from the face of the moon, and as the pale light fell upon the upturned faces of those sleeping boys, and I realized the terrible fact that they were absolutely home-less and destitute, and were almost certainly but samples of many others, it seemed as though the hand of God Himself had suddenly pulled aside the curtain which concealed from my view the untold miseries of forlorn child-life upon the streets of London.'[1]

This incident occurred in 1867. The doctor placed Jim with a motherly woman in lodgings near his own; he frequently went out at night with the lad as his guide gathering together desti-tute boys and gradually providing for fifteen or sixteen of them by this rough method of fostering. Lord Shaftesbury became interested in the work and soon Barnardo received a letter from a well known member of Parliament, Samuel Smith, who offered to provide a thousand pounds for rescue work if he would give up, even temporarily, the plan of going to China. This letter decided Barnardo's future, he accepted the offer, and in 1870 opened the first Home for Destitute Boys at No. 18 Stepney Causeway, a little house in a mean street, but a shelter for twenty-five neglected children, which he and a few of his fellow students repaired and decorated and made ready.

A few years earlier, when unexpectedly, and in default of a missionary speaker who had been delayed, he had addressed impromptu a large assembly on his experiences in the East End, the doctor had received his first public donation towards his work, a servant girl's gift of an envelope containing twenty-seven farthings. But he began his residential work in a business-like way, determined to avoid debt and to take in only as many boys as could be provided for. This tidy administrative

[1] Quoted in A. E. Williams, *Barnardo of Stepney*, Guild Books, 1953. pp. 60–61.

51

principle was soon exploded, however, by the circumstances of the little red-haired waif John Somers, known as Carrots, with whom the doctor came in contact. Barnardo found the eleven year old Carrots with several other boys sleeping out in Billingsgate. From among them he chose five to fill the vacancies in his Home, and though Carrots begged to be included Barnardo had no extra room and so could only give him a few coppers for food and promise him the next vacancy.

A day or two later, a porter, who, in the early morning, was moving a large sugar barrel lying with its open end to the wall, disturbed a sleeping boy by whom there lay another boy also apparently asleep. The child disturbed made off in a twinkling but when the porter touched his companion he did not move, and, lifting the lad up in his arms, he saw that he was dead. This boy was Carrots who, according to the Coroner's inquest later had died 'from exhaustion, the result of frequent exposure and want of food.' This incident, and the remorse which followed it, cut deep into Barnardo's heart and truly changed him from an eager philanthropist to a fiery crusader. Over the door of his Home he fixed a signboard NO DESTITUTE CHILD EVER REFUSED ADMISSION. He extended his premises and went out at night and in the early hours of the morning, carrying a lantern, in hovels, shacks and waste places, seeking out derelict children and prevailing on them to accept the shelter of his Home. Indeed he found now that persuasion and constraint became necessary in his work, for the recently introduced Education Act of 1870 compelled London children below thirteen to attend school regularly, and many of the street children preferred their wild mature freedom and the shelter of their temporary lairs to the thought of compulsory school and discipline linked with the shelter of a Home.

After his marriage in June 1873 Barnardo opened a Home for girls attached to his own home, Mossford Lodge at Barkingside, but he soon learnt that any errors in principles of care had much more serious effects on girls than on boys. 'My first attempt', he says, 'really took shape as a small institute on what would now be called the barrack-system. Forty little girls were housed simply in a remodelled coach-house, with a single upper-floor added to it at the back of our own dwelling Mossford Lodge. The forty soon grew to sixty; and then the seriousness of the situation was borne in upon me with such overwhelming force, that one night I came to the conclusion that I must stop it all! I felt that the system was a bad one, though I still knew of no better.'

Disturbed at the degraded and exceptional behaviour of the girls he thought hard about the problem until at last 'I saw at a glance what I ought to do. Instead of a big house with sixty girls clad in dull uniform, I would arrange for a number of little ivy-clad cottages to arise, each presided over by a kindly Christian woman who would be the "Mother". The children should be of all ages, from the baby-in-arms to the girl well on in her teens training for service. They should be dressed as simply and with as much variety as possible, and there should be nothing in the way of uniform. Anything approaching institutionalism would be scrupulously excluded. In such a home, and in such an atmosphere, the affectionate ties of family life and family love would have a chance of being created and fostered in the experience of the children, while the daily performance of commonplace duties would tend to fit them for their future career. Surely the family is God's way, for "He setteth the solitary in families' "[1]. So in the family traditions encouraged in the Rauhe Haus at Hamburg, and at Mettrai, and pleaded for by Mary Carpenter, Barnardo effectively carried the principle of cottage homes into the voluntary child care service and in July 1876 thirteen of the planned cottages at Barkingside were formally opened. They were later known as the Village Homes and their most beautiful memorial is found in the story of the girl who passed her childhood there and proudly vindicated it in *The Likes of Us*.[2]

The work of Thomas John Barnardo was based wholly on the power of new environment and teaching. 'If the children of the slums,' he said 'can be removed from their surroundings early enough, and can be kept sufficiently long under training, heredity counts for little, environment counts for everything.' He established the ever-open door, made it known to the police and all who dealt with destitute children. His policy was admit the child first, in the extremity of his need, and

[1] Quoted in A. E. Williams, *Barnardo of Stepney* pp. 95-6.
[2] G. V. Holmes. *The Likes of Us*. Frederick Muller Ltd. 1948.

afterwards investigate before the admission was made permanent. He believed in lifting the children out of their native environment and giving them another life where work, self control and religious teaching were their guiding stars. The policy of all his Homes was first to bring up the children as Christians and then to make them useful, reasonably well-educated citizens. For this purpose he regarded industrial training as very important and established his own schools on the Home premises in which he introduced a broader education than was to be found in the average outside school. For boys he established well equipped work-shops with professional craftsmen in charge to teach a trade, for the girls he ensured a careful domestic training lasting three months before placing them as servants or nannies with respectable families.[1]

He had begun his lifework with a tentative attempt at boarding out, for he had no alternative, but in 1886 he established a systematic boarding out scheme which he favoured for appropriate children between the ages of five and nine years. Later he included younger children and paid a higher rate for those under three, because they require special care. His system differed from that of the poor law in that he recalled the children from the foster parents to the Children's Home at the age of twelve or thirteen in order to give them a training to earn their own living. The Victorian doctrine of work and trade, on which the nineteenth century based its independence, was the justification of education for rescued children.

But Barnardo also attempted to deal with the growth of deprivation by cutting at some part of the root. He saw the social ostracism of the unmarried mother and her financial inability to keep her child as part of the whole problem, the child often being sold or given away to unscrupulous women. In 1889, by financial grants, he began what is still known as a system of auxiliary boarding-out to enable a young unmarried mother to provide proper care for her child. A condition of the grant was that the mother was otherwise respectable, and employed, or willing to be employed, in domestic service where the employer was therefore in close contact with the girl. Barnardo's Homes then helped the girl with a sufficiently large grant to enable her to place the baby with a reliable paid

[1] See Norman Wymer, *Father of Nobody's Children*, pp. 71, 73.

foster mother. The grant was paid at monthly intervals direct to the girl's employer, as long as a satisfactory report could be given on the girl and an assurance that proper care was being given to the baby. The employer thus accepted some responsibility for welfare. As a safeguard against a too autocratic employer a Barnardo worker visited from time to time.[1]

The mean common lodging houses of the time, which children and young girls frequented, were notorious for their immorality, and collective centres for thieves and prostitutes, if not actually brothels for children. In 1887, at the time when the public conscience was stirred by the conditions disclosed by the notorious Jack the Ripper murders in Whitechapel where the victims were unprotected girls who frequented these common lodging houses, Barnardo decided to set up two himself, which he licensed under the Common Lodging Houses Act, and opened, one for women and children, and one for children alone, at a cost of a penny a night. These lodging houses attempted to give some protection to the more hardened and mature child and adolescent who refused to enter Barnardo's Children's Homes. As yet there was no legal machinery to provide compulsory care or protection through the courts for this type of boy or girl.

An examination of the work of Dr. Barnardo shows it to be that of an individualist and an inspired autocrat.[2] The other great rescue societies of the nineteenth century, the National Children's Home, the Waifs and Strays Society and the Crusade of Rescue are, in contrast, works of a community each of which originated with a denominational church.

The beginnings of the National Children's Home were almost contemporary with the foundation of Barnardo's work, the first Home being opened in London in 1869 through the efforts of Thomas Bowman Stephenson, a young Wesleyan

---

[1] 'Some auxiliary schemes of Dr. Barnardo's Homes' by Barbara Bagwell, *Child Care Quarterly*, July, 1956, p. 104.

But legal provision, where effective, was actually more enlightened. The Bastardy Laws Amendment Act 1872 enabled a mother to obtain an order for maintenance of the illegitimate child against the putative father before the child was born, and this support could enable the mother to keep the child rather than foster him. See *post* p. 99.

[2] For the first ten years he worked alone without any committee. A committee was formed as a result of recommendations made in 1877 by a public enquiry after his work had been attacked and vindicated.

minister. Dr. Stephenson came to London in 1868 after six
years of experience of ministry in the industrial districts of
Manchester and Bolton. He became the minister of the
Waterloo Rd. Chapel in the Lambeth slums and here too the
sight of poverty, the pinched faces of the children and their
staring, too bright eyes, made him wretched and moved him to
action. He made contact with two young men, Francis Horner
and Alfred Mager, who were spending their spare time preach-
ing to tramps and thieves in a disreputable district in South
London, and asked them to help him to take a house and provide a home and training for a small number of boys. This they
agreed to do and rented a small house—No. 8 Church St.,
Lambeth—to take twenty boys. The stable at the back of
the house was turned into a dining room and the loft over the
stable became a dormitory. Here the first two boys were
admitted on the 9th July, 1869. Almost immediately afterwards
a public meeting was held in support of the rescue work, at
which twenty-five people were present and six interested friends
agreed to subscribe £20 each to a Foundation Fund.

Like Dr. Barnardo, the founders of the Home sought out their
children at night, sometimes with the help of policemen, from
the shelter of warehouses and casks, in waste land and on the
wharves near London Bridge where, when the police lifted the
tarpaulins and turned on their bull's-eyes, the boys 'swarmed
from their holes like rats from a sewer'.[1] Dr. Stephenson
himself described his work with these wild lads very simply,
'they needed a friend and a home—someone to tell them of
God and to teach them a trade.'[2]

But from the very beginning Dr. Stephenson based the work
of his Homes on certain definite principles. In the forefront was
the religious value of the Home, to him the work was above all
else a mission 'to seek and save' among destitute children. He
had also been much influenced by a description which he had
read of the work of Emmanuel Wichern and his mother at the
Rauhe Haus near Hamburg, in which the workers identified
themselves with the destitute children as a family. His Homes
were intended to conform to the family idea, mixed homes of
boys and girls together with a mother and father in charge.

[1] *Golden Links* by Cecil F. Walpole, Epworth Press, 1950, p. 9.
[2] Quoted in *The Silver Stream*, by Cecil F. Walpole, 1947, pp. 39–40.

In addition vocational training was to be provided for the children to fit them for a livelihood.

In 1871 when he was appointed to the Victoria Park Church in South Hackney he was able to take on new premises where it was possible to build up a system of industrial training, and instruction in printing, carpentry, shoemaking, laundry work and sewing was provided for the boys and girls. After this as branch Homes were opened one by one each tried to become specialised and to deal with a different particular need experienced in the work. An interesting development followed when in the same year a Mr. James Barlow bought and presented to Dr. Stephenson an old house with a hundred acres of land on the moors at Edgworth near Bolton. The conditions were bleak and primitive, but here the boys, experienced, mature and hardened by their London street life, found an expression for their independence and maturity in building a small village home. They cut the stones from the quarries, built new houses and transformed the wild moorland into a farm so that this Home became a self-contained village with accommodation for several hundred children.[1]

Stephenson was enlightened in his approach to the problem of child rescue and care in that he tried to undertake preventive work with the families. The training of Sisters for work in the Homes as a religious vocation has always been a strong feature of the National Children's Homes, and he established mission centres from which he himself, and the members of the Sisterhood, visited the homes of families in the slum areas, in the same spirit of ministry and evangelism which inspired their work for the children.[2]

Meanwhile the problems of poverty and destitution in London and the big cities had been increased by the entry of

---

[1] This form of treatment for the deprived child is no longer appropriate in contemporary England. But it was interesting to see it arise again under similar conditions spontaneously among the rescue work for street arabs of war devastated Europe, culminating in the various children's communities of Gaudiopolis, Civita Vecchia, etc. Such organisation seems to be acceptable to the older adolescent who is delinquent and mature beyond his years and unable to bear authority from someone with less experience of life. The principles of the children's villages, modified, are used to some extent in Approved School work to-day among just this type of boy.

[2] See 1954 Convocation lecture of the National Children's Home by John H. Litten, C.B.E., 'I sat where they sat.'

large numbers of poor immigrants from Ireland where the disastrous failure of the potato harvest in 1845 drove young men and women with their families to look for a better life in a new land across the water. Leaving a homogeneous community in their native island they found in England a much less organised religious society, for the penal laws of the previous centuries had circumscribed the activities of Roman Catholics here and so rendered them apathetic about social reform. Though they were drawn together as a minority group they were divided in interest among themselves, being made up of those who were Roman Catholics by inheritance and had held their faith impoverished and with penalties over the centuries, and those from the educated ranks of society who were converted mainly by the influence of the Oxford movement. To these now a third stream, that of the poor Irish immigrants, was joined, but it was some long time before the three streams coalesced. So in the field of Roman Catholic rescue work in London, after the restoration of the hierarchy, we find the first steps taken as a private charity, rather than a collective responsibility of the Church, when a few gentlemen, in December 1859, opened St. Vincent's Home in Brook Green Lane, Hammersmith.[1] The home was for twenty boys who had to be orphans or destitute or in danger as to their faith or morals. Members of the committee attended the Courts to pick out appropriate boys for admission and they were then nominated by patrons who paid four shillings a week for their keep. It was not until 1876 that the system of patronage was brought to an end. The Home was then formally transferred by the committee to a priest, Father Douglas, whose policy it was to take in those whose need was greatest, and in this way, and through the growing organisation of the Church, he was able by a vigorous campaign in the Roman Catholic press to rouse a sense of personal responsibility in members of his faith. In this way more orphanages were founded in London as well as in the other great cities of Liverpool, Birmingham, Manchester and Leeds, but the work was not integrated;

[1] *These my Little Ones, The Origin, Progress and Development of the Incorporated Society of the Crusade of Rescue and Homes for Destitute Catholic Children.* Edited by the Rev. N. Waugh. Sands & Co. 1911. Some earlier isolated work of various religious orders did exist, see *Catholic Child Care in England* by I. R. Hoskins, Catholic Truth Society, 1956.

it remained subject to parochial or diocesan interests until Cardinal Manning's conflict with Dr. Barnardo in 1889[1] brought the inadequacy and insufficiency of its rescue organisation into prominence. After Manning's death Cardinal Vaughan co-ordinated the charitable work done by Roman Catholics for children of their faith; himself a soldier's son he founded the Crusade of Rescue in 1899 and called his community to arms by rousing words, 'God hath given to every man a commandment concerning his neighbour, and no man can angrily object, when his brother is dying in need, "Am I my brother's keeper?" without branding himself with the mark of the race of Cain.' Five years earlier the aims of the work had been defined 'to provide for homeless and destitute children, to rescue the children of dissolute and degenerate parents, to afford aid to poor parents struggling to keep out of the workhouse by sheltering their children to enable them to work, and to serve children in danger of losing their faith.' In the conditions of the time the receiving of children in order to enable their parents to work was regarded as preventive as well as rescue work and as preserving infant life. By 1899 a more organised Roman Catholic community also saw the society as protective of the children's faith and the Cardinal made a public pledge which recalls Barnardo's policy of the ever-open door, 'that no Catholic children, really destitute or in danger with regard to their faith, and for whom no other provision could be made, would be refused admission to our Homes.'

The Waifs and Strays Society[2] (now known as the Church of England Children's Society) was founded by a group of clerical and lay gentlemen and arose out of the Sunday School experience of two brothers, Edward and Robert de Montjoie Rudolf, of the South Lambeth parish of St. Ann's. There two little boys, who had regularly attended the Sunday School at which the brothers taught, disappeared and were later discovered, destitute and neglected, begging food from the men at a nearby gasworks. It appeared that their father had died, and the widow, who had seven children, refused to enter the workhouse, so relief was withheld and the boys were forced to fend for themselves. When the Rudolf brothers made efforts to find

[1] See *Post*, p. 63.
[2] *The First Forty Years. A Chronicle of the Church of England Waifs and Strays Society, 1881–1920.* S.P.C.K. 1922.

a place for the boys in a Church Home or orphanage they found that in every case payment or election by subscribers was required, and eventually the boys had to be admitted to an undenominational home which accepted them without payment, on grounds of need. Edward Rudolf felt keenly this failure on the part of a national Church, and suggested in a circular letter to a number of clergy a plan he had for setting up a central Church home for the poorest and most neglected children in the Church of England. At a meeting held on the 21st March, 1881, it was decided to proceed with the plans, and later the Archbishop of Canterbury agreed to encourage the work by his patronage. On December 16th, 1881, the first home, No. 8 Stamford Villas, Friern Road, East Dulwich, was rented on a yearly tenancy. The society from the first was interested in work with girls and in providing mixed homes. Among the early letters of the society is one dated June 1881 from an experienced social worker, Marcia Rye, a pioneer of the emigration schemes, advising them to appoint a woman to work amongst girls.

'I want to press upon you very strongly the importance of making the *girls* a first point; I am sure looking after them while young is nationally a matter of vital importance. If we never do meet, remember that is my message to you—a young worker, commencing from where I shall soon have to retire, or, at any rate, go softly. People will tell you the girls cannot be helped, or cannot be found, but this is all nonsense and they need the help a thousandfold more than the boys.'

The first children to be accepted were a mixed group of two boys and three girls. The Society early adopted the practice of boarding-out very young children with foster-parents, and besides opening Homes of its own, placed children in private Church Homes for which payment was made. In November 1882 a woman visitor and correspondent was appointed to be responsible both for the children boarded-out and for those placed in other Church Homes. The children eligible for admission to the Society's care were defined in 1883:—

1. Any child who shall have lost both parents, and also shall have no relatives or friends able to maintain it.
2. Any child whose parent, or surviving parent, shall be physically incapable of supporting the child.

3. Any child whose mother shall be a widow having other young children, and who shall be doing her best to support them upon insufficient means; the action of the Executive to be in co-operation with the Guardians when desirable.

4. Any illegitimate child whose mother shall be striving to retrieve her character, upon the understanding that a contribution be made by the parents towards its maintenance if possible.

5. Any child seriously neglected or ill-treated by its parents or guardians, or subject to immoral influences.

6. Any child whose parents, or surviving parent, shall be undergoing a term of imprisonment, provided it has no other available means of support.

The utmost care to be used in order to avoid encouraging natural guardians in idleness, or evil courses, and every legal step to be taken to compel parents to discharge their responsibilities.'[1]

Although the term 'Waifs and Strays' was originally chosen to make clear the Church's intention to receive the most friendless and destitute children who could not gain admission to the older orphanages, of which so many required payment, it will be seen that the admissions were carefully regulated. And as the Society grew, and branch Homes were opened up and down the country, it was the policy of the society that each Home should become part of the town or village, and the children should not be segregated in any way. Local committees were attached to each branch Home and people nearby were encouraged to take an active interest in the children who attended their parish church and local school.[2] In this integration of the children with the community they were greatly helped by the reality of the parish organisation of the Established Church within which they worked.

All the Rescue societies used emigration fairly extensively and selected boys and girls were sent overseas, mainly to Canada, but some also to Australia, New Zealand and South Africa. There was a large demand for boys to work as helpers on the farms of the new countries and for girls to help with the

[1] *The First Forty Years*, op. cit., p. 22.
[2] *Everybody's Children. The Story of the Church of England Children's Society*, Mildred de M. Rudolf, O.U.P. 1950, p. 11.

domestic work of the farm. The great overseas continents provided an opportunity for pioneering agricultural life denied to adolescents at home by the failure of British farming, and emigration was looked on both as a medium of self expression and initiative for a boy, and a means of separating him entirely from his former bad family surroundings to which, in the mother country, he was very likely to return after leaving the children's Home. Special receiving Homes were set up in the new countries to which the children could go and stay for a short while to become acclimatised and to get to know the agent who would supervise them in their new home.[1] It was, however, a difficult and tricky business and, by the loneliness and isolation, laid the child open to grave abuse. For a time also it was the subject of protests by the Canadian Government because so many unsuitable delinquent children had been included in the emigration schemes.

Experiments in care were wholly the work of the voluntary organisations which were thought to be in a better position than the boards of guardians to administer small specialised homes or village communities. In the first place, the voluntary bodies could choose whom they received and could discriminate about the age and sex of the children they placed in their various type of homes, whereas the poor law had a continual problem in the fluctuating numbers of the children in care and the admissions of children of vagrants, described in the reports as 'ins and outs'. The voluntary bodies also retained the children in care for two or three years longer than the children in pauper schools and could therefore give them more effective industrial training. Their committees too, usually consisted of people who were specially interested in the particular form of care and training given to destitute or delinquent children. This was not generally true of the boards of guardians who were responsible for the whole field of poor law duties and administration, and were not specialists in the problems of the deprived child. And it is, of course, much less open to objection if voluntary bodies experiment with public money they have

---

[1] A fairly comprehensive description of emigration as practised by one of the rescue societies is found in *These My Little Ones*. See also the *Report on the Emigration of Pauper Children to Canada* presented in 1875 by Mr. A. Doyle, local government board inspector.

raised for that purpose, than if statutory bodies attempt to 'risk' money provided from the rates.

The last quarter of the nineteenth century sees the development of legislation for the protection and custody of the deprived child. Some of it arose through a clash between the zeal of Dr. Barnardo and the increasingly organised work of the Crusade of Rescue, in 1889.

Until this time the power of custody of deprived and delinquent children was vested in three acts of parliament, an Act for the care and education of infants convicted of felony passed early in Victoria's reign, in 1840, and apparently little used, the Reformatory Schools (Youthful Offenders Act) 1854 and the recent Poor Law Amendment Act of 1889. The Infant Felons Act of 1840 empowered the Court of Chancery, where an infant was convicted of felony, to assign his care and custody to any person who might be willing to take charge of him under terms and regulations laid down by the Court, the natural father or lawful guardian thereby losing his power of control over the child. The Reformatory Schools (Youthful Offenders) Act gave Reformatory schools powers to detain children in them against the wishes of their parents, the Poor Law Amendment Act gave boards of guardians powers to assume parental rights.[1]

Rescue societies, had, however, no rights of custody over the children and were forced, under threat of a writ of *habeas corpus* to return children to parents, however neglectful, if they wished to have the child back. This, however, Barnardo consistently refused to do, thereby acting illegally, and at the same time openly admitting that, in the absence of any legal care or protection procedure, he abducted children from neglectful parents in order to give them the care and shelter of his Home. The position came to a head when the Crusade of Rescue, now more effectively organised to deal with its own children in need, attempted to reclaim from Barnardo the Roman Catholic children he had admitted in default of an organised denominational arrangement for their care. In March 1889 Barnardo wrote in his magazine *Night and Day* that the Roman Catholic authorities were trying to get him to hand back to disreputable relatives the children of mixed marriages whom he had

---

[1] See page 93 *Post.* But see also p. 102 *Post* for powers conveyed under the Prevention of Cruelty to Children Act 1889.

received. It so happened that six months earlier Barnardo had received into care just such a child, Harry Gossage, whose cruel and drunken mother had sold him for a few shillings to a couple of foreign organ grinders who left him destitute in Folkestone. Brought by a police officer to London Barnardo admitted him, and then, after discovering the mother's whereabouts, wrote to her, seeking and obtaining her consent to the boy's entry. Barnardo then posted his standard form of agreement which, among other things, contained a clause granting him the right to arrange the child's emigration if suitable. These agreements, though formal, were not, however, legally binding on the parent.

Before this form was returned a Canadian gentlemen called on Dr. Barnardo wishing to take back to Canada one of the doctor's boys whom he proposed to educate in his own background. For this reason he made the condition that the boy should have no further contact with relatives and that he should be allowed to take the lad away without disclosing his future home. To these conditions Barnardo rashly agreed and as fate would have it Mr. Norton's choice fell on Harry.

It had apparently never entered Barnardo's calculations that Harry's mother would wish to have him back. While the lad was on the high seas, however, the mother had taken the form of agreement to a priest for help in completion and Barnardo received a letter asking for the lad's immediate transfer to a Roman Catholic Home. As he did not comply the letter was followed by a writ for *habeas corpus*.

The litigation, lasting ten months, which followed eventually led to an agreement between Dr. Barnardo's Homes and the Roman Catholic Homes which persists to-day whereby both organisations agreed to advise each other about applications for admission to their Homes by children of the opposite faith, and to be guided, in the case of mixed marriages, by the religion of the father, or, in case of illegitimacy, the mother. But of greater administrative significance was the disclosure that all the great rescue organisations alike had no authority to protect children in care against even actively cruel parents who wished to reclaim them. The workhouse and the reformatory alone had the legal right of asylum. Accordingly, the House of Lords appointed a standing committee of three judges who eventually drafted a Bill which, known as the Barnardo Bill, received Royal Assent in 1891 as the Custody of Children Act. This Act gave authority for rescue to benevolent institutions and curtailed the responsibilities of neglectful parents. Judges were given power of discretion to reject applications for writs of *habeas corpus* from parents who abandoned, neglected or ill treated children and to deny the issue of a writ to anyone seeking to remove a child from a trustworthy institution or benevolent society. A pattern was set, underlined by the poor law authority to assume parental rights bestowed in Acts of 1889 and 1899[1], by which the neglectful home and the substitute home became exclusive of each other, a pattern which remained dominant in child care until the changing social conditions of the second world war tore it apart.

The pattern of rescue from the environment, rather than rehabilitation within it, was a consequence of the social conditions of the time. Rehabilitation only becomes possible when the standard of social services ensures a level where the family's material environment is adequate for health and subsistence and the services can therefore support and educate within an accepted minimum standard.

This standard had not been reached when the need of the destitute and neglected children grew so great, and those who heard their cry answered it in the only possible way they knew. The great voluntary organisations brought back into the field of degradation and failure that dearness founded on esteem for every human soul which is the heart of charity. In their work for the inarticulate child they made concrete the compassion felt by many men and women who, in new industrial communities, could only express their charity by indiscriminate alms. The sincerity and beauty of this charity is well described in much of the literature of the time,[2] and there are passages where, as often in the diary of Francis Kilvert, the young curate of Clyro, one comes face to face with the thoughts which seemed to motivate men: 'As I was sitting in a confectioner's shop, . . . I saw lingering about the door a

---

[1] And by the Prevention of Cruelty to Children Act of 1889 by which Courts were given power to transfer parental rights of children to other guardians.

[2] Particularly the 'improving' literature for children—see *Ministering Children* by Maria Louisa Charlesworth, Seeley, Jackson and Haliday, 1854.

barefooted child, a little girl, with fair hair tossed and tangled wild, an arch espiègle eager little face and beautiful wild eyes, large and grey, which looked shyly into the shop and at me with a wistful beseeching smile. She wore a poor faded ragged frock and her shapely limbs and tiny delicate beautiful feet were bare and stained with mud and dust. Still she lingered about the place with her sad and wistful smile and her winning beseeching look, half hiding herself shyly behind the door. It was irresistible. Christ seemed to be looking at me through the beautiful wistful imploring eyes of the barefooted hungry child. I took her out a bun, and I shall never forget the quick happy grateful smile which flashed over her face as she took it and began to eat. She said she was very hungry. Poor lamb. I asked her name and she told me, but amidst the roar of the street and the bustle of the crowded pavement I could not catch the accents of the childish voice. Never mind. I shall know some day.'[1]

Yet this help was so often only palliative, for society as a whole is far from being permeated by altruism, nor was its almsgiving always infused by such concepts of charity. The rescue societies canalized the expression of charity, but the change in social philosophy towards those in want and suffering hardship, when it came, was in the nature of a development of democratic rights and was only partly influenced by the philanthropic movement.

---

[1] *Kilvert's Diary*, edited by William Plomer, and published by Jonathan Cape, 1938–40. The entry is for Thursday, 4th June, 1874. Kilvert was on a visit to Bristol at the time.

CHAPTER FIVE

THE POOR LAW CARE OF CHILDREN

THE development of the voluntary child care societies in the nineteenth century, and the experiments in care which they pioneered as a result of their ideologies, profoundly affected the administration of the poor law towards the pauper child. Since the Poor Law Amendment Act of 1834 the policy of the Poor Law Commissioners was one of education of the children to fit them for employment and independence in later life, and they aimed first at separating the children from the adult inmates of the workhouses and improving the quality of the workhouse schools. In their fourth annual report issued in 1838[1] is a description of the parish workhouse children before the formation of the unions in 1834. 'The children, who were for the most part orphans, bastards and deserted children, continued to remain inmates of the workhouse long after the period at which they might have earned their subsistence by their own exertions;[2] and those who obtained situations, or were apprenticed by means of the parish funds, turned out as might be expected of children whose education was utterly neglected or at best confided to the superintendence of a pauper. They rarely remained long with their employer but returned to the workhouse—which, so far from being to them an object of dislike, they regarded as their home, and which they looked forward to as the ultimate asylum of their old age. In this manner the workhouse, instead

---

[1] *P.L.C. Report 1838*, p. 89.

[2] This in spite of the fact that in 1697 a poor relief act (8 and 9 William III c.30) compelled even unwilling masters to receive and provide for parish apprentices from the age of nine to twenty-one. Masters could, however, pay a fine to secure exemption. An examination of the registers of parish apprentices at Leeds shows a rise in the numbers of masters buying exemption from approximately 14% of the total attempts to place in the period 1760 to 1769 to 38% in the period 1800–1808, and may be some indication of their unsatisfactory service.

of diminishing, increased pauperism, by keeping up a constant supply of that class of persons who most frequently, and for the longest period, became its inmates. Pauperism, however, was only one of the evils which resulted from the neglect to provide proper means of instruction for destitute children. Those who have ascertained the early history of persons who in a greater or less degree have offended against the laws, have found that a large proportion have passed their infancy and youth in the workhouse, and can trace the formation of the habits which have led them to the commission of crime to the entire want of moral training in these institutions.'

The poor law therefore tried to cut the problem of pauperism at its root, by ensuring for the children in its care moral and industrial training, if possible separated from the workhouse itself. The first orders and regulations for the management of workhouses, issued under the amended poor law in 1835 by the Poor Law Commissioners, provided for the appointment of a schoolmaster and schoolmistress who were to instruct the boys and girls 'for three of the waking hours at least every day, in reading, writing and the principles of Christian religion, and give them other instruction to train them to habits of usefulness, industry and virtue.'[1] Educational efforts in the workhouses, however, were hampered by the backward state of the national education of the time and by the difficulty of obtaining good teachers and of giving suitable industrial training to the small numbers.[2] An example of the standard is seen at Salisbury, where the schoolmistress could not write and the schoolmaster was a pauper who had found his way into the workhouse through excessive drink, while at Southampton the schoolmaster was a deaf old man completely unable to control his class.[3] The units of administration were too small and local, even under the revised poor law, to attract and pay sufficient people of the calibre required for the right quality of teaching.

The attention of the public and the Government was first drawn to the inadequacy of the workhouse school system in

---

[1] Quoted in W. Chance, *Children under the Poor Law*, Swan Sonnenschein & Co. Ltd., 1897, p. 4.
[2] Numbers ranged from about five upwards and rarely exceeded fifty.
[3] *9th P.L.C. Report, 1843*, p. 137, p. 309.

1837 by a Mr. Hickson and Dr. Kay (afterwards Sir James P. Kay-Shuttleworth) who suggested that the unions should combine to form schools in which a better quality of education could be provided. Dr. Kay, by insisting on the even greater importance of education to the pauper child than to the child of poor parents, broke away from the original principle of less eligibility which was characteristic of poor law administration. The schools, serving a larger district and separated from the workhouse, were to provide a more efficient and economical system of education and attract a better type of teacher.[1] An example had been found in the private establishment of a Mr. Aubin at Norwood which contained a thousand children and which was well known to Dr. Kay and visited later by the Manchester board of guardians. As a result of further enquiries and investigations made by the Poor Law Commissioners[2] legislation was passed in 1844 giving authority for parishes and unions to combine into districts for the setting up of separate or district schools with boards of managers representing the several parishes. In 1846, in order to improve the standard of education of pauper children in the small workhouse schools, Parliament voted £15,000 towards the payment of their teachers' salaries, the continuation of the grant being dependent on their maintaining a standard of efficiency. For the purpose of checking this, separate inspectors of workhouse schools were appointed, under the control of the Committee of Council of Education.[3]

The growing emphasis on education as well as public

[1] In a report by Dr. Kay on the training of pauper children, published in 1839, the aim of the industrial training to be given in these schools was defined. 'The great object to be kept in view in regulating any school for the instruction of the children of the labouring class is the rearing of hardy and intelligent working men, whose character and habits shall afford the largest amount of security to the property and order of the community. . . . In mingling various kinds of industrial instruction with the plan of training pursued in the model school, it is not proposed to prepare the children for some particular trade or art, so as to supersede the necessity for further instruction; it is chiefly intended that the practical lesson, that they are destined to earn their livelihood by the sweat of their brow, shall be inculcated.'

[2] See *Report from the Pr· Law Commissioners on the training of pauper children, 1841.*

[3] Complaints were later made because these inspectors were classical graduates of Oxford and Cambridge. Lady inspectors with experience of scholastic, domestic and industrial training were considered more appropriate for workhouse schools. From 1863 the Poor Law Board controlled its own inspectors of Poor Law Schools.

awareness of the dangers of exploitation in the apprenticeship system led to a revision in 1847 of the regulations governing the binding of pauper apprentices. By these regulations a child under the age of nine (other than a deaf and dumb child) who could not read and write his own name, was forbidden to be apprenticed by the guardians. In future apprentices were not to be bound for more than eight years and there were restrictions on the qualifications of people to whom a child might be bound, and on the payment of premiums.[1] The guardians now turned their attention from an emphasis on apprenticeship to devising their own industrial training and education for the children, and this was a major change in their expressed policy over the last hundred years. Meanwhile, by 1849, six districts had been formed in the south and midlands for the setting up of separate schools.[2] At first the idea of these residential district schools was favoured, for they had obvious advantages; they were built away from the workhouses and in country surroundings and the separation of the children from the adult paupers reduced the chance of undesirable associates and removed them from the stigma of the workhouse. The country air and fresh, natural surroundings did much to benefit the children, often puny and delicate and mentally dull. The large size of the schools also made it possible to improve the educational standard and so attract a better type of teacher.

In 1861 the Royal Commission on Education reported very unfavourably on the schools in the workhouses, and attempted

[1]'No child shall be so bound to a person who is not a housekeeper, or assessed to the poor rate in his own name;

'or who is a journeyman, or a person not carrying on trade or business on his own account;

'or who is under the age of twenty-one;

'or who is a married woman;

'No premium, other than clothing, for the apprentice shall be given upon the binding of any person above the age of sixteen years, unless such person be maimed, deformed, or suffering from some permanent bodily infirmity, such as may render him unfit for certain trades or sorts of work

'Where any premium is given, it shall in part consist of clothes supplied to the apprentice at the commencement of the binding, and in part of money, one moiety whereof shall be paid to the master at the binding, and the residue at the termination of the first year of the binding.'

See Articles 52–74 of the General Consolidated Order of 24th July, 1847.

[2] In the areas of south metropolitan, central London, north Surrey, Farnham and Hartley Wintney, Reading and Wollingham, south east Shropshire.

to encourage the establishment of district schools, with their greater educational advantages, by recommending they should be made compulsory. The report emphasised that the cure and prevention of pauperism lay in education, and in ending the children's association with the workhouse, which they grew up regarding as their home. In fact, however, district schools were not largely adopted; from 1870 onwards the alternative systems of boarding-out and cottage homes began to gain favour, and their large size, however effective for educational purposes, proved in the end to be their downfall. Several of them held more than a thousand children[1] with nothing in common but their pauperism, and the inability of such institutions to cope with the needs of parentless children was soon apparent. The new constructive educational policy of the poor law as it was expressed in the district schools was found to be ineffective both in developing intelligence and in forming character, while in 1872 serious outbreaks of ophthalmia occurred among the children in several of the London schools. In fact, ophthalmia and skin eruptions began to distinguish the institutionalised child. The cost was found to be higher in the district schools than in any other form of provision for the children, and it was only on the outskirts of the large towns such as London, Manchester, Liverpool and Leeds, that they were used as an expedient method of care.[2] The trend towards widespread adoption of district schools was halted incidentally by the compulsory Education Act of 1870. This Act, by making education of the poor a national duty, thereby made it possible for guardians to provide alternative forms of care under which the children could be sent out to schools in the general community. And education by itself was seen to be no answer to pauperism and the delinquency which so often accompanied it. 'We all know from unhappy experience' said W. E. Forster, the prime mover in the 1870 Act, 'that knowledge is not virtue, much less is elementary

---

[1] Among the metropolitan schools, for example, the four establishments at Sutton, Hanwell, Anesley and Ashford, accommodated respectively 1,543, 1,148, 900 and 790 children and covered areas of 92, 136, 60 and 69 acres. See *Report of the Mundella Committee on Poor Law Schools, 1896*, p. 7.

[2] The majority of the large barrack homes, which some of the rescue societies inherit, date from their pioneering attempt to build on the educational principle before the district schools finally became discredited.

education, and that education alone does not give the
power of resisting temptation.' Something more than the
principle of education was needed in the care of pauper
children.

The Local Government Board (which from 1871 onward
controlled the Poor Law) was so concerned about the difficulty
of attempting to train, educate and care for the pauper children
so that they grew up into normal and useful citizens that in
1873 it asked Mrs. Nassau Senior,[1] later one of its women
inspectors, to make a report to them with particular reference
to the education and training of poor law girls. Her conclusion sounded the death knell of the large institutional traditions and began a gradual move away from the administratively convenient device of the barrack home to the family
system we have to-day. Her conclusions were: 'That the
massing of girls together in large numbers was bad and must
issue in failure: that their physical condition when in the
schools and their moral condition on leaving them was dis-
appointing and unsatisfactory; and that, while the scholastic
training of both boys and girls in the Metropolitan pauper
schools was first rate, on all other points the system of education did not answer in the case of girls, even at the very best
separate and district schools, and that many of them were, in
general intelligence, below children of the same class educated
at home.'[2]

Mrs. Nassau Senior had herself made certain recommendations which attempted to classify the different needs of the
children and meet them; these were: an extension of boarding
out, but only for orphan children, the separate education of
deserted children and casual children in schools of a more
homelike character on the Mettrai system, each family cottage
containing not more than twenty to thirty children of all ages,
separate training for permanent and casual inmates, and a

[1] The daughter-in-law of William Nassau Senior, Oxford Professor of Economics,
who was one of the authors of the 1832 report on the reform of the poor law and
one of the original poor law commissioners. Mrs. Nassau Senior was appointed
inspector of workhouses and pauper schools in 1874 and was the first woman to
hold such a position. An account of her work is given in *The Spectator* of the 31st
March, and 7th April, 1877, following her death.

[2] *Report on the Education of Girls in Pauper Schools, 1.1.1874*, quoted in *Chance*, op.
cit., p. 35, and in *Report of the Royal Commission on the Poor Law and Relief of Distress,
1909*, Part IV, c. 8, p. 235.

system of after care for girls when they were placed out in the world.[1]

It was in this climate of opinion that the guardians, while not abandoning the district schools for another twenty years, turned their attention to the alternative systems of boarding-out and cottage homes.

The idea of cottage homes, seen at first as smaller schools on the family system with agricultural training, based on the continental experiments at Hamburg and Mettrai, had been advocated for the poor law in a paper submitted by Mr. Joseph Fletcher in 1851 to the Statistical Society of London— 'Statistics of the Farm School System of the Continent, and of its applicability to the Preventive and Reformatory Education of Paupers and Criminal Children in England.' He thought that England could learn from the continental experiments the value of moral and industrial education based on family life and farm training, which could be provided at a fraction of the cost required to keep the children in workhouses with such unsatisfactory results. 'Labour', he said, 'must be the staple of the poor man's training. To live is the first necessity ... And in all the best continental institutions for these classes, therefore, labour on the land and industry in the workshop is the first desideratum, religious and moral training on example realised in daily life the next, and intellectual culture ... used rather as a relief from other occupations than as the greatest feature of a pauper school.'

After Mrs. Nassau Senior's report the introduction of the cottage home system into the poor law appears to have been due to the suggestion of a government inspector, Mr. Andrew Doyle, who, on the 9th April, 1877, wrote a letter to the Swansea board of guardians suggesting that the Swansea Union should join with the two neighbouring unions of Neath and Bridgend to provide for their children by a district school established on the cottage home principle. In the end each Union built a separate establishment but in the Report of the Local Government Board for 1877–78 there is approval for

[1] This led in 1876 to the foundation of a voluntary association of ladies who looked after the girls in London, known as the Metropolitan Association for Befriending Young Servants, which undertook for the poor law the after-care of girls in service. An organisation with similar aims for boys was founded in 1893.

plans for three more unions (West Derby, West Ham and Bolton) to build district schools on cottage home lines. The establishments were large communities, broken down into groups of children in cottages; for example Bolton, 300 children in groups of 30, Swansea, 80 children in groups of 20, Neath, 44 children in groups of 20 and 12, Bridgend and Cowbridge, which joined together, 60 children in groups of 10. It is interesting to compare the family groups with the size of the average Victorian family, which at this time consisted of 5 or 6 children.

As the system seemed likely to develop the Local Government Board now turned its attention to the pioneer experiments of the voluntary organisations into the cottage home and family group system and arranged an investigation into the work of six voluntary homes all based more or less strictly on the family system and aiming 'to bring up destitute or criminal children in habits of religion and virtue.'[1] The investigators described in detail the architectural lay out of the grouped cottage homes, their staffing, organisation and finance. In Princess Mary's Village Home at Addlestone 'The unit adopted for the family is ten. Each little household is complete in itself, with its general living room, its dormitory or dormitories, its kitchen, larder and suitable out offices. Each is ruled over by a housemother, assisted by one of the elder girls ; and all the ordinary household duties naturally involved in the charge of a family of ten children are discharged by them. Every child as it advances in age, and becomes fitted for the work, takes a part in the management of the household, and in the care and training of the younger children. . . .

'The whole system being based on the family group, the housemothers are the pivot on which it turns. In the selection

---

[1] *Education of Children (Poor)* Return to an Order of the Honourable the House of Commons, dated 15th July, 1878, for 'copies of Report of F. J. Mouat, Esq., M.D. Local Govt. Board Inspector and Captain J. D. Bowley, R.E., on the Home and Cottage System of Training and educating the Children of the Poor and of the reports of H. G. Bowyer, Esq., and J. R. Moseley, Esq., Inspectors of Workhouse Schools, upon the education of pauper children in their respective districts.' The voluntary organisations were (1) Princess Mary's Village Home, Addlestone, (2) The Home for Little Boys, Farningham, Kent, (3) Dr. Barnardo's Village Home for Girls, Ilford, (4) Stockwell Orphanage, (5) The Children's Home, Bonner Rd., Victoria Park.

of these important officers, Mrs. Meredith [the founder] as a rule, prefers widows, with or without children as best calculated to gain the hearts of the children, and to represent the nearest approach to the natural mother. The salaries are small (£6–£12 per annum) but the advantages of healthy habitations, together with the privilege which the mothers possess of having a child of their own in the school free of expense are sufficient to secure an ample supply of candidates for the vacancies that from time to time occur.'

The basis of the whole system of the Farningham Home for little boys 'is to make it as much as possible a home and to introduce as much of family life as can be attained by means of paid agents. . . . As the name implies, so is the institution, in fact, a home; it is in truth, a series of homes; like any pretty country village, the home may be taken . . . for a picturesque group of detached villas with its village church, and other buildings, indicative of active life. . . . In the home are "father and mother"; for at the head of each of the ten families of thirty boys, into which the institution is divided, are a Christian man and his wife. . . . The "housefather" is also an industrial trainer, and gives instruction in one of the trades' (i.e. bread-making, printing, shoe-making, tailoring, gardening, painting and glazing, engineers' work, carpentering and farmyard work).

Of the Children's Home, Bonner Road, it was said that 'it was resolved to begin upon the home principle, originated and exemplified by Dr. Wichern at the Rauhe Haus. Its peculiarity is this, that instead of gathering many hundreds of children into a huge institution, half barrack and half workhouse, it divides them into "families", each family living in a separate house, maintaining its own intimate special relations and interests, and being connected with the other families by the common school, the common workshop, and the common superintendence.'

In making their report on these examples of villages of cottage homes Dr. Mouat and Captain Bowley recalled the earlier findings of the late Sir James Kay-Shuttleworth who believed that the degraded condition of pauper children made it imperative that they should receive special care in education and training to correct defects which were considered in-

separable from their birth and upbringing. They thus believed
that a corrective environment must be provided through
vocational education which should concentrate on physical
improvement, on moral instruction and on industrial training
to fit them to become independent by their own labour. Formal
education was to be in harmony with their future position in
life, and to give them no visions of dreaming spires. This
philosophy was really a return to the early Elizabethan system
of providing for destitute children, but with something more.
The education and training were thought to be best fulfilled
through the cottage home or farm school system where the
family unit approximates within economic limitations to the
natural family, and for this the investigators recommend a
family size of 12 to 20 children, boys and girls being brought up
together until the boys reached the age of ten. A great
advantage of the system was the possibility of appointing
married staff with children of their own of both sexes. Formal
education was to be carried out in a mixed central establishment corresponding to an ordinary village school; industrial
training was to be as varied and comprehensive as possible
and be not only vocational 'but also to fit both boys and girls
to become healthy heads of families, and the progenitors of
children free from the hereditary traits now common to their
class.'

One can see at once the tremendous appeal of the cottage
home system, after the long search for an effective means of
care. The new system spread and was adopted by boards of
guardians as a great improvement both on the large district
school and on the old workhouse where the children 'stood
about like moulting crows.' The family life with its more
individual attention to character and health, industrial training and greater freedom and variety of life within the village
community was, at best, still artificial, but brought, perhaps
for the first time, brightness and expectation of love into the
poor law establishments for children. In time, however, the
system developed disadvantages, perhaps as a result of a too
enthusiastic adoption. The villages became too self-contained,
the cottages, in the zeal of their administrators too frequently
became villas, and the community, composed of children of
one class and their 'caretakers', out of touch with the outer

world and unable to learn by joining in the experiences of other people.[1]

The isolated and scattered Home system therefore developed as an improvement on the idea of the village communities, and was an experiment of the Sheffield board of guardians.[2]. They, by 1896 had set up nine scattered homes, ordinary working class houses indistinguishable from other houses in the different districts in which they were placed. The homes took mixed families with babies in the same home, and the children attended the local board school with children from normal families. An account of the beginning of the experiment is given by Mr. J. Wycliffe Wilson, the Chairman of the Sheffield Board of Guardians: 'A great many years ago we went very carefully into the question of the association of the children with the adult paupers. We came to the conclusion that it was most important that they should be removed—that was in 1883— and we made some inquiries into the different systems that existed. We visited the Swinton (Manchester) Barrack Schools, the Marston Green Cottage Homes, and we went to Leeds to see the boarding-out as it was carried out there, and I think we unanimously came to the conclusion that it was desirable that the children should be removed and our wish was at that time to introduce the double system of boarding-out and a cottage homes village. We had not then thought of this plan of isolated homes. Later on we decided to adopt boarding-out, both within the union and without, and we put a number of orphan children out. We came to the conclusion at that time that no system that was in existence was exactly what we wanted, that the boarding-out was not universally applicable—that though it was an excellent system where good homes could be obtained, and where it was applicable, namely, to orphans and deserted, yet that, we thought, it would not be likely to be successful with 'ins and outs', and we began to think whether anything else could be done. Well, then we saw the disadvantages, or some disadvantages, of the cottage homes village, and we said to ourselves, 'Can we not obtain a system which would be a combination of the two, which will have a good many of the best features of boarding-out in family life, mixing with the

---

[1] *Report of the Mundella Committee on Poor Law Schools 1896*, p. 104, c. 8027.
[2] Ibid, p. 128.

outside population, and yet where we shall be able to select our own mothers and our own localities, and where we shall be able to deal with children of all sorts?' And this idea of isolated homes as a means of meeting the two difficulties appeared to us the best. But we were in this position, that we had built very good schools; we had no immediate use for them, and when we made application to the Local Government Board to allow us to carry out this scheme they said 'No, you have got good schools; you must not go trying some new experiments and wasting the money that has been spent on these schools.' Therefore the matter stood over until recently, three years ago, when we were getting so full in the workhouse that we saw we might advantageously use the old school buildings. We then made a fresh application. A deputation of us came up and saw Sir Walter Foster, and permission was given to us to carry out our scheme.'

The Sheffield Board of Guardians also set up a 'headquarters' or receiving-house into which, instead of the workhouse, all the children were received on admission and from which they were drafted into the scattered homes. It was quite possible to meet the child's religious needs by providing some of the scattered homes for Roman Catholic and some for Protestant children and to situate them within ready distance of their denominational schools. It was claimed by the originators of the experiment that the system was 'the most complete and efficient system in existence for dealing with the children of paupers . . . is the nearest approach to family life, and in no other system is the "workhouse taint" so completely removed.'[1] It proved a precedent of high promise for other authorities in the field of child care.

An interesting development at this time was the gradual blending of the voluntary and statutory services, the guardians were beginning to use some of the voluntary homes for the reception of pauper children. This arrangement became legalised in 1862 when an Act of Parliament[2] was passed by which poor law children could be sent to voluntary institutions

[1] Ibid., p. 129.
[2] 25 and 26 Vict. c.43, Poor Law Certified Schools Act. See Florence Davenport Hill, *Children of the State*, 1889, Macmillan & Co., p. 10 ff. and *Chance*, op. cit., p. 237 ff.

certified by the Poor Law Board. Payment was made by the guardians to the managers of the home at a maximum rate laid down by the board. Certification of the home implied inspection by the central department. Many small homes were made use of in this way, sometimes denominational in character, sometimes serving the special needs of handicapped children or of boys and girls requiring treatment because of physical, mental or moral disabilities, or needing further training before they could go out to earn their own living in the world. By this means the voluntary homes were used to cater for the special needs of individual children and to provide a training alternative to the old apprenticeship system.

The last thirty years of the nineteenth century also saw the revival of boarding-out, which, with the scattered home system, was not only an attempt again to accept and bring up the children within the community, instead of within specialised institutions, but an acknowledgement by the community at large of a collective responsibility for the children of the state. Boarding-out also was linked in importance with the provision of education and one of the arguments which at first discouraged the Local Government Board from giving its approval was the difficulty of ensuring an interest in education among the sort of people thought most likely and suitable to offer homes for the children.

The system was revived first within the unions and in rural areas, in Warminster Union, for example about 1849, in Sandbach about 1852[1] and in Ringwood about 1857[2] and was influenced by the fact that existing poor law institutional methods of care were proving so unsatisfactory for girls. In 1861 Mrs. Archer, the wife of an ex-officio guardian who was for many years chairman of the Highworth and Swindon board, published a pamphlet enlisting the interest of other women in the pauper child.[3] She proposed that in each union as many women as were able should form themselves into a Society for the supervision of orphan girls. 'It is not', she said, 'that the little girls in the workhouses are not fed and clothed properly, or that they have not a proper amount of school teaching, about which

---

[1] See Appendix IV, p. 222.
[2] *Chance*, op. cit., p. 28. Florence Davenport-Hill, op. cit., p. 175.
[3] *A Scheme of Befriending Orphan Pauper Girls*, Hannah Archer, Longmans, 1861.

I am now raising a question; but I would wish it to be understood that under the workhouse system of bringing them up their minds are contracted and their affections stifled to such a degree that they are unfitted for being placed out in those situations of life where they would be most likely to make a favourable impression, and gain the goodwill of respectable employers. To remedy this evil I would propose that we should use our influence with Guardians to get all such children placed with trustworthy cottagers under whose care they may have the same advantages as other children, and the opportunity of gaining a proper knowledge of life before being thrown on their own resources.' Attendance at a good elementary school was made part of the scheme. Mrs. Archer in the same year obtained permission in her own union to try out the scheme, the Guardians granting two shillings a week for board and lodging, and ten and sixpence a quarter for clothing. These sums did not cover all expenses but Mrs. Archer hoped some of the cost would be met by gifts, the combination of state aid and voluntary help was an important feature of her plan.

In Scotland the system of boarding children in an area outside the union having responsibility for the child was almost universal; children from the densely populated cities were boarded out in rural districts with the small occupiers and crofters where there was more chance of employment, and also, even in country districts, a well established system of education.[1] Knowledge of the effectiveness of the Scottish system spread to England and in 1868 for the first time we hear of Boards of Guardians applying for leave to board certain classes of pauper children outside their own areas. In 1869, the Poor Law Board, which had been doubtful of the expediency of boarding-out, agreed to a fair trial of the system and directed poor law inspectors to report on how far boarding-out prevailed in their various districts. At the same time they requested a Mr. J. J. Henley, inspector for the Poor Law Board, to investigate and report on the Scottish system by which children were boarded-out in the areas of other unions. Their cautious attitude

[1] The respect given to education in Scotland is well illustrated by the story of the English visitor to the Highlands who, after surveying the barren, mountainous country, turned to the shepherd at his side and asked 'In God's name what does this country produce?' The shepherd first removed his cap and then replied, 'Sir, in God's name it produces educated men.'

was expressed in a letter of that year sent to the Evesham Board of Guardians in which they said they had been against the system because of the difficulty of exercising control and supervision over children removed from the workhouse, and because of the responsibility imposed on the guardians, and the danger of placing children in charge of those 'whose main object in taking the children would be to make a profit out of the sums allowed for their maintenance.'[1] Another strong objection raised was the difficulty of ensuring regular education for the children. The inquiry into the system in England and Wales showed that only 21 Unions practised boarding-out within their areas and that 347 children were boarded-out in this way, under the control of the guardians and supervised by the relieving officer.

The position in Scotland was very different for here the many small crofters with their bit of land and cattle and poultry were able and ready to provide a home and good food to children from the industrial cities in return for the boarding-out allowance. Mr. Henley quotes in his report an account of children boarded-out in Arran in 1862. 'Throughout the island there are a number of crofters or small farmers paying from £5 to £25 rent and upwards, having one or more horses, cows, sheep, etc. The houses on these small farms are on the whole good of their kind, and their sleeping accommodation is generally sufficient to enable the tenants to take two or three children as boarders without inconvenience. In the houses of these crofters or small farmers there is usually a roughness, as it is called, that is a plentiful supply of oatmeal, barley meal, butter, potatoes, poultry and other wholesome provisions. The addition of two or three children makes no very material or perceptible difference in the family consumption of food, and their board, paid regularly in cash, is of considerable importance to the crofter in helping him to pay his rent.

*　　*　　*

'The last family visited is a fair specimen of the rest. The house consisted of the byre, the kitchen, with two beds, and the inner room with two beds. The rent of the croft was £5; there were a horse, three cows, poultry, etc. There was ample

---

[1] Quoted in *Chance*, op. cit. p. 28.

show of provisions in the house of all kinds, sacks of meal, oat-meal, peasemeal, bread, eggs, butter, potatoes and hams hanging in the kitchen. The beds and general furniture good and substantial of their kind. In short, there was all the appearance of a substantial and well-stored house.'

There were from time to time cases of neglected and ill-treated foster children and not all the material accommodation was so good. In Western Scotland Mr. Henley himself came upon a foster home where a young girl slept in the dark, flagged kitchen among the herring tubs, potatoes and hogwash. His report stated that the selection of foster mothers was the key-stone of the whole edifice, and that, if introduced in England, a system of boarding-out would not be successful unless there were careful selection of foster-mothers, liberal payments, and supervision by paid officers. Not all his recommendations were followed. In November 1870, however, the Poor Law Board issued an Order[1] sanctioning the boarding-out of children beyond the boundaries of their own unions, under the care of certified committees of voluntary workers. Within a year thirty of these certified committees had been formed to obtain homes and place and visit children sent to them by guardians into whose care they had been received. Boarding-out was confined to certain groups of children, namely to orphans or illegitimate children deserted by their mothers, legitimate children deserted by both parents or by one parent, the other parent being dead or under sentence of penal servitude, or suffering permanently from mental disease, or out of England. The explanatory letter accompanying the Order said that this was done as 'it is most important on all grounds to avoid severing or weakening in any way the ties of the family.' Boarding-out was therefore regarded as making a complete break with the natural family, and it is clear that parental contact was regarded as something which would have interfered with the success of the arrangement. The Order limited the weekly sum payable for the child's maintenance to four shillings. Payments for clothing, school money and medical attention were left to the discretion of the individual boards of guardians. The greatest importance was attached to securing

[1] See Appendix V. Orders and Regulations of the Poor Law Board for the Boarding Out of Pauper Children, p. 224.

proper school arrangements for the children and regular school reports were required which would also act as a guarantee against ill-treatment going undiscovered. The foster home had to be within a mile and half of a school, and within five miles of the residence of some member of the boarding-out committee, and the child had to be visited every six weeks by a member of the committee who must then report in writing on his condition. No child under two could be boarded-out and a certificate of his good health must be provided before he was placed. He could not be boarded-out with foster parents of a different religious creed. Instructions about over-crowding and accommodation of children in the foster home were also contained in the explanatory letter issued with the orders. Six main recommendations were made :—

'1. That children should not, save in special cases, be boarded-out with relations or with persons in receipt of relief out of the poor rates.

2. That children should not be boarded-out in any home where the father is employed in night-work; and that in every case the foster-parents should be by preference persons engaged in out-door, not in sedentary, labours.

3. That in choosing the home special attention should be paid to decent accommodation and the proper separation of the sexes in the sleeping rooms. Children over seven years of age should never be allowed to sleep in the same room with married couples.

4. That no child should be boarded out in a house where sleeping accommodation is afforded to an adult lodger.

5. That particular attention should in all cases be paid to the schoolmaster's quarterly report; and if after two warnings to the foster-parents the report continued unfavourable, the child should be instantly withdrawn, and either transferred to another home or sent back to the union from which it came.

6. That great care should always be given to providing the children with good ordinary clothing. No child should ever be sent by the guardians to be boarded out of their union or parish without a suitable outfit, for the repair and renewal of which a quarterly allowance, not exceeding 10s., should be made to the foster-parents by the guardians. Anything resembling a "workhouse uniform" should be most carefully avoided.'

These orders and recommendations were issued only to unions and parishes in large, populous towns to enable them to carry out a system of boarding-out in country areas where foster parents were more plentiful and conditions better for the children.[1] Since the choice of home and placing and inspection of the children were in the hands of lay committee members the fairly tight regulations seem designed to minimise the difficulties from the administrative point of view. At the same time the early boarding-out was based on a policy of utilising and canalising maternal sympathy, and of enabling the poor to co-operate in a work of charity rather than to be the recipients of it. It was, therefore, though perhaps unconsciously, linked with the democratic growth of the self-help movements which began to gain strength about this time. At its best it provided the most satisfactory form of child care the poor law could devise. How natural and happy this could be is well illustrated by a description of a foster child told simply in the words of his foster mother.

'Little Dicky was a queer little chap when he first came, with sore eyes and so rickety and sickly he couldn't walk no distance, and he was so funny too in his way, running in and telling all the neighbours what we'd got for dinner, and shouting out when my husband came home that *he'd* got a father now. Anyone could see he hadn't been brought up like other children, but he came all right in a year or so.'[2]

Boarding-out within the union, which was not so popular, was brought under regulation in 1877. In 1885 the Local Government Board appointed an Inspector, Miss Mason, whose duties were to visit all the children boarded-out in unions other than their own, and to inspect the work of the boarding-out committees, helping them with advice about the placing and supervision of children. In May 1889 two revised boarding-out orders were issued to replace the regulation of 1870 and 1877 and which now applied to all unions and separate parishes in England and Wales; boarding-out committees could now be set up for the boarding-out of children within the union, and

[1] It is possible that the widespread adoption of the ugly term 'boarding-out' in place of the more homely 'fostering', arose historically from the emphasis on the revival of fostering outside the unions at this time. 'Boarding-out' within the union was referred to at first as 'out relief', later as 'boarding of children in unions'.

[2] Quoted in Florence Davenport-Hill, op. cit., p. 193.

every committee had to consist of not less than three persons of whom at least one must be a woman. This was regarded as an improvement on previous arrangements within the unions where supervision was undertaken by the poor law officers who were men, and who continued the poor law association or 'stigma' in the foster home placing; the supervision by members of a voluntary committee was thought preferable in ending this association, and giving the child the opportunity of meeting someone who could befriend him in a less official way, while the girls particularly benefited by women visitors.

The Committees were required to appoint one of their members to act as secretary and their joint responsibility for the welfare of children was emphasized in a circular letter addressed to them by the Board. 'The Board desire that the members of a boarding-out committee should bear in mind that they are jointly responsible for all children entrusted to the care of the committee, and that the visitation of each child should not be entirely left in the hands of an individual member of the committee. The Board have reason to believe that in some instances persons have consented to become members of committees under a misapprehension as to the responsibility they would thereby incur.'[1]

The advantages of the boarding-out system to the children were well described in evidence given before the departmental committee appointed in 1894 by the Local Government Board to inquire into the existing methods of care for poor law children.[2]

'One advantage to the child of boarding out is that it provides home training and allows development of personal affections. Of course, the home training is what has made an English working class as good as they are. Home training involves a great many things which perhaps men know less of than women; it is the small details of every day home life that bring out the character of a child, and that, as it grows up, enable it, though unconsciously, to develop self-dependence,

[1] Appendix A to *The Nineteenth Annual Report of the Local Government Board*, p. 35.
[2] *Report of the Departmental Committee appointed by the Local Government Board to inquire into the existing systems for the maintenance and education of children under the charge of managers of district schools and boards of guardians in the metropolis and to advise as to any changes that may be desirable*. C. 8027, referred to as the Report of the Mundella Committee on Poor Law Schools. 1896.

resourcefulness, thriftiness; it learns by the example of its elders. This is a perfectly unconscious influence, and no amount of teaching by direct information could give a child that particular class of experience which it gets in the every day home life—the rubs and frictions that come from brothers and sisters and elders and youngers; the self-denial that it sees its parents going through when times are bad, the happiness when times are better; the need for forethought; the dependence for success on industrious habits; the value of money and clothes— from all these the boarded-out child learns and realises what the life that is coming to it will be. Then there is another thing; home life draws out the personal affections, and I think it is one of the most terrible things in workhouses or in very large schools, that a child who can elsewhere be trained, up to a certain age, through its affections, has that particular item in its human character perfectly undeveloped, and I believe that is the reason that so many of them in after life fail. I am not speaking against the officers of the schools. I think they do good work as far as they can, but it is a sheer impossibility that they can do what can only be done in the ordinary every day home.

'Then another point is that they are educated in a family of mixed ages and both sexes, which is most important. Of course it is impossible in a large school, or a large workhouse, to allow the boys and girls to mix together, and they never see each other from one year's end to another. This is a serious drawback in after life, especially with girls ; they have not been accustomed to receive the respect which a boy ought to give to a girl in his own cottage home, they do not know how to treat boys, they have never seen them; consequently they do not know how to treat young men, nor do the young men know how to treat the girls when they meet them'.[1]

The success of the system was believed to depend on an efficient regular inspection to ensure high standards by the boarding-out committee whose duty it was to place and super-vise the pauper children from other areas.[2] In 1896 there were 157 of these boarding-out committees in England and Wales,

---

[1] Evidence of Miss Brodie Hall quoted in *Report of the Mundella Committee on Poor Law Schools*, op. cit., p. 91. 'Minutes of evidence' p. 11, 344.
[2] ibid., p. 96, para. 395.

caring for 1,802 children of whom 968 were in the care of the metropolitan board of guardians.[1]

Among the advantages of the committees, was the use of women members, instead of men relieving officers, to make regular contact with the children, and to advise the foster-parent, valuable because in the condition of the time, supervision of the children was thought to be best ensured by means of surprise visits and periodical 'check ups', the child being partially undressed and examined for lice, bruises, skin diseases, and this women could do without any objection. Writing in 1889 Miss Florence Davenport-Hill commented on the extreme difficulty of laying down a common standard of requirements for foster homes in the widely different parts of the country with their varying local conditions. The most one could do was to try to ensure that the boarded-out child should be brought up as well as, and no better than, the most respectable poor in the locality in which he was placed[2], and she commented on the need to avoid over inspection. 'Equally with the inspector the committee must avoid, individually and collectively, becoming a court of appeal against parental authority in the foster-home, or by word or deed impairing the filial respect of the child. If the parents accept the labour and responsibility of the relationship, they must also be endowed with its rights and powers; and if not worthy of the trust, the child must be removed from their keeping. Supervision must, then, be as quiet and unobtrusive as possible, though not therefore the less vigilant. Experience shows that over-inspection and fuss are apt to excite rebellious feelings in the child, leading to disobedience and failure of due deference to the foster-parents. To aid it to forget its alien birth and to merge it in the foster family is a cardinal principle in Boarding-Out[3]'. Miss Mason gives an idea of the quality of supervision considered necessary and at the same time, the need to interpret findings in the light of the standard of child care among the poor at the time.

'Persons living on the spot and seeing the children every day may yet have no idea of the treatment if they do not, by

[1] ibid., p. 98.
[2] F. Davenport-Hill, op. cit.   p. 205.
[3] ibid., p. 2.

partly undressing them from time to time, and by surprise visits, ascertain their bodily condition. I do not myself completely undress each child as does the lady who inspects for Dr. Barnardo, although I think her precautions are on the safe side, because dirt and neglect do not so much show where the body is well protected by the clothing. The feet are a better guide than anything else to the treatment of the child, for it is in the hollows of the ankles that strata of dirt accumulate most visibly, and having now seen some thousands of children's feet, I am generally able, by taking off one stocking, to tell the date of the last bath to a week, if it is only weeks since. There is very little visible difference between dirt of some month's and a year's standing. The human skin cannot retain strata of more than a certain thickness. The removal of a stocking also often reveals broken chilblains, blisters, and sores, nails uncut and broken below the quick, or growing into the foot. The neck, shoulders, and upper part of the arms also show dirt, bites and marks of vermin, skin complaints and blows. Beating is generally begun on the upper parts of the arms. I sometimes find bruises there, evidently made by sticks, and where this is the case I undress the child as much further as necessary. I have thus now and then found a child covered with bruises.

'An examination underneath also shows whether the underclothing is sufficient, and the linen and stockings clean and in good repair. All tidy labouring people change and mend their children's linen weekly, but many of them disregard the washing of their bodies after they are quite young. Taking this into consideration, if I find a child clean I always report the fact to the foster parent's credit, whereas I do not report dirt of months' standing if the case is otherwise satisfactory, and there is no other trace of neglect and ill-treatment, and if I can get the matter set straight by pointing it out to the committee. Whenever my reports are silent on this point, it is not because I have not investigated and do not know the facts, or that I do not consider them of importance, but because I draw a distinction between the dirt of mere ignorant custom and that of wilful neglect. It cannot be said therefore that I am unduly severe towards the foster parents, or that I do not make allowances for the habits of a labouring people.

'The choice of a home is no doubt a matter of the highest importance. An improper selection is inexcusable, as showing either a want of care or of judgement. But selection is not the only thing necessary; supervision should come afterwards, and it is neither safe nor right to trust to even the best selected foster parents. As I have pointed out, continual or daily visiting may reveal nothing of the true condition of things. The Denmead Committee were living unsuspectingly among a number of children covered with itch and body lice, seeing them daily at the school, and one of the Committee was walking hand in hand with one of the worst cases on the day before my visit and its revelations. There may be even too much supervision and visiting: continual interference in detail only tends to shift the responsibility from the foster parents who have the actual care of the children to the committee, whose duty it is to see and ascertain that the foster parents are treating them properly. A thorough examination from time to time of the children's bodily condition is the only way to know this for certain. Quality, not quantity, is to be desired in supervision.'[1]

The efficiency of committee members to maintain the necessary standards of the boarding-out system was soon called in question. Miss Mason's visits and reports provided guidance, but too often the committees lost interest and dwindled in size or individual members placed children with villagers whom they knew, as a form of patronage. Money allowances were made at an adequate level for the time and the children placed among the respectable poor, so that in the first instance the motive in taking them was often one of profit, but this did not exclude the possibility of affection and real concern for the child in the home and could mean that he was less likely to be exploited for his labour than if the allowance had been inadequate. The situation did, however, then as now, call for knowledge in assessing the deeper motives of foster parents and in placing and matching children, and this largely unexplored field of psychology was the responsibility of voluntary committee members.

The system was full of difficulties, as it is to-day; but the difficulties were accentuated by lack of people with sufficient skill to make assessments of foster parents and to supervise

[1] 21 *L.G.B.*, p. 195. 1892.

afterwards. The supervision was much more in the nature of inspection than of support in a situation where powerful emotional drives are involved, but this approach was forced on the worker by the social conditions of the time. As a skill, boarding-out was an empirical, chancy piece of work, and it was realised that more attention needed to be given to it. Constructive criticism was moving towards better and trained administration as the answer. As late as 1909 the majority report of the royal commission on the poor laws was recommending that boarding-out should be placed in the hands of competent women officers and, both within and without the union, should be brought under Local Government Board Inspection.

The alternative systems of child care under the poor law in the last quarter of the nineteenth century were a developing experiment to attempt to meet the individual needs of deprived children in care. They were all the time efforts to discover ways of substituting personal care for the administrative machinery of an institution. The able men and women who concerned themselves with the question of the poor law care of children showed often in their reports an enlightened understanding of the child's emotional needs, but the social conditions of the time made it difficult for this understanding to be given effective expression in the administration. The recommendations of the Report of the Mundella Committee on Poor Law Schools emphasised the need to emancipate the children from their pauper associations and assimilate their lives more closely to those of the self-respecting working classes. They saw that variety was needed in the treatment of children, some responding to boarding-out, care in a scattered home or voluntary home, or finding their best hope of success in emigration. Much headway was made, and by the beginning of the twentieth century the new methods of care were being widely used. Of 69,030 in poor law care in 1908 less than a third were in workhouses or infirmaries.[1]

[1] The figures were : Boarded-out 8,659 ; in Workhouses and infirmaries 21,498 ; in separate establishments (district schools, cottage homes, scattered homes) 27,698 ; other institutions 1,906 ; and in establishments not provided by the poor law, being hospitals, homes for the handicapped, training and industrial homes and schools and training ships 9,319. See *Children under the Poor Law. A Report to the President of the Local Government Board* by T. J. Macnamara*. 1908. Cd 3899.
  * Parliamentary Secretary to the Board.

So, together with the emphasis on education and a corrective environment, we see an effort based on the experiments of the voluntary societies, to give to the child more individual care and some sense of belonging to a community, first developed in the cottage and later in the scattered homes system. Independently came the revival of boarding-out for selected groups of children, at first adopted hesitantly because of the prevailing emphasis on industrial education, and later encouraged because it tended to eradicate the stigma of pauperism and absorb the children naturally in the local population. Administered on a commonsense and experimental basis, children boarded-out within their own unions often remained in the foster homes without any supervision at all, while there were many cases of ill-treatment among those boarded-out outside the unions and inspected by the Local Government Board Inspector.[1] In the successful cases the mental, moral and physical development of the children was considered to be more satisfactory than in other forms of care, but in the conditions of poverty and absence of standards of child welfare which existed at this time, boarding-out had very real dangers and abuses which the administration could not control and it was said by those who opposed it that its principal merit in the eyes of the representatives of the ratepayers was that it was cheap.[2] Children were fostered in the homes of the respectable poor, and because these were the early days of the public health movement, with prevailing low standards of child care and dangers to child health from infections in an industrial community, the relationship of the more skilled visitor to the child and foster parents was that of an inspector, watchful guardian of the child's health and treatment, who paid surprise visits to the foster home. Assessment of the needs of foster parents and knowledge of the complicated dynamics of the fostering relationship and of the supportive part to be played by the visitor is a twentieth century development.

The policy which lay behind the care given to the deprived child was treatment through education for work, but this was

[1] Evidence of Miss Mason before the Mundella Committee on Poor Law Schools, Q. 14,377—14,385.

[2] See Chance, op. cit., p. 392. Writing in 1897, after the Mundella Report, Chance is concerned to make a case against indiscriminate boarding-out.

not meant to be as punitive as at first it may appear. Deprivation was seen as a product of destitution and pauperism which must be cut out at the root. To do this, the child had to be made to rise above the conditions which had brought him to the workhouse, and this he could do only by the value of his labour. The Victorian doctrine of hard work, which permeated society and was responsible for the country's prosperity, was as much in the interests of the child as of the citizens who paid the bill for his training. Of course, such a doctrine was open to abuse, and much menial and degrading work was given to the children by those whose job it was to care for them, and against whom there was no effective protection, but the poor law pressed forward with its work of education, believing this to be the answer. This persisted until the development of the new child care service after 1948 led to a different policy of treatment.

In all the planning of the various systems of care for the deprived child, the natural family, where it existed, remained a problem which, if it was not being treated, was certainly to be reckoned with. Separating the child and the unfit parent or relative of bad influence was a definite attempt to prevent pauperism reproducing itself in the next generation, but the policy was often difficult to effect even if it was considered ethically sound. The constructive work which the poor law attempted by providing a better environment for the child was frequently brought to nothing by what was described as the 'pernicious influence of the child's relations' particularly when the children passed out of the guardians' care at sixteen. Two solutions were found for coping with this problem, both of them based on a drastic tightening up of the policy of separation; the first method was the emigration of children, in order to sever their connections with their native surroundings, and the second method was the assumption by the state, in the person of the poor law, of the parents' rights.

Boards of Guardians were empowered under the Poor Law Amendment Act of 1850 to emigrate orphan or deserted children under the age of sixteen years, provided the child gave his consent. There were real opportunities, particularly in Canada where there was a shortage of labour and where food was cheap, and the guardians made use of these opportunities, though not to any great extent.   In general voluntary organisations, such as Dr. Barnardo's Homes or the Roman Catholic Emigration Agency, were used as agents, the fittest and most promising of the eligible pauper children being chosen for this new life.

The more difficult problem of the child and the unfit parent was grappled with by Acts of 1889 and 1899.   These gave the boards of guardians in England and Wales authority to assume complete rights and responsibilities of a parent over a child in care until he reached the age of eighteen. Such rights could be assumed only in respect of deserted children at first, but in 1899 their application was widened to include orphans and children of parents who were disabled or in prison, or unfit to have the care of them. This power to assume parental rights by the state was an expression of the public interest in the welfare of children and was intended to lay down a definite standard of parental care; failure to reach this standard by individual parents gave to the state authority to intervene and assume responsibility till the child became eighteen and to require the parents to contribute to the cost of the children's maintenance. These powers are still in force to-day, but with far more agencies now working to support the family and raise standards of parental care.

CHAPTER SIX

THE GROWTH OF STATE OBLIGATION TOWARDS THE CHILD

IN an earlier chapter we saw the development of legislation to protect the deprived child. In the last thirty years of the nineteenth century we can now begin to trace the growth of measures intended to protect the child neglected within his own home, or whose circumstances of birth and illegitimacy were exploited as a means of private profit. This was a grave problem requiring public attention and was brought into the open by the development of the new public health movement with its emphasis on the prevention of mortality by attention to environmental hygiene and social conditions.[1] The inadequate support given to unmarried mothers under existing bastardy laws, and the poor law policy of refusing out-relief to mothers with illegitimate children, also encouraged the practice of baby-farming whereby children were placed out with 'professional' foster mothers for payment of a lump sum or for weekly allowances. The mortality among infants under a year put out to nurse in this way was estimated to be between 40% and 60% in rural areas and between 70% and 90% in the large towns with their sanitary conditions so detrimental to infant life.[2] Many of the mothers, particularly in the manufacturing districts of Lancashire and Yorkshire, placed their children in good faith with 'professional' foster mothers or nurses either in the day time or by the week, so that they could carry on with their employment; but many

[1] See *Report on the sanitary conditions of the labouring population of Great Britain.* Edwin Chadwick, London, 1842. The unhygienic conditions of industrial towns in the middle of the century were a scientific and administrative challenge accepted by the medical profession in the persons of their first Medical Officers of Health. It was a surgeon, Mr. John Brendan Curgenven, honorary secretary to the Harveian Medical Society, who, in March, 1867, stimulated public interest in infant life protection by reading a paper on the waste of infant life among illegitimate children before the Health Department of the Social Science Association. In July 1870, with another surgeon, Mr. Ernest Hart, editor of the *British Medical Journal,* he helped to found the Infant Life Protection Society which promoted a Parliamentary Bill.

[2] Illegitimate children suffered heavily. Of a total of approximately 50,000 illegitimate children born annually 30,000 were said to die in the first year—See *Hansard,* 6th March, 1872, Col. 1,486.

also placed them out with the deliberate knowledge, and even intention, that they would be sure to die.[1] The exploitation and despair of the unmarried mother is movingly described in George Moore's novel *Esther Waters*, published in 1894, but twenty-two years earlier legislation attempted, not entirely successfully, to deal with the evil first made notorious by the trial of Margaret Waters and Sarah Ellis. These women had been in the habit of advertising in the press for a child to adopt,[2] and arranging with applicants for a premium of four or five pounds to be paid over with the child. The children were afterwards neglected and many died. At the trial the conditions of the house were vividly described by a police sergeant who had visited and insisted on seeing a particular child who had been 'adopted' in this way:

'It was very emaciated, and very dirty, in fact, filthy. It was wrapped up in some old clothes and was a mere skeleton, mere skin and bone. It was quite quiet and did not appear to have power to cry or make any noise. I asked her (Mrs. Waters) if she had got any more children in the house and she said "A few". I said I should like to see them and she said I could. I went downstairs into the front kitchen and at first saw nothing. But I thought I could see something that looked like the shape of a head under some black clothes on a sofa, and, on moving them, there lay five infants, all huddled up together. Three of the infants were lying on their side along the sofa, all close together, the other two laid on their backs with their mouths open, at the lower end of the sofa. They were all quiet and appeared to be asleep from some cause. They all had some clothing on, infants' clothes and very dirty indeed, saturated with wet, and smelling very offensively. I did not see any appearance of food about. Two of the infants appeared to me to be dying, the two that were lying on their backs. They were in an emaciated condition. I went into the backyard and there found five more. They appeared in better condition and one boy was a very fine child. I said to Waters, "Those children

---

[1] Writing in 1845, Disraeli, in his novel *Sybil*, gives a harrowing description of the early life of such a child who grew up unknown, and was given the name of Devilsdust. 'Infanticide,' he wrote, 'is practised as extensively and legally in England as it is on the banks of the Ganges.'

[2] An adoption in fact, but not in law. Legal adoption did not become possible until the Adoption Act of 1926.

look better. How do you account for that?" and she said, "We have so much a week for these ".'[1]

All but one of the children, who was claimed by his grand-father, were removed to the workhouse two days later. They were numbered from one to nine since nobody knew their names. Four of the youngest babies died shortly afterwards.

Mrs. Waters was executed for murder and the Government set up a select Committee on the protection of Infant Life whose report was printed on the 20th July, 1871.

'According to the evidence, which seems to be indisputable', ran the report, 'there are in all parts of London a large number of private houses, used as lying-in establishments, where women are confined. When the infants are born, some few of them may be taken away by their mothers; but if they are to be "adopted", as is usually the case, the owner of the establishment receives for this adoption a block sum of money, sometimes as little as £5, sometimes as much as £50 or £100, according to the means of the party who goes to be confined. The infant is then re-moved (generally immediately after birth) to the worst class of baby farming houses, under an arrangement with the lying-in establishment, by which the owners of the baby-farming houses are remunerated, either by a small round sum, which is totally inadequate to the permanent maintenance of the child, or by a small weekly payment varying from 2s. 6d. to 7s. 6d., which is supposed to cover all expenses. In the former case, there is obviously every inducement to get rid of the child, and, even in the latter case, unless the mother should come to look after it (which she seldom does), improper and insufficient food, opiates, drugs, crowded rooms, bad air, want of cleanli-ness, and wilful neglect, are sure to be followed in a few months by diarrhoea, convulsions and wasting away. Where the child has not been brought from a secret lying-in establishment, the knowledge of those houses, to which other children are taken, was, until lately, acquired by advertisements in the public news-papers; but since the more respectable of these newspapers have declined any longer to insert such advertisements, it is now obtained, though with more difficulty, by private circulars,

---

[1] L. G. Housden. *The Prevention of Cruelty to Children*, Jonathan Cape. 1955. p. 130 ff. The same information is given in a rather different form in the minutes of evidence of the *Report of the Select Committee on Protection of Infant Life*, 1871.

secretly distributed in various ways, through the post or otherwise.

'It will be seen that nothing can be worse than this class of houses, or more reckless than the conduct of those by whom they are kept. The children born in the lying-in establishment are usually illegitimate, and so are the children taken from elsewhere to the worst class of baby-farming houses. Nobody except the owners of the houses knows anything more about them; their births are not registered, nor are their deaths;[1] some are buried as still-born children, some are secretly disposed of, many are dropped about the streets. In illustration of this, it may here be noted, that the number of infants found dead in the metropolitan and city police districts during the year 1870 was 276. The returns made up to the 19th May in this year (1871) show that there were 103: a very large number of these infants were less than a week old.'[2]

A sergeant in the metropolitan police, who had been ordered by the District Superintendent to make inquiries into the practice of baby farming, in giving evidence before the committee described the practices of a baby farmer, Miss Hall, and said, 'There must have been great profit in the trade, because in an old hat in Miss Hall's garden, I found bonds and securities to the value of about £800 '.[3]

The Select Committee recommended that there should be a compulsory registration of all births and deaths and compulsory registration of all private houses used habitually as lying-in establishments. They also recommended registration for all persons taking for hire two or more infants under one year of age to nurse for a longer period than a day, and suggested that, where nurses were not required to register compulsorily, voluntary registration should be encouraged. Parliament at the time felt unable to deal with the preventive recommendation about the lying-in establishments, because of the changes and reconstruction taking place in the Public

---

[1] The Registration of Births and Deaths Act of 1836, though mandatory, contained no machinery for enforcement.

[2] *Report from the Select Committee on Protection of Infant Life, 1871.* The detailed information about the practice of nursing for reward and its abuses is found in the minutes of evidence.

[3] Minutes of evidence taken before the Select Committee on Protection of Infant Life, 808.

Health Department which made the duties of registration and inspection impossible. Legislation was therefore concerned with legal protection and directed towards the main recommendations made to end the abuses of baby farming. The Act for the better protection of Infant Life, which was passed on the 25th July, 1872, required professional foster mothers, taking for payment two or more children under one year of age, to prove their fitness for the work by registering with the local authority.[1] The local authority could refuse to register any house thought to be unsuitable, and could strike off the register the name of any person guilty of serious neglect, or incapable of providing the children with proper food and attention. If a child, fostered for reward, died while with the foster mother, notice must be given to the coroner who was to hold an inquest unless he was satisfied, by a certificate from a doctor who had personally attended and examined the child, about the cause of death.

The provisions of the Act tried at the same time to avoid a system of too stringent registration which would fetter the goodwill of relatives and guardians who rallied round to help. They were deliberately excluded from the application of the Act as were institutions, such as the foundling hospitals, 'established for the protection or care of infants', or people fostering children under the poor law provisions.[2]

---

[1] Local authority for the purposes of the Act was :—

  (a) In the case of counties (except Metropolis and City of London), Justices in petty sessions.

  (b) ,, ,, ,, Metropolis, Metropolitan Board of Works.

  (c) ,, ,, ,, City of London, Common Council.

  (d) ,, ,, ,, Boroughs, Council.

[2] Other changes in the law were suggested to the Committee in the course of their investigations. They were not incorporated in the recommendations as these changes lay outside the scope of the immediate inquiry, but were noted, and some early became the subject of fresh legislation. The suggestions were :— (1) That the provisions of the criminal law as to the seduction of very young girls should be extended to a somewhat later age ; (2) That the affiliation of illegitimate children to their putative fathers should be permitted before birth ; that greater facilities should be given for ascertaining and enforcing the father's liability for the maintenance of the child; and that liability should be extended in amount. ; (3) That all illegitimate children should be under the supervision of the poor law medical officer; (4) That no midwife should practice unless examined and registered; (5) That no infant or very young person should be entered in a burial club or become the subject of life insurance.

Because the problem of maintaining and caring for the illegitimate child lay very largely at the root of the practice of baby-farming the Bastardy Laws Amendment Act was passed in the same year to enable the unmarried mother to have more financial support for her child. Only since 1844 had she been able to apply to the court for maintenance, but experience had shown that the putative father frequently disappeared, or left the country at the time of the birth. The new law enabled the mother to make a claim against the putative father before the child was born or at any time within a year of the birth, and raised the maximum amount payable for maintenance.[1] Although passed nearly ninety years ago this remained the principal Act dealing with the custody and maintenance of the illegitimate child until 1957.

In the same year a bill for the compulsory registration of births and deaths was introduced into Parliament and became law in 1874.

The infant life protection legislation was repealed in 1897 and a new Infant Life Protection Act was passed, following another scandalous murder trial of a foster mother, Mrs. Dyer of Manchester. The need for greater protection of the illegitimate infant was illustrated by the statistics of the medical officer of health for Manchester, Dr. Tatham, who stated in his return for the years 1891 to 1894 that the mortality in the first year of life of infants illegitimately born was more than twice that of the legitimate child.[2] It was felt, too, that the relieving officer or women members of the visiting committees of the boards of guardians were more suited to undertaking the infant life protection inquiries than the police who had previously been responsible. The new Act raised the age limit of children subject to protection from one to five years, and laid a duty on local authorities to inquire in their areas whether there were persons fostering for reward. The inspectors of the local authority were given powers to apply for authority to enter a house where they were refused entry and had reason to believe an infant was being nursed, and to remove the child to a place of safety.

---

[1] From 2s. 6d. to 5s. weekly.

[2] Legitimately born 174‰. Illegitimately born 392‰, quoted in *Hansard*, 29th March, 1897, Col. 1,529 ff.

Improper care was defined in the Act as a state where an infant was

'(*a*) Kept in any house or premises which are so unfit or so overcrowded as to endanger its health; or

(*b*) retained or received by any persons who, by reason of negligence, ignorance or other cause, is so unfit to have its care and maintenance as to endanger its health.'

In fact the child life protection legislation begins to move from the single motive of protection from neglect and murder towards the preservation of infant life in a vulnerable group, though it did not link up with the administration of public health until 1929. At the beginning of the twentieth century concern for general infant welfare was becoming a significant movement owing to the declining birth rate and high mortality among babies in the first year of life.[1] The change in the balance of population set a premium on the life of children and had repercussions upon the care given even to those formerly most neglected or exploited.

While economic motives furthered the cause of state protection, concern for the well-being of all children whose lives were vulnerable is seen in the growth of the voluntary societies aiming at the prevention of cruelty towards them. As early as 1868 boards of guardians had power to prosecute parents who wilfully neglected to provide for their children so that their health was endangered,[2] but this legislation, though it could be described as preventive of injury and cruelty in that the likelihood of injury and not the fact alone was made a punishable offence, was limited to children with whom the poor law became directly concerned, its chief object being to prevent

---

[1] The birth rate fell from 35.5 births p. 1000 population during the period 1870–75 to 29.3 p. 1000 population during the period 1896–1900. In 1899 out of every thousand children born 163 died within the first year of life. This was the highest infantile mortality rate ever recorded. From this began the emphasis of the public health services on maternity and child welfare by better sanitation of towns and houses to minimise infection, and by the development of clinics with personal attention to the feeding and health of infants.

[2] 'When any parent shall wilfully neglect to provide adequate food, clothing, medical aid or lodging for his child being in his custody, under the age of fourteen years whereby the health of such child shall have been or shall be likely to be seriously injured, he shall be guilty of an offence . . . and the Guardians of the Union or parish in which such child may be living shall institute the prosecution and pay the costs thereof out of their funds.' Poor Law Amendment Act 1868. 31 and 32. Vict. C.122, sect. 27.

further pauperism arising from the conditions of neglect.[1] There was no effective method of discovering and repressing cruelty until the formation of the voluntary societies for this purpose.

The movement towards the prevention of cruelty to children took shape from the example of pioneer work in New York, Boston and other great American cities, which had been observed by Thomas Agnew, a Liverpool merchant and banker, while visiting that country in 1881. On his return to Liverpool the following year he discussed the experiments with his member of Parliament, Mr. Samuel Smith. The result of the member's support was that, a few weeks later, at a meeting organised by the Society for the Prevention of Cruelty to Animals, an appeal for a Dogs' Home became extended into an appeal for the protection of children.[2] So, in April, 1883, was formed the Liverpool Society for the Prevention of Cruelty to Children. Similar societies were formed in most of the large towns, Bristol and Birmingham each founding a society in 1883, and London, Glasgow and Hull two years later. In London the Reverend Benjamin Waugh, a congregational minister of dynamic personality,[3] was made honorary secretary of the society, and it was largely owing to his untiring efforts that the impact of the regional associations became united and coherent. Thirty-one cities and towns had formed organisations by 1889, many of which were making separate representations to Parliament for legislation to protect the unguarded child. In May of that year, therefore, the London society amalgamated with the branches in some of the large towns, so forming the National Society.[4] In the late summer of that year their work was crowned by the passing of the first Act for the prevention of cruelty to, and better protection of children.[5]

The powers of protection for the inarticulate child conveyed by this Act were new in English social history and the legislation

[1] In fact it was little used—see *Minority Report of the Royal Commission on the Poor laws* 1909, p. 150.
[2] 'I am here for the prevention of cruelty and I can't draw the line at children'. See Housden, op. cit., p. 367.
[3] See *Life of Benajmin Waugh*, by Rosa Waugh. T. Fisher Unwin, 1913.
[4] The Birkenhead and Wirral Branch did not amalgamate until 1953, nor the Liverpool branch until 1954. Some—Dundee, Aberdeen and the Isle of Man—still remained independent, even then.
[5] 52 and 53 Victoria. c. 44.

was referred to in Parliament as the Children's Charter[1]. It expressed the public desire to try to prevent cruelty to any child before it actually occurred, and to prevent excessive suffering and overwork which still existed in the many kinds of employment open to children and not regulated by the factory acts. The work of Waugh and of the National Society was of great importance in helping the public to become aware of the cruelty and ill-treatment which existed, and of the machinery by which they could help to play their part in preventing and controlling it.[2] Many local boroughs had asked for, and obtained, powers of control over the employment of children at night, in the streets, in public houses and places of entertainment, for example, and the Act attempted to provide uniformity of the law. With regard to the offence of cruelty, the Act, like the Poor Law Amendment Act of 1868, intended action to be taken before actual injury had occurred, but it attempted also to be a deterrent measure by making cruelty a punishable offence. 'Any person over sixteen years of age who, having the custody, control or charge of a child, being a boy under the age of fourteen years or being a girl under the age of sixteen years, wilfully ill-treats, neglects, abandons, or exposes such a child, or causes or procures such a child to be ill-treated, neglected, abandoned, or exposed, in a manner *likely to cause* such child unnecessary suffering, or injury to its health, shall be guilty of a misdemeanour.'[3] Punishment, it will be noticed, was confined to *wilful* cruelty, that is, to acts of criminal intention, and not to cases of neglect due to ignorance, poverty

[1] Until this time prosecutions could only be made for offences listed in the Offences against the Person Act 1861 and which had actually occurred. These included the neglect of masters to provide necessary food, clothing, and lodging for servants and apprentices, and the abandonment or exposure by anyone of a child under two so that his life was endangered or health permanently injured, assault of children under 14, child stealing or receiving a stolen child, and abduction of a girl under 16. Actual cruelty and neglect of children by their own parents and guardians were not included among the punishable offences, unless the prosecution was undertaken by the poor law.

The term Children's Charter was later again applied to the great consolidating Children's Act of 1908.

[2] Waugh published, on the 1st January, 1887, the first number of *The Child's Guardian* which later became the official journal of the National Society, describing the kind of problems with which they dealt, and the success of their work.

[3] Act for the Prevention of Cruelty to, and better Protection of Children, 1889, section 1.

or any of the other prevailing social evils of the time. Important legal changes enabled necessary evidence to be put before the courts, and strengthened the work of those concerned with the child. A spouse became a competent (though not compellable) witness against the other spouse, and the evidence of a child of tender years, though not given upon oath, could be received by the court. Two important powers of a new kind now became exercisable; firstly, the magistrates, on the sworn evidence of any person having reasonable cause to believe a child was being ill-treated or neglected, could issue a warrant to be executed by a police officer to enter a house and search for the child and take him and detain him in a place of safety until he could be dealt with by the court. This clause was inserted to enable representatives of the rescue societies or the societies for the prevention of cruelty to act quickly, but this right of any person to initiate action is still carefully preserved as a safeguard for the child in current legislation,[1] though rarely exercised by members of the general public. Secondly, the courts were given power to take a child out of the care of a parent convicted of neglect and ill-treatment, and to commit him to the charge of a relative or other fit person until the age of fourteen, if a boy, or sixteen if a girl. The term 'fit person' covered industrial schools and charitable institutions. When the child had been committed the court could still order the parent to contribute towards his maintenance, a measure intended to emphasize the parental responsibility which the committal order might have seemed to destroy. It is interesting that this constructive, rather than punitive attitude towards contributions, is emphasized in the parliamentary debate at the time.

In the five years following the passing of this Act 5,792 persons were prosecuted for cruelty and 5,460 of them convicted, while 47,000 complaints were examined by the National Society for the Prevention of Cruelty to Children. Mainly as a result of the work of its energetic secretary Benjamin Waugh, new legislation was passed in 1894[2] by which committal orders

---

[1] Children and Young Persons Act 1933, Sect. 28.
[2] 57 and 58 Victoria c. 27. This and the previous Act were consolidated one month later in 57 and 58 Victoria c. 41—An Act to consolidate the Acts relating to the Prevention of Cruelty to, and protection of, Children.

were made operative to the age of sixteen. The original 1889 Act made a punishable offence the illtreatment of boys up to 14 and girls up to 16. The age limit for boys was extended to 16 under the new legislation. Cruelty was now widened to include assault and the terms 'suffering' and 'injury' were more clearly defined.[1] In dealing with offenders the Act made some notable alterations. In the first place it underlined the deterrent nature of the legislation by extending the length of maximum imprisonment, but it provided some new powers to deal with offenders who were habitual drunkards. Experience had shown that the majority of cases of cruelty were committed when the adult was drunk and uncontrolled and the magistrates were now given powers to send such offenders not to prison but to an inebriates' home, where constructive treatment could be given without the branding of a prison sentence. The offender's consent was required before such an order could be made. This marks a positive step forward in constructive work towards the prevention of further cruelty. Other clauses in the Act controlled the employment of children in places of public entertainment or in occupations with risk of danger to them, such as those of acrobat or contortionist, and factory inspectors were given powers to inspect and examine premises where the children performed, and courts were enabled to issue licences before they performed, after satisfying themselves of the health and kind treatment of the children.

Thus we see how, through the later years of the nineteenth century, the voluntary organisations, by their rousing of the public conscience and their work of protecting minorities, achieved legal rights for the inarticulate and exploited child. His primary needs of shelter and protection were won very largely by the activities and example of the rescue and preventive

---

[1] The words now were: 'If any person over the age of sixteen years who has the custody, charge, or care of any child under the age of sixteen years, wilfully assaults, ill treats, neglects, abandons, or exposes such child—or causes or procures such child to be assaulted, ill-treated, neglected, abandoned, or exposed in a manner likely to cause such child unnecessary suffering, or injury to its health (including injury to or loss of sight, or hearing or limb or organ of the body, and any mental derangement), that person shall be guilty of a misdemeanour.'' 57 and 58 Victoria, c. 41, sect. 1(i).

societies.[1] But from this same period onwards a significant change began to take place in social attitudes towards the depressed groups which culminated in nothing less than a new view of society. This change in attitude was mainly due to the growth of scientific ways of thought which were applied to the study of poverty, pauperism and assistance, both practically and academically.

On the practical side immense importance must attach to the work and influence of another voluntary body, the Charity Organisation Society. Founded in London in 1869 the society attempted to tackle the problem of indiscriminate and palliative almsgiving by providing a centre through which the resources of various charities could be mobilised to provide constructive help. Particularly after the appointment of Charles Stuart Loch as secretary in 1875 their policy was to deal with the need or hardship in such a way that they built up the resources of the individual and made it less likely that the hardship would recur. This, of course, meant the need to analyse the cause of the difficulty in each individual case and to plan help with a view to eradicating the cause. Providing grants and gifts in any other way, they believed, eventually destroyed the individual's independence and self-respect. The Charity Organisation Society, therefore, changed the concept of relieving distress by alms, while at the same time scientific surveys into the nature of poverty changed society's attitude to pauperism as a personal fault and emphasized the social factors which caused it.[2] The academic studies of Charles Booth and Seebohm Rowntree were scientific works, based on carefully analysed facts, and as such commanded a wide influence. They showed how widely prevalent was poverty in the society of the time and that the major causes of it were not personal factors or fault of character but low wages, the cost of maintaining large families of young children, and the enforced idleness which comes from sickness,

[1] See the chapter by Miss R. M. Wrong 'Some voluntary organisations for the welfare of children' in *Voluntary Social Services*, edited by A. F. C. Bourdillon. Methuen & Co. Ltd., 1945.

[2] See (a) Charles Booth, *Life and Labour of the People in London*, Macmillan 1890–1900. The eighteen volumes describe the conditions of industrial poverty in contemporary London; and (b) B. Seebohm Rowntree, *Poverty. A Study of Town Life*, Macmillan 1901, in which conditions in York are described. The two independent works show striking similarities in findings on the amount of poverty, 30% of all the population in Booth's survey, 27.9% in Rowntree's.

old age, unemployment, or the death of the chief wage earner.[1]
The disclosure that such a large proportion of poverty prevailed, and that so much of it was due to causes beyond the
individual's control, led to a demand for a state policy to
prevent the causes of poverty arising, and with this came a new
attitude towards the pauper. In the light of the new evidence
punitive policies were no longer acceptable and social reformers demanded that, where destitution did exist, relief should be
given as a right. Knowledge of the causes lying behind poverty
and disease led to a call for social justice and an emphasis
on the rights of the individual to minimum conditions of subsistence and health in which he had freedom to exercise responsibility for himself and his own life.[2] Besides this, the falling
birth rate made it imperative to preserve the lives of children
and provide for them adequate standards of nutrition, health
and moral training to ensure their social usefulness in adult
life. The large percentage of rejections on physical grounds of
recruits for the army was a cause of much concern and led to
Government inquiries into the conditions under which children
were reared.[3] In the early twentieth century, therefore, legislation was passed to deal with the relief of poverty. This
was done in a piecemeal yet constructive kind of way,
by building up social services to support the family in its
period of greatest need and to provide a social environment

[1] Rowntree, for example, found 9.9% of the total population of York (15.46 of
the wage earners) living in primary poverty whose causes he analysed as follows:—
low wages (51.96% of the cases), large families (22.16%), death of the chief wage
earner (15.63%), illness or old age of the chief wage earner (51.11%), unemployment (2.31%), irregular work (2.83%). He found 18% of the total population
(28% of the wage earners) living in secondary poverty, i.e. poverty which could
have been avoided if the money had not been spent on drink, betting, or some im-
provident way, or misused by ignorant or careless housekeeping. Rowntree's
scientifically calculated measurement of primary poverty was a very stringent one.
He defined it as a state where the total earnings of the family were insufficient to
obtain minimum necessities for the maintenance of merely physical efficiency. It
is for consideration how far the social conditions of the industrial towns promoted
discouragement and the misuse of money among the poor to bring them into
secondary poverty.

[2] The development of this responsibility had begun earlier with the friendly
societies with their death and sickness benefits, the trade unions with their out of
work pay, and the co-operative movement.

[3] See the *Report of the Committee on Physical Training (Scotland)*, published in 1903.
Cd. 1507, and of the *Royal Commission on Physical Deterioration* published in 1904.
Cd. 2175.

in which it would be easier to maintain a minimum standard of life and subsistence. Early and tentative as the legislation was, it laid the foundation of the present welfare state.

In the field of general child care, social services were provided which could not fail to reduce the amount of sickness and neglect and consequent poverty. Notable measures were the permissive power of local education authorities to feed children at school,[1] and the duty laid on them to provide for the medical inspection of all children attending public elementary schools,[2] while the preservation of infant life and health was safeguarded by provision for the notification of all births to the local medical officer of health, in addition to their registration, in order that the skilled advice and help of the health visitor might be available at the earliest and most crucial period.[3] The new attitude also spilled over into the field of juvenile delinquency and we find legislation to emphasize and make possible the reform, rather than the punishment of new offenders.[4]

It was in this atmosphere that, on the 10th February 1908, Mr. Herbert Samuel introduced into the House of Commons a Bill designed to consolidate the legislation dealing with the protection of children and the training and treatment of child offenders. The existing law was spread over a large number of statutes, thirty-nine of which were repealed, in whole or in part, when the Bill became law as the Children Act on the

[1] 6. Edward VII c. 57 Education (Provision of Meals) Act, 1906.

[2] 7. Edward VII c. 43 Education (Administrative Provisions) Act 1907.

[3] 7. Edward VII c. 46 Notification of Births Act 1907 (permissive). Compulsory powers of notification were obtained in 1915.

[4] 50 7 51 Vict. c. 25 Probation of First Offenders Act 1887 had enabled courts to bind over first offenders to be of good behaviour for a specified term, instead of imprisoning them.

64 Victoria c. 20. Youthful Offenders Act 1901 enabled a child or young person to be remanded or committed on remand to a place other than prison and extended the powers of committal to industrial schools instead of prisons. 7 Edward VII c. 17 Probation of Offenders Act 1907 allowed offenders to be placed on probation. The Act was not confined to juvenile offenders but the fact that the court were, as in the 1887 Act, to have regard to the character, antecedents, age, health, or mental condition of the person charged, made it inevitable that juveniles were found more suitable for probation. Reformation rather than punishment of the offender had been advocated long ago by penal reformers. Acceptance of this concept was influenced by the new growth of criminology, the scientific study of the social and personal factors which lie behind crime.

21st December, 1908.[1] While this was a humanitarian measure, it was also a necessary step taken by the state to ensure its own economic well-being. Indeed in the twentieth century the movements for social reform show a blend of motives in which humanitarianism is justified by insistence on democratic rights to a recognised standard of living, and by the necessity of the state to ensure the vitality and efficiency of its citizens in a highly competitive society. While the state ensures a common standard of life below which no one need fall, it is left to the people themselves and to their democratic organisations to ensure its individual quality.[2]

The Children Act of 1908, was a great and fundamental step in child protection, not so much because it was new, or clarified any matters which were controversial, but because for the first time it gathered together into one statute a host of amending laws and piecemeal legislation which publicly emphasized the social rights of children.

The first part of the Children Act 1908 embodied the earlier infant life protection legislation, extending its application to the fostering for reward of only one child instead of two or more as previously. The second part of the Act was intended to strengthen the law to prevent cruelty to children, and now imposed penalties not only for wilful cruelty, but for negligence, as, for example, where a child is overlaid and suffocated, or burnt or scalded by being left in a room with unguarded fire. It also became an offence for anyone in charge of children to allow them to beg in public places[3] or to be in brothels. As a protective measure of child health the Act went on to prohibit children from smoking in the streets, and fixed penalties for those who sold tobacco to them. Nineteen statutes which contained the law relating to reformatory and industrial schools were consolidated and the Secretary of State given power to transfer youthful offenders from reformatory to industrial

---

[1] 8 Edward 7 c. 67. An Act to consolidate and amend the law relating to the protection of children and young persons, reformatory and industrial schools, and otherwise to amend the law with respect to children and young persons.

[2] This ensures the importance of the voluntary organisations in the welfare state.

[3] As distinct from any person causing or procuring them to beg, thereby underlining the duties of guardianship.

schools thus enabling the now largely artificial distinction between them to be broken down,[1] managers of such schools were enabled to board out children sent to them under the age of eight. The Act showed an enlightened approach to juvenile offenders and their treatment by the Courts. 'The Courts', it was said in parliamentary debate, 'should be agencies for the rescue as well as the punishment of children.'[2] Children were to be kept separate from adult criminals at their trial and, afterwards, were to receive treatment suited to their special needs, and not punishment fitted to the crime. For the first time juvenile courts were set up in which young offenders and non-offenders were charged and heard in a separate room or at a separate time from the adult court, and the public not actually concerned with the hearing were excluded. The imprisonment of children under sixteen was abolished, and special places of detention, remand homes, aided by Treasury grants, were to be set up to avoid any child being sent to gaol before his trial. While the Act moved away from punishment of the child towards his treatment and care it did not aim at undermining parental authority. It drew the parent into the problem and underlined his share in responsibility. He was required to attend in court when a child was charged with an offence, and courts were given wider powers requiring parents to pay fines for their children's offences. Finally, the Act tried to bring under some control the large number of small voluntary homes which received poor children but were not subject to inspection as certified poor law homes or industrial schools. Provided these homes were supported wholly or partly by voluntary contributions the Secretary of State was empowered to arrange for them to be visited and

[1] Until 1899 boys or girls sentenced to detention in a reformatory served a period of preliminary imprisonment. 62 and 63 Victoria c. 12 ,the Reformatory Schools Amendment Act of 1899, abolished this and so removed the landmark which had always distinguished the reformatory from the industrial school. The distinction between the two schools was now becoming largely artificial, except that only offenders went to reformatory schools.

[2] Section 58 (i) of the Act gives seven categories of children who could be brought before the Juvenile Court as non-offenders. If the Court thought fit it could send such children to a Home Office school (industrial school) or place them in the care of a relative or fit person with or without the supervision of a probation officer (section 58(7) and 60). Children beyond the control of parents or guardians or refractory children maintained in workhouses or poor law schools could be sent to an industrial school (section 58(4) and (5)).

inspected.[1] There was, however, no system of registration of voluntary homes at this time, many were unknown to the central government department, and, unless gross neglect or cruelty was found, no steps could be taken to compel improvements or close the Home if the Inspector's advice and warning were not heeded.

In the light of the developing reforms it now becomes necessary to examine the concepts and social theory on which the principles of the poor law administration were based. Conditions of twentieth century England were vastly different from those in 1834 when the deterrent policy of less eligibility was framed. The gradual extension of the franchise since the Reform Act of 1832 had shifted the balance of political power to the majority of the people ; working men with democratic experience obtained through the co-operatives, trade unions and friendly societies brought their views before the country, prepared to exercise their responsibility in collective bargaining. Against this background of growing and of wider understanding of the causes of destitution the poor law methods of dealing with distress called for examination. In 1905 the Government set up a Royal Commission into the working of the poor laws which reported in 1909. The Commission was not unanimous and produced majority and minority reports which were of great significance in the future history of social welfare and the administration of services for the deprived child. The majority report was conservative and essentially British in character in that it tried to build on the existing poor law structure, improving the character of its administration and supplementing it by voluntary aid. In this way an improved poor law authority would be responsible for providing the necessary services for the destitute child at a standard in keeping with more enlightened knowledge and care. The minority report on the other hand, a burning piece of invective against what it stated was the failure of a destitution authority to relieve destitution, recommended nothing less than the breaking up of the poor law and the transfer of its functions

[1] Section 25 (i). The First Report on the Work of the Children's Branch published by the Home Office in April, 1923, though written fifteen years later, says (p. 76) that the object of this was not to establish any regular system of inspection but to provide a method of investigation where allegations of ill treatment or lack of care were made.

on a specialised basis to appropriate departments of the local authorities. Its signatories pointed out the anomalies and over-lapping which existed in the care of children under different rival authorities—the poor law caring for the destitute, the Home Office responsible for the inspection and grants in aid of industrial and reformatory schools, and the education authority now forging ahead with the medical inspection and treatment and feeding of all school children. Because these functions of the local education authorities invaded so effectively the sphere of the destitution authority, the minority report recommended that the duties of the poor law towards destitute children should cease and that they should be superseded by the local education authorities. 'The failure,' they said 'of the Boards of Guardians in the great centres of population . . . to relieve so much of the child destitution, is rooted in the very fact that they are Destitution Authorities, with a long established tradi-tion of "relieving" such persons only as voluntarily come for-ward and prove themselves "destitute." What is required is some social machinery, of sufficient scope, to bring automatic-ally to light, irrespective of the parent's application, or even of that of the children, whatever child destitution exists. . . . An Authority dealing with the child, or with the family, merely at the crisis of destitution, having no excuse for intervening before or after this crisis, can never cope with the conditions here re-vealed. What is required is the steady and continuous guidance of a friend, able to suggest in what directions effective help can be obtained where help is really needed, which will gradually remedy parental ignorance or neglect. In many cases friendly advice and warning will suffice. Such an organisation for systematic friendly visiting can, we think, only be supplied by voluntary effort, working as part of the machinery of the Local Education authority and enabled in ways that we shall sub-sequently describe to bring to bear the material aid that the children, in some cases, are found actually to require. These Children's Care Committees, under one title or another, are now becoming part of the machinery of the Local Education Authority. They were, for instance, required by the Act of 1906, and their establishment has been expressly called for by the Board of Education.' They therefore recommended 'That the only practicable way of securing this unity of administration, and also the most desirable reform is, in England and Wales, to entrust the whole of the public provision for children of school age (not being sick or mentally defective) to the Local Education authorities, under the supervision of the Board of Education; these Local Education Authorities having already, in their Directors of Education and their extensive staffs of teachers, their residential and their day feeding schools, their arrangements for medical inspection, and treatment, their School Attendance Officers and Children's Care Committees, the machinery requisite for searching out every child destitute of the necessaries of life, for enforcing parental responsibility, and for obviating, by timely pressure and assistance, the actual crisis of destitution.'[1]

The propaganda and publicity arranged for the minority report by one of its signatories, Mrs. Sidney Webb, created active agitation for poor law reform during the next two or three years, but no direct legislation followed as a result.[2] Instead the president of the Local Government Board undertook what he called 'revolution by administration' and in this way many of the proposals of the minority report, which had been so much more actively publicised, were gradually put into practice. Certainly this report was responsible, for good or ill, for the growth of a more specialised and departmental approach to the social services. What is mainly important, however, and agreed in the two reports is the way in which their authors clearly and wholly discarded the principles of deterrence and less eligibility shown towards those who were less independent members of society, and if on the one hand they could not prevent them coming into existence, on

[1] *Separate Report of the Royal Commission on the Poor Laws and Relief of Distress* (*Minority Report*) *1909*, pp. 163, 164, 169. The recommendations differed slightly for Scotland. For Ireland they interestingly foreshadow the principles of the Curtis Committee in 1946. As no local education authorities existed in Ireland it was suggested that the work might be entrusted to County and County Borough Councils, acting through special Boarding-out Committees, on which there should be women members, and sending children to the existing day schools.

[2] The National Insurance Act of 1911, for example, introduced by the Liberal administration under Lloyd George, was the government's alternative to the proposal of the Minority Report for a comprehensive system of reform for dealing with the unemployed by organising the national labour market.

the other they tried to emphasize their right, even in destitution, to care, support and treatment as the acknowledged birthright of a common humanity.[1]

[1] See Una Cormack's Loch Memorial Lecture 1953 on the *Royal Commission and the Poor Laws, 1905–1909, and the Welfare State,* published by the Family Welfare Association.

CHAPTER SEVEN

THE EMANCIPATION OF THE CHILD

THE strength of the original conception of poor law administration had been its comprehensiveness, the ability of one administrative body to provide care for the destitute individual according to his need, whether it be sickness, deprivation or old age. In fact, however, the history of the poor law shows how this original conception became destroyed by philosophies and techniques which in the twentieth century were out of keeping both with the developments in knowledge, and with the spirit of responsibility in the people. Gradually the duties of the poor law became enfeebled and powers which had previously belonged to it were laid on the newly developing departments of local authorities.[1] These departments specialised in particular needs requiring service, making no distinction between the client who was destitute and the client who was able to pay. In this way the comprehensiveness of the poor law was finally destroyed and there developed a series of services based on specific needs of the general public in the treatment of which a high degree of knowledge and efficiency was sought. Many of these needs became clear for the first time, or were emphasized, in the changing climate of social thought and greater statistical and scientific information, while the 1914–1918 war, which broke down so many social and economic distinctions, forced some problems to the public notice in an atmosphere of greater responsibility and understanding.

Among these problems was the increased number of illegitimate children born in the war years and their high mortality

---

[1] This is seen in the increasing number of acts and orders dealing with, for example, education and ancillary services 1902–09, housing and town planning 1909–26, mental deficiency 1913–27, venereal disease 1916, maternity and child welfare 1918 and tuberculosis 1921.

rates.[1] By 1918 illegitimate births were 6.26% of all live births in England and Wales, and the death rate of illegitimate children in the first year of life was 186 per thousand, compared with 91 per thousand among babies legitimately born, and represented a serious wastage of precious infant life. This high death rate could also be taken as indicative at that time of a high sickness rate among those who survived, with consequent risk of impaired physical and emotional growth, while the economic insecurity and thinly-veiled contempt which was the background to so many of the children's lives provided sometimes an excuse for the parent to desert them, or for the children to find satisfaction in a pattern of maladjustment or delinquency.

By this time, however, the creative thought of the humanitarians and philanthropists in the late nineteenth century was beginning to be effective. Among the voluntary organisations working in this field there had developed a tradition of personal understanding and individual care towards the unmarried mother on which it was possible to build a policy of reconciling both her and the child to her own family[2]. In this way the origin of much future deprivation could be destroyed. The growth of the moral welfare organisations since 1883, and the formation of the National Council for the Unmarried Mother and her Child in February 1918, were positive and preventive steps taken on a large scale to provide supportive care within the family, rather than to seek to improve the care given to children when they became deprived.[3] This attitude was greatly helped by the growth of the infant welfare services throughout the country, the setting up of maternity and infant welfare clinics with staffs of skilled health visitors and midwives

[1] See Helen Best, *The War Baby. A discussion of the special problems raised by illegitimacy during the Great War.* Stanley Paul & Co., 1915.

[2] See the article on 'Moral Welfare' by Barbara Reeve and Ena Steel with bibliography in *Social Casework in Great Britain*, edited by Cherry Morris, Faber & Faber (2nd Edition) 1955.

[3] See *Twenty one Years and After. The Story of the National Council for the Unmarried Mother and her Child*, by Lettice Fisher. Published by the Council 1937. The functions of the Council were :—(1) to obtain reform of the existing Bastardy Acts and Affiliation Acts, (2) To secure the provision of adequate accommodation to meet the varying needs of mothers and babies throughout the country, with the special aim of keeping mother and child together, (3) To deal with individual enquiries from, or on behalf of, unmarried mothers.

working with the family, which had developed gradually from 1899 and in 1918 became the responsibility of the local authorities[1]. Yet in some cases reconciliation could never be possible, and for the child the problem of his illegitimate existence, with its legal, economic and social disqualifications remained and became often the origin of circumstances which brought him into poor law care.

It was now for the first time that steps were taken to destroy the fact of illegitimacy by creating a legal status for a child through the process of adoption. In law such a thing had never previously been possible, though adoptions in fact were common. Though friends and foster parents had taken over the permanent care of a homeless child by arrangement and though adoption societies were started during the Great War to provide homes for 'unwanted' children there had never been the protection of legal status either for child or adopter. Boards of Guardians since 1889 had been able to 'adopt' children by assuming parental rights until the age of eighteen[2] and then often placed them for fostering, but this did not give a legitimate status to the child. There now grew up a demand for some more permanent safeguard for the illegitimate child which was embodied in the first Adoption Act of 1926[3]. The Act was a cautious one, concerned with the legality of the adoption procedure and change of legal status of the child and

[1] In 1899 the first milk centre in England was set up in St. Helens, Lancashire. The origins of the clinics were mainly voluntary. See G. F. McCleary, *The Early History of the Infant Welfare Movement*. H. K. Lewis & Co. London, 1933. The Maternity and Child Welfare Act of 1918 gave local authorities powers to set up maternity and child welfare clinics and authorised government grants to them. The growing emphasis on ante-natal care of the mother and on skilled midwifery reduced maternal mortality and so attacked one source of deprivation.

[2] Frequent use was made of this power. In 1908 12,417 children were so 'adopted'.

[3] This did not come easily upon the statute book. Between 1920 and 1926 two Committees of inquiry into adoption were set up and six bills were introduced in Parliament. Support for adoption came from two angles, firstly the desire to regularise the position of orphans or unwanted children adopted by private persons and to protect them from exploitation and ill treatment, and secondly the desire of persons having no children of their own and wanting to adopt a child, to secure their position from interference by natural parents. For a history of adoption legislation, etc., see Margaret Kornitzer, *Adoption in the Modern World*. Putnam. 1952, and the Report of the Departmental Committee on the Adoption of Children. Cmd. 9248.

natural and adopting parents[1]. It is interesting to see later the development of thought behind adoption procedure which is embodied in the legislation to-day.

In the same year was also passed the Legitimacy Act by which illegitimate children could be legitimated and re-registered by the subsequent marriage of their parents[2]; in this way a child, although already assured of a home and affection, was given protection from the psychological damage which often resulted from society's attitude to his illegitimacy.

These steps were important in giving expression to the modifications of society towards minority groups which had previously carried a severe social stigma and in consequence of which many dissatisfied and frustrated individuals had become a source of danger and distress in society[3]. While the work of treating and curing the problem of delinquency and poverty and pauperism went on, these acts of parliament were true preventive measures and heralded a new enlightened approach in general towards problem groups.

The gradual emancipation of the poor law child from the stigma and principle of less eligibility applied more generally to the adult pauper has been traced in the chapter on poor law care in the first half of the nineteenth century.[4] The emancipation continued in the twentieth century, while public attitudes to the poor law were moving towards its reorganisation, and the child had a specially privileged position in poor law administration. This is seen in the development of regulations governing boarding-out and the alternatives to workhouse care. The Royal Commission in 1909 had recommended that 'effective steps should be taken to secure that the maintenance

[1] During the first fifteen months after the Adoption Act came into force the demand for a system of legalised adoption was seen to be justified. A total of 4,386 applications were made to the Courts. About two-thirds of the adoptions were of illegitimate children, and among these were a small number whom one or both of their parents sought to adopt. See the *Fourth Report on the Work of the Children's Branch*. Published by the Home Office, Nov., 1928.

[2] 16 and 17 Geo. V c. 60, sect. 1, provided that, at the time of the child's birth neither parent was married to a third person, and that at the time of marriage the father was domiciled in England and Wales.

[3] See for example the chapter on home environmental conditions in *The Young Delinquent*, by Cyril Burt. University of London Press. Revised edn. 1944.

[4] A summary of the conditions at the beginning of the twentieth century is found in the Macnamara Report, op. cit.

of children in the workhouse be no longer recognised as a legitimate way of dealing with them' and a more active policy of boarding them out, placing them in certified schools and institutions, in scattered or cottage homes, in poor law schools or of emigrating them abroad was now developed. The boarding-out orders of 1889 were replaced in 1905 and 1909 by fresh regulations governing the boarding-out of children beyond and within the Unions respectively by which boarding-out committees became obligatory and in 1911, again under the tidy and efficient influence of the Royal Commission, a single unifying order was issued to cover both methods of boarding-out. Among its more important provisions were the now universal requirement that one-third of all boarding-out committees shall consist of women, and that relieving officers were excluded from the duties of making weekly payments to foster parents as part of a policy to exclude them altogether from dealing with boarded-out children. There was now no minimum age for boarding-out, and maximum payments were fixed by the Local Government Board. Insurance of the lives of such children was now prohibited.

The Board encouraged the setting up of comprehensive boarding-out committees, known as Children's Committees, with salaried women visitors who, besides visiting the boarded-out children in foster homes and widows with dependent children who were receiving out relief, supervised the conditions under which poor law children were working in service or as apprentices, and undertook the infant life protection visiting which had been laid as a duty on the poor law officers under Part 1 of the Children Act 1908[1]. Where there was no salaried visitor the committee members undertook the boarding-out visiting. The Boarding-out committees themselves could be of two kinds, either committees of guardians appointed by guardians for a definite period, subject to re-appointment (appointed committees), or independent voluntary committees which were authorised by the Local Government Board (authorised committees). In the last full annual report made by

---

[1] The infant life protection duties laid on the poor law were : to receive notice where a person undertakes for reward the nursing and maintenance of an infant under 7 apart from his parents; to appoint visitors to inspect such children; to limit the number in any dwelling: to remove such infants improperly kept; to receive fines imposed for offences.

the Local Government Board, just before the outbreak of the Great War, Miss Ina Stansfield, the superintendent woman inspector, reported on the system at the time. There had been a great increase in the number of children boarded out, both relatively in relation to children in care, and absolutely, the figures having risen from 2,799 on the 1st July 1885 to 11,596 on the 1st January, 1914.[1] The greatest increase had been in boarding-out within the Union, and the total figure represented roughly 14.5% of all children in care (excluding those children receiving medical relief only, and those on the out relief lists). It was remarked, however, that Boards of Guardians seemed reluctant to employ salaried visitors, by 1913 only 80 of them having made such appointments.

However, considerable progress was now being made in removing children from the ordinary wards of the workhouse and finding accommodation for them elsewhere as the following figures show.[2]

	Children over 3 in workhouses	Total number of indoor children
31st March 1906 ..	11,072	58,991
1st Jan., 1913 ..	8,206	70,676

In 1913 the emancipation of the child from the historical punitive aspects of the poor law was recognised by the Poor Law Institutions Order of that year which prohibited children from the age of three up to sixteen years from being maintained in a general workhouse for more than six weeks. The Great War, which followed, naturally made it impossible for Guardians to proceed with any building plans, but we find that by 1918 50.2% of the indoor poor law children were in separate institutions provided wholly for the reception and maintenance of children.[3]

At the end of the war the departmentalisation of services previously unified in the poor law was the subject of a com-

---

[1] Appendix pp. 78 ff. *Forty-Third Annual Report of the Local Government Board, 1913-14.* The increase showed

		1885 1st July	1895 1st Jan.	1905 1st Jan.	1913 1st Jan.	1914 1st Jan.
Children boarded out—						
(*a*) Within the Union	..	1,774	3,778	6,814	9,128	9,272
(*b*) Beyond the Union	..	1,025	1,794	1,086	2,269	2,324
Total ..	..	2,799	5,572	7,900	11,397	11,596

[2] *Forty-Second Annual Report of the Local Government Board, 1912-13.*
[3] Compared with 45.8% in 1908.

mittee set up under the Chairmanship of Sir Donald Maclean, K.B.E., M.P., 'to consider and report upon the steps to be taken to secure the better co-ordination of Public Assistance in England and Wales and upon such other matters affecting the system of Local Government as may from time to time be referred to it.'[1] The report enumerated eleven different public authorities dispensing assistance out of rates and taxes, frequently with little co-ordination between them. Their recommendations for the unification of the existing services were not entirely followed but resulted in 1918 in the absorption of the Local Government Board in the Ministry of Health which now became responsible for the administration of the poor laws. Almost immediately afterwards economic distress and unemployment disturbed and agitated the country and is reflected in the impaired vitality of the progressive work with children which had been proceeding over the last seventy years. In contrast with the living vivid reports of the Victorian era the arid pages of the economy-ridden Ministry of Health reports give no interpretation of what the administration meant to those who lived within it. While this moved steadily towards a greater safeguarding of the child's freedom to develop a normal life, the provision of skilled, not to say trained, staff, continually lagged behind enlightened policy. Extended boarding out, removal from the workhouse, the provision of scattered homes were excellent techniques of administration, but the staff able to carry out the techniques with understanding of their purpose hardly existed. In Lucy Sinclair's account of her life in a group of cottage homes between 1920 and 1933 we are fortunate in having a first hand picture of institutional life as it seemed to the perceptive child.[2] In many such places it seems that the original concept which lay behind the cottage homes had been submerged under a smooth administrative procedure. The homes were no longer run by pioneers to whom the vision of cottage family life was dynamic because the reason behind it was clear to them. They were often now run by people who knew only how to keep them going. So the children lived in groups and went to bed in

[1] See *Report on Transfer of Functions of Poor Law Authorities in England and Wales. 1918*. Cd. 8917.

[2] Lucy Sinclair, *The Bridgeburn Days*. Gollancz 1956.

groups, and, justifying their daily bread by work, sighed for the free life in the world of childhood. 'Besides all the work in the Matron's house and the boys' and girls' cottages, there were the mats to be made. Miles of knitting they must have done in their day when the other jobs were finished, and miles and miles of clippings they must have cut up and prodded into the hessian with its nasty bitter smell. Ah, the tedium of spending the school holidays at this hated task. In our house we had the most, the thickest and the newest mats of all. But what a price they cost in weariness and sad longing to be free. Free to rush about and play, free to tear up one drive and down the other, free in a dozen little things that make for gladness, like the runaway horses belonging to a farmer in the village which every now and then would break loose and come galloping round the cottage homes, till, with manes flying, they would dash away up the hill road, the sound of their going like strange, exotic music, a joyous tattoo that echoed and re-echoed long after the horses were lost to sight. It was the music of the wild and free. Our Ma alone remained unmoved by their coming and going. But the girls would return to their work with sparkling eyes and happy hearts, and when the next morning came there was always one to say wistfully, "I wish this was yesterday when the horses came." '[1]

From time to time the changes and movement in the poor law are reflected in the pages of this autobiography, and when a new Matron came normality burst upon the children of Bridgeburn in the shape of new clothes. 'New cotton frocks were the next to come, with gay checks and stripes in what was felt to be the latest fashion, cross over bodices and two flappy pieces at the sides. Coat pinafores, instead of the apron type worn for so long. And then the coats! They came ready made in various shades of wine and navy and green and brown, with deep cuffs and stand-up collars. As for the hats, excitement reached fever pitch. Hats with bows, hats with feathers, hats with cherries that looked good enough to eat, and flowers so realistic that the girls took it in turns to smell them. Dainty forget-me-nots, marguerites and roses adorned the now giddy heads of the Bridgeburn girls.'[2]

[1] Lucy Sinclair, op. cit., p. 22.   [2] p. 8.

But the development of the various social services and the higher standards required by them, in education, in the medical and dental attention given to children, and in the care of young babies, emphasized the need for more skilled poor law staffs, particularly in the appointment of women visitors to work with the children. An entirely new concept of the education of the poor law child is seen developing in which his own aptitudes and abilities are becoming of paramount importance. 'All the Inspectors emphasize' says the first report of the Ministry of Health in 1920, 'the value of school reports and co-operation with the teachers as a means of discovering special talent indicating the occupation in which children are likely to succeed.' And a code issued in 1919 by the Board of Education for the use of public elementary schools had defined the purpose of these schools as 'to form and strengthen the character, and to develop the intelligence of the children entrusted to it, and to make the best use of the school years available, in assisting both boys and girls, according to their different needs, to fit themselves practically as well as intellectually for the work of life.' As theories of education became more and more child-centred, the poor law was able to share in the greater freedom for individual self-expression which education was securing for the child.

But more progressive in their vision at this time than the administrators of the now dying poor law were those responsible for the care of children in the reformatories and industrial schools. They saw their work of education as a training of the children's character, mind and body, and a treatment of the offenders to prevent them from growing up to be a source of unhappiness to themselves and a menace to others.[1] They developed progressively the practice of boarding-out the young children committed to the care of managers in industrial schools[2], and in them we see the seeds of constructive work

[1] *First Report on the Work of the Children's Branch,* published by the Home Office, April, 1923, p. 7 and p. 26.

[2] In contrast, the *Sixth Annual Report of the Ministry of Health* for the year 1924/25 says that foster parents cannot be expected to provide for children below average standard and with special needs, and that these children should as a rule be provided for in suitable institutions. Examples of those not considered suitable for boarding-out included children of arrested development or lowered vitality, those anaemic or with a tendency to phthisis, the feeble minded, and those needing careful medical or other supervision or special teaching.

to restore the child to his own family which is so vital a part of the children's service to-day. The real secret of work for the care of boys and girls after they had left the schools was seen by them 'to establish with the decent parent a strong bond of sympathy and co-operation whilst the boy is in school, to make the matter of disposal one of mutual agreement and to make the home fit for the return of the child if possible.'[1] This was indeed a great and enlightened development.

This whole period of the twenties was marked by a growing interest in the treatment of the offender. The Home Office inspectors themselves pleaded for greater facilities, in the places of detention, for children, in order that more and better information could be collected on which a diagnosis of the delinquency could be made. In this field too, the effect of welfare legislation, education, clinics, medical inspection and treatment, and school meals led to a reduction in committals, though a growing reluctance to commit children to an expensive training was no doubt an operative factor too. Between 1915 and 1925 committals of boys to reformatories were halved and committals to industrial schools fell by an even larger proportion.[2] The more difficult type of child was now being sent to the Home Office schools, the less difficult being placed on probation or dealt with by fines or binding over. Of the two types of school the reformatory was used for young people who had committed offences against the law and generally were above school leaving age. The industrial schools were for younger offenders and for those children neglected or brought before the Court in their own interests.[3] Gradually the distinction between them was breaking down and it was becoming apparent that a better procedure would be to match the child, rather than the offence, to a particular type of school.

[1] Ibid., p. 49.
[2] *Third Report of the Work of the Children's Branch*, Published by the Home Office, July, 1925, p. 25.
[3] I.e., under one or other of seven categories of children under 14 needing protection, being found (a) begging in the streets; (b) wandering and having no proper guardian; (c) destitute with parents, or surviving parent, in prison; (d) in the care of drunken or criminal parents; (e) the daughter of a father convicted of the carnal knowledge of any daughter under 16; (f) frequenting the company of a reported thief or prostitute; (g) living in a house frequented by prostitutes or living in circumstances likely to lead to the seduction or prostitution of the child.

In this period of active interest and concern the Government set up two departmental committees to deal with questions of importance, the prevalence of sexual offences against young persons which caused so many of them to be in need of protection,[1] and the treatment of young offenders generally.[2] Both these committees showed concern that many young people were found in undesirable surroundings without any guardianship being exercised by their parents and were therefore drifting into bad associations. They could not, however, be brought before the Court for protection as they had committed no offence neither did they come within any of the categories justifying Court protection under the Children Act of 1908. The problem was first focused by the Committee on Sexual Offences and two recommendations were later made by the Young Offenders Committee to cover this need. It was recommended that the Juvenile Courts should consider and take appropriate measures in the case of two groups, i.e. :

(1) Children and young persons under seventeen who have no parents or guardians, or parents or guardians who are unfit to take care of them, or who do not exercise proper guardianship, where the Court is satisfied that the children or young persons are falling into bad associations, or exposed to moral danger, or beyond control.

(2) Children or young persons under seventeen, in respect of whom specified offences (such as cruelty or sexual offences) have been committed, or who are living in homes where such offences have been committed in respect of other children or young persons, and the Court is satisfied that they require special protection.

The Young Offenders Committee was also concerned about the different ways in which neglected children were dealt with administratively, some being brought before the Courts and committed to industrial schools (where they might be boarded-out) or to the care of fit persons, and others, by far the largest number, whose unsatisfactory parents were destitute, being received into the care of the poor law where they were boarded

[1] *Report of the Departmental Committee on Sexual Offences against Young Persons 1924-5.* Cmd. 2561 and the similar report for Scotland 1926, Cmd. 2592.
[2] *Report of the Departmental Committee on the Treatment of Young Offenders 1927.* Cmd. 2831.

out, placed in workhouses or infirmaries, in poor law schools, cottage or scattered homes, or certified voluntary homes. Twenty years after the Minority Report of the Royal Commission on the poor laws proposals for the unification of the children's care were still being made. 'We have referred to children under the Poor Law in some detail because it appears to us as an integral part of the whole question of neglected children. It is not within our functions to make any recommendations as regards the administration of the Poor Law. We would point out, however, that if under any proposals for the reform of the Poor Law the powers and duties of Boards of Guardians are transferred to the ordinary local authorities, the separation of Poor Law children from other classes of neglected children would tend to disappear, and it would be possible to secure a greater measure of unity and consistency in this treatment.'[1]

The proposals for reform of the poor law referred to in the report, and which had been developing and gathering strength since 1909, finally became embodied in the legislation of 1929 by which the boards of guardians were abolished and their duties taken over by the Councils of the Counties and County Boroughs. This aided the break-up of the poor law into administration by separate specialist departments. The duties of the poor law to visit child life protection cases, under Part 1 of the Children Act 1908, now became the responsibility of the local authority health departments,[2] and the care of destitute children, who were physically or mentally handicapped, but educable, became an educational provision.[3] So effective had the legal provisions been against the mischievous practice of

[1] *Report of the Departmental Committee on the Treatment of Young Offenders*, op. cit., p. 116.

[2] Section 2 of the Local Government Act of 1929 enabled the authority for maternity and child welfare to have the powers conveyed under the relevant part of the Children Act of 1908. The general intention was now as far as possible to vest all powers connected with the health of children, from the ante-natal care of the mother to the care of the child at school, in the same authority, and to split up the health functions of the guardians among the public health authorities, as had been recommended by the Royal Commission on the Poor Laws twenty years ago.

[3] Successive education acts had given local education authorities powers to board and lodge, as well as educate, handicapped children. The protection of employment of children and young persons had also become the responsibility of the local education authorities.

baby farming that it was now considered to be largely eradicated. The supervision had developed into an infant and child welfare service for which the public health departments, with their specially trained health visitors, were more appropriate administrators.[1] By the Poor Law Act of 1930 every county council and county borough was required to set up a Public Assistance Committee. This continued the administration of services for children in poor law care, but was also given powers to delegate its functions to other appropriate Committees of the Council.[2]

In 1933 there was passed a consolidating act of great importance, whose main provisions were based upon the recommendations of the Young Offenders Committee of 1927.[3] The Children and Young Persons Act of 1933 now forged much closer the link between work for neglected and delinquent children and the work of the local education authorities, and further separated the care of neglected children from the poor law. The main important changes in the law which were provided dealt with the constitution and procedure of the juvenile courts, the duties and responsibilities of local education authorities in this field, and the treatment of boys and girls brought before the courts.

The Act defined a child as one up to the age of fourteen, and a young person as between fourteen and seventeen. Parts of it are still operative to-day and it is worth looking at it in some detail since its gathering ground is still the source of all cases which come into the children's departments through the courts. The Act is divided into six parts, the first of which defines the criminal offence of *wilful* cruelty and *wilful* neglect committed against a child by which the perpetrator could be dealt with and the child brought before the juvenile court for care or protection. (It was not until 1952 that a child could receive the protection of the court where there was ignorant neglect other than wilful).[4] The second part consolidated the

---

[1] See *Eighth Annual Report of the Ministry of Health 1926–27*. Section on Infant Protection.

[2] In some cases the care of destitute children was delegated to other committees of the Council, being divided between the education committee, public health committee or maternity and child welfare committee, see *Curtis Report*, para. 14.

[3] 23 and 24 Geo. V. c. 12. Children and Young Persons Act 1933.

[4] See *post* p. 178. Section 1 of the Children and Young Persons (Amendment) Act 1952. 15 and 16 Geo. VI and I Eliz. II c. 50.

legislation restricting the employment of children, and regulating their street trading and employment in entertainment. Part III of the Act dealt with the constitution and machinery of the juvenile courts first set up under the Children Act of 1908 and now extended to include boys and girls up to the age of seventeen. The powers of protection for children were enlarged by extending the age range of children and young persons, governed by the Act, from sixteen to seventeen, and by widening the definition of the need for care or protection which now covered the important points raised by the two earlier departmental committees. A person can now be defined as in need of care or protection if he is 'a child or young person who, having no parent or guardian or a parent or guardian unfit to exercise care and guardianship or not exercising proper care and guardianship, is either falling into bad associations, or exposed to moral danger, or beyond control or is ill treated or neglected in a manner likely to cause his unnecessary suffering or injury to health.'[1] Here two conditions must be fulfilled ; the failure of guardianship and the danger to the child must both be present.

The object of the juvenile court was now to be not punishment alone—'the Court shall have regard to the welfare of the child'—but rehabilitation and even social service, and justices were to be specially selected for it on the grounds of experience and interest.[2] Local education authorities had a duty now to provide the magistrates with information about the family and school background of the boys and girls who appeared before the Court, and on them, not on the police or ' any person', was laid the primary responsibility for bringing before the Courts children and young persons in need of care or protection. Emphasis on the constructive and educational purpose of the remand home is now seen in the transfer of the duty to provide them from the police to the local education

[1] Section 61.   Children and Young Persons Act 1933.

[2] In the metropolitan police court areas juvenile courts were to consist of a metropolitan police magistrate, who acted as chairman, and two lay justices, one man and one woman, drawn from a panel of London justices appointed by the Secretary of State. Outside this area the justices of every petty sessional division were required to form a juvenile court panel which was to consist of those of them specially qualified for dealing with juvenile cases. The members of the juvenile court are selected from this panel.   The court is to be constituted of not more than three justices, including one man, and so far as practicable, one woman.

authorities[1], and the fact that remand homes could now be used as places of safety for boys and girls in need of care or protection, the use of public assistance institutions for this purpose being prohibited by Remand Home Rules issued after the Act. This definite separation of public assistance from protective work is further seen in the powers given now to the local education authorities to act as a fit person to whose care, if the authority gave its consent, boys and girls could be committed by the court. Moreover the local authorities now had a duty to board out children committed to them and the Home Secretary was empowered to make rules governing the method of fostering. The fourth part of the Act dealt with the treatment of children after the court had made a decision about them. The distinction between the reformatory and industrial schools was abolished, and they both became schools 'approved' by the Home Office for giving short-term training to enable boys and girls to take their place as useful, happy citizens in society. They thus became known as Approved Schools and a maximum period was determined and laid down for the detention of children and young persons in them. Boys and

---

[1] The four main purposes of the remand homes are well summarised in the *Fifth report of the Children's Branch of the Home Office* published in 1938, p. 14.

(1) If the juvenile court has any doubt whether, after an adjournment of a case, the boy will re-appear before it, he can be sent to a remand home to ensure that he shall.

(2) If the offence is serious he can be sent to a remand home to ensure that he shall not have the chance of repeating the offence during the period of remand.

(3) If a boy does not seem to realise that he has broken the law, in a remand home he can be given an opportunity of reflecting upon his conduct in the interval between the first and second hearing of the case. Moreover the separation from home and friends involved by removal in custody generally amounts in *itself* to a punishment for the normal child—a punishment which is incidental rather than designed, but which sometimes proves salutary in cases where home discipline is lax.

As for a boy who has started to earn, the loss of liberty, the separation from home and companions, the cessation of pocket money, and the realisation that the family income is being reduced by the amount of his wages, has a wholesome effect in some cases not only on the boy but also on his parents.

(4) After guilt is proved in cases of boys charged with offences, remands for further inquiries into home surroundings, school record, health and character are usually essential in all but trivial cases. The juvenile court remands on bail any suitable cases, but where the court needs additional information to enable it to decide on the best course to adopt for the welfare of the child, a remand in custody is often more helpful as medical and psychological reports can thus be obtained, as well as a report from the head of the remand home.

girls in need of care or protection because they were beyond
control at home could now, as an alternative to being sent to an
approved school, be placed under the supervision of a probation officer or other suitable person.[1]

The Act, in its fifth part, then dealt with the care given to
neglected or homeless children by the voluntary homes, or
orphanages, and preventive, rescue and other voluntary children's homes. For the first time a voluntary home was defined[2]
as a home supported wholly or partly by voluntary contributions for the boarding, care and maintenance of poor children,
and for the first time they were required to send annually to
the Secretary of State certain prescribed particulars.[3] This
enabled a record of such Homes to be kept by the central
government department whose inspectors could help with
advice on diet, clothing, fire prevention, medical standards
and sleeping accommodation, while there were powers to
remove children from those Homes considered unsatisfactory
where the Home Office directions for improvement had not
been carried out.

The sixth and final part of the Act dealt with the administrative provisions. They were somewhat unusual, in that the
Central Government department, responsible for inspection
and exchequer grants to local authorities, was the Home
Office, while administration of the care of children at the
local level was the responsibility of local education committees
who normally worked with the Board of Education. Voluntary
organisations received exchequer grants for the administration

[1] As these children were not charged with an offence the provision of the Probation of Offenders Act 1907 did not apply but section 58(4) of the Children Act
1908 had enabled a court—where a child *under fourteen* was brought by the parent
or guardian as beyond control—to deal with the child in the same way as if he
had been charged with an offence, and so place him on probation. The Children
and Young Persons Act 1933 made possible the use of supervision by the probation
officers to all under the age of seventeen. The use made of this measure is shown in
the following figures :
1933 probation orders for beyond control cases numbered 24 ; 1934—261
supervision orders were made ; 1935—402 ; 1936—490.
The Children and Young Persons Act 1933 gave the Courts new powers to
commit such cases to a fit person as an alternative to supervision or to approved
school care.

[2] Section 92, Children and Young Persons Act 1933.

[3] In fact, however, many did not appear to know of the legislation and did not
comply and remained un-inspected. See *Fifth Report of the Children's Branch 1938*,
p. 103.

of approved schools, but not for orphanages or rescue or other voluntary homes.

But the Act is memorable in setting a standard of welfare and rehabilitation for the delinquent and the neglected children and those in need of care which had never previously been approached. Ideas and philosophies which had required treatment of social failures and problems to be justified by hard work and stigma were now finally discarded and a constructive concept of social training in the best interests of the child took its place. The welfare of the child, and not the judgement of society, was now paramount.

Yet it is interesting to see how firmly the concept of training by alteration of the environment had permeated the legislation of the time. In providing for the group of neglected children whose home life had proved so inadequate the Children and Young Persons Act of 1933 could offer only substitutes for the natural family. A committal order to a fit person remained in force till the child became eighteen. There is no real and positive concept of the eventual return of such a child to his own rehabilitated home.[1] Indeed the increased powers of committal to the local authority with a duty to board out in a foster home bringing with it new ties of close personal affection increased the likelihood of the child's final break with his unsatisfactory family, and the authority of the court verdict strengthened his integration with the new foster home. Although the emphasis on rehabilitation of the child is forward looking, the concept of care is still nineteenth century, based on removal from the degrading environmental conditions of squalor and poverty, and provides a substitute family for the home which has failed. Furthermore the Act expressly dissolves doubts about the propriety of sending a child of good character away for years. The court can now justify such action by the welfare of the child 'Every court in dealing with a child or young person who is

---

[1] The two sections bearing on this are firstly, section 75(4). 'The person to whose care a child or young person is committed by any such order as aforesaid shall, while the order is in force, have the same rights and powers and be subject to the same liabilities in respect of his maintenance as if he were his parent, and the person so committed shall continue in his care notwithstanding any claim by a parent or any other person.', and section 84(4) 'The Secretary of State may at any time in his discretion discharge a child or young person from the care of the person to whose care he has been committed, and any such discharge may be granted either absolutely or subject to conditions.'

brought before it, either as being in need of care or protection
or as an offender or otherwise, shall have regard to the welfare
of the child or young person and shall in a proper case take
steps for removing him from undesirable surroundings, and
for securing that proper provision is made for his education
and training.'[1] This attitude is perhaps not remarkable if one
examines the circumstances of the time in which the legislation
was passed. Many things encouraged the legislators to think
that the strength of family life was breaking down, the mass
unemployment with its poverty and the break up of families
caused by the means test and the search for work and lodging
elsewhere, the sickness and high maternal mortality rates now
known to be aggravated by conditions of poverty, the lack of
free medical treatment for mothers exhausted by coping with
families in conditions of overcrowding and undernourishment,
the rising numbers of separations in the matrimonial courts,
the falling birth rate and loss of status of family life at this
time because of the economic disadvantages of numbers of
small dependent children.[2] In these circumstances the task of
rehabilitating the unsatisfactory family was too great, the
numbers of available family caseworkers too small, for the
legislation to encourage a different approach. The problem
really called not for caseworkers, but for a policy of economic
support for the family expressed in legislation.

It is in the care for the delinquent child with its control of
the duration of sentence and system of after care, that the work
of restoration and co-operation with the natural parents is first
seen. The reports of the inspectors of Home Office schools
had drawn attention to this considerably earlier in connection
with the care of boys and girls after they had left the schools.
'The real secret of after care is to establish . . . with the
decent parent a strong bond of sympathy and co-operation
whilst the boy is in the school . . . and to make the home fit

[1] Sect. 44 Children and Young Persons Act 1933.

[2] For a graphic description of family life affected by poverty and unemployment in the thirties see the study of Margery Spring Rice, *Working Class Wives. Their Health and Conditions*. Pelican Books, 1939, and *Men Without Work*, published for the Pilgrim Trust by Cambridge University Press, 1938. This last study showed that the chronic unemployed man with a large family was often financially better off receiving unemployment assistance than when he was working. This tended to lower the value of the large family in the eyes of society because of its burden on the exchequer.

for the return of the child if possible.'[1] and 'The old theory, once very strongly held, that the parents having failed with their children, should be more or less ignored, has now given way to a realisation that whenever possible the co-operation of the parent in the training and disposal of the child is advisable and very helpful .'[2]

By 1938, those experienced in the work of the Approved Schools were beginning to wonder whether the elaborate administrative machinery was too heavily weighted on the side of institutional and substitute family care, and too little emphasis put on the preventive social services. Too often the solution to a child's problem of need was only found through the juvenile court when the boy or girl had reached the age of fifteen or sixteen and committed one or more serious offences. 'Everything therefore points to a pressing need for machinery for the ascertainment and recognition at an early age of those children who will require special supervision and care and for effective steps to be taken to give such help as is necessary before they become victims of neglect and social failure."[3] In spite of this preventive approach the cure was still to be effected through the institution. The approach to cure within the family had not yet come.

Ten years, made memorable by war and a silent social revolution, were to pass before the social conditions of the people made this new attitude either acceptable or possible.

[1] *First Report of the Children's Branch 1923.*
[2] *Fifth Report of the Children's Branch 1938.*
[3] *Fourth Report of the Children's Branch 1928.*

CHAPTER EIGHT

THE STATE AND THE IMPORTANCE
OF THE FAMILY

IT was the personal experience of the whole population of Great Britain whose lives were directly affected and disrupted by the conditions of war which rediscovered for the nation the value of the family. Up to this time, its importance, from the period of the industrial revolution, had been undermined by powerful economic and social factors, and this loss of status was reflected in its smaller size and the lack of support given to it in social legislation. When society had been agricultural the family had been able to work together as a productive unit, the oldest and the youngest could be found some work to do in the house or on the land near by, but the individual competition and struggle for survival which came with industrial conditions weakened its cohesive nature, and economic need sent even the very young children out from the home into long hours of unsupervised factory labour. Even the ameliorating legislation when it came, brought also problems to the poor, for the early factory and education acts prolonged the period of a child's dependency, and families were unable to make up the loss of wages. The family with young children became itself a cause of poverty and this is clearly shown in the study made by Rowntree in 1901. Children, once a financial asset, now became, during their long dependency, a liability. The smaller family with less mouths to feed had more chance of security, for it was less liable to the vicious circle of poverty and consequent hunger and ill health. It thus became more desirable economically and the large family began to disappear, even became a source of irritation to administrators because of its economic dependence ; and with the going of the large family there also went the special protection to childhood offered by the kinship group of different members and generations.

The changing social conditions and the improved position of women as individuals in their own right also diminished the status of the family. During the first forty years of this century general advances in living conditions were applied more to social opportunities and to leisure and less to planning or improving domestic conditions in the home which would make it easier for the mother to cope with the responsibilities of a family. Conditions in the home lagged behind commercial and industrial advances and women recognized that in these circumstances an unlimited family threw an excessive burden on them, which they refused to tolerate. All these factors led to the spread of family limitation, the loss of prestige of the family and the concentration of social reform in a way organised to meet the difficulties outside the family circle. The problems created by neglect, delinquency and deficiency were removed out of the family background and the individual treated in an institution as one of a protected group in a specialized setting.[1] In this way the problem child and the problem parent had become separated, instead of connected entities.

In this new and uncertain pattern of the family it had been left to the studies of anthropologists and of psychologists to demonstrate the extraordinary strength, tenacity and satisfaction found in the family group.[2] As a social concept this does not seem to have been accepted until the wartime disruptions between 1939 and 1945 demonstrated its truth, the fact that the family still preferred to cling together as a fundamental unit in the face of every obstacle. In spite of carefully contrived plans to evacuate mothers and young children, and school children, to safer areas, they refused to remain divided and gradually, in ones and threes and then in groups and crowds, they returned to their homes and family circle, preferring to stay together under danger than to be separated

---

[1] i.e. the neglected child in the children's Home, the delinquent in the approved School, the mental defective in the institution, the destitute in the workhouse, the sick person in hospital, the criminal in prison. The institution is a convenient administrative device for treatment. But it contains in it also an element which is not treatment but prevention of contamination. It is an attempt to remove the infection from society, and, sometimes, to punish the individual too.

[2] See the contemporary article and bibliography on the *Family* in the *Fourteenth Edition of the Encyclopedia Britannica* published in 1929.

and safe.[1] This was the way that human nature actually worked, and the administrators' well meaning plans were powerless against it.

At the same time the conditions of war had once again resulted in an increase in illegitimate births.[2] Adoption or placing the children in an institution was often resorted to in despair, for few unmarried mothers were able to obtain skilled local help and advice in the difficult early days of making a decision. So much was this a matter of concern, that the Ministry of Health in 1943 called on a sub-committee of the advisory Committee on Mothers and Young Children to report on the problem of caring for the illegitimate child, and to suggest some action. The Committee's recommendations, in a problem historically the province of the poor law, illustrate the new social pattern. They asked for the appointment of carefully selected social workers for whom each local authority should be responsible, in order that personal care and skilled attention could be given to the problem of the unmarried mother and her child. The government circular which followed embodying their recommendations brought to an end the old association of the poor law with illegitimacy.[3] Henceforth the local authorities, acting through their public health committees, either appointed special health visitors or social workers or made use of denominational moral welfare workers, part of whose salaries they were empowered to pay. The historical emphasis of these workers on the natural family meant that this problem, at least, was moving away from its institutional setting, and a domiciliary service of prevention and rehabilitation was to attempt its solution. Shortly afterwards the introduction of a shortened form of birth certificate, to be generally

[1] The history of the effect of the war on civilians is described by Professor Richard Titmuss in *Problems of Social Policy* in the History of the Second World War United Kingdom Civil Series, edited by W. K. Hancock and published by H.M.S.O. and Longmans Green & Co., 1950. The Ministry of Health in 1949 published a survey of its evacuation scheme in which it drew attention to the impossibility of providing children with any adequate substitute for the family.

[2] The numbers rose from 25,942 in 1939 (4.19% of all live births) to 43,216 in 1943, and 64,064 (or 9.35% of all live births) in 1945. An account of the problem of illegitimacy in the war is found in Sheila Ferguson and Hilde Fitzgerald's *Studies in the Social Services*, Chapter III and IV, History of the Second World War United Kingdom Civil Series, etc., 1954.

[3] Ministry of Health Circular 2866, dated 1st October, 1943.

used, attempted to give to the illegitimate child equal acceptance within the community.

But the partial mobilisation of women, the need for many of them to spend a large part of the day working in the factories, the absence of fathers on service, of relatives at work, and the destruction of houses by bombing required the state to intervene in another way by providing residential nurseries where young children could be given the care and attention impossible where family life had become non-existent, and where they could be protected from enemy attack.[1] Many of these nurseries were opened up and down the country under the control of voluntary organisations or of the local authorities in areas outside the bombing ranges, at first with financial help from America, and later supported by Treasury grants. Exclusive of public assistance children, it was estimated that 15,000 residential war nursery places would be needed by the end of 1942. In fact, 13,000 places were achieved, and of the 415 residential nurseries which came into existence in reception areas, five-sixths were for children evacuated from the London region.[2] It became possible to observe on a fairly extensive scale, therefore, the effect upon small children of complete separation and of life without a family, and to measure its influence upon their development at various stages of growth. Studies of this kind were made by Dorothy Burlingham and Anna Freud, the daughter of the psycho-analyst, in the Hampstead Nursery.[3] Here many of the children had gone through a long experience of air raids before they were admitted to the nursery, but the writers found that the suffering the young children experienced most personally was that of sudden separation for which they were unprepared. The intensity of their fear in bombing was the same as that of the parent with whom they shared the experience ; the separation they suffered alone. The detailed observation on the nature of separation and the child's reaction to it was carefully examined by scientific observers of integrity with conclusions which

[1] See S. Ferguson and H. Fitzgerald op. cit., c. VII.
[2] Ibid, p. 231.
[3] Dorothy Burlingham and Anna Freud: *Young Children in War Time. A year's work in a Residential War Nursery.* George Allen and Unwin, 1942, and *Infants without Families. The Case for and against Residential Nurseries.* George Allen and Unwin, Ltd., 1944.

challenged the practice of most child care workers at the time.

'Our case material shows that it is not so much the fact of separation to which the child reacts abnormally as the form in which the separation has taken place. The child experiences shock when he is suddenly and without preparation exposed to dangers with which he cannot cope emotionally. In the case of evacuation the danger is represented by the sudden disappearance of all the people whom he knows and loves. Unsatisfied longing produces in him a state of tension which is felt as shock.

If separation happened slowly, if the people who are meant to substitute for the mother were known to the child beforehand, the transition from one object to the other would proceed gradually. If the mother reappeared several times during the period when the child has to be weaned from her, the pain of separation would be repeated but it would be felt each successive time in smaller doses. By the time the affection of the child has let go of the mother the new substitute-object would be well known and ready to hand. There would be no empty period in which the feelings of the child are completely turned inward and consequently there would be little loss of educational achievement. Regression happens while the child passes through the no-man's land of affection, i.e. during the time after the old object has been given up and before the new one has been found.

'Mothers are commonly advised not to visit their children during the first fortnight after separation. It is the common opinion that the pain of separation will then pass more quickly and cause less disturbance. In reality it is the very quickness of the child's break with the mother which contains all the dangers of abnormal consequences. Long-drawn-out separation may bring more visible pain, but it is less harmful because it gives the child time to accompany the events with his reactions, to work through his own feelings over and over again, to find outward expressions for his state of mind, i.e., to abreact slowly. Reactions which do not even reach the child's consciousness can do incalculable harm to his normality.'[1]

It will be seen that an examination of this kind of the

[1] Burlingham and Freud. *Young Children in Wartime*, op. cit., pp. 75 ff.

traumatic effects of separation was of major importance in centering the thought of those whose responsibility it was to care for the homeless child on the satisfying of his need for personal attachment, security and continuity, and on his ability to understand also what is happening to him, to take part in it, to talk about it consciously as far as he can, and not to be treated as a child to whom things happen and are done. The true rights and true responsibilities of the child as an individual are being recognised. The second study by the same writers later tried to evaluate the importance of the family, to weigh the advantages and disadvantages of institutional life at different phases of the infants' development in order to measure the usefulness of providing residential nurseries for the very young child after the war. This study emphasised the correlation between the child's emotional satisfaction and normal development and showed that in the first two years the child in a good institution has advantages over the family child in those spheres of his life which are independent of the emotional side of his nature. At stages when the emotional tie to the mother or the family is the mainspring of development, he is at a disadvantage.[1]

It becomes therefore important now to examine for a moment the purpose of the family and the reason why, on rational grounds, social policy needed to move towards its support rather than the extension of the institutional device. It is here that the work of the psychologists and anthropologists is vindicated, and can be seen as the sifting of generations of human experience, explaining in scientific terms what is expressed in the practical wisdom of the people.[2]

In all forms of society the family appears to be a naturally accepted pattern for safeguarding and protecting the growth and physical health of the child through the strength of the affection which binds its members together. Because of this affection it is also the most powerful force by which behaviour, or the qualities of an accepted way of life, can be handed on to the next generation. The very young child does not learn

[1] Burlingham and Freud. *Infants without Families.* Op. cit.

[2] A study of the earlier work on the importance of the family is found in the report, *Maternal Care and Mental Health,* prepared by John Bowlby for the World Health Organisation and published in 1951. Reference to it and its influence belongs to a later chapter.

only by imitation, his true learning is the result of restraint which he imposes on his impulses under the influence of praise or disapproval from those he loves. Within the family, therefore, with its powerful natural ties of affection, is found most abundantly and most exclusively the power to teach the child behaviour, self discipline, values and the code of society. The whole art of living is interpreted and handed on to the child by his parent in the way most acceptable to him. And family life to be understood must be experienced. The experience of the family has a different quality from the sum of experiences of the individual alone; it is a special form of group experience which cannot be learnt by theory but only by apprenticeship. Family life, therefore is perpetuated of itself and by no artificial teaching, and if it is to be kept alive this can only be done by deliberate fostering of its vitality. On its vitality depends the significance of human institutions, and the success of human relationships expressed in living together in society. Within the family there is provided a range of emotional experience which, rightly handled, can immunize the child against the major crises of later life, and by its constitution it provides the most effective method of training which enables the child to grow and adjust to the wider group of society.

This early training, so dependent on personal feeling and possessive care, cannot be provided, as it is meant to be provided, by uninvolved personalities, nor can the state supply any substitute for individual standards of maternal competence and care. The individual art of motherhood within the family, the mother's strongly motivated personal wish to learn and her personal application of the growing knowledge of child care and training, has been shown to be the major factor in reducing the diseases and deaths so prevalent in infancy fifty years ago, and not, by themselves, the improved social conditions and growth of the child welfare services.[1]

Moreover the enlightening studies of a group of social biologists at Peckham in the years immediately preceding the war showed how important to the individual was the status and acceptance of the family within society. The family as a family has a real relationship with its environment, with the

[1] See Sir James Spence *A Thousand Families in Newcastle-on-Tyne*. Oxford University Press, 1954.

neighbours, the church, the club, the school, and this relationship as a group affects the abilities of individual members within it. If a family is well and happy within itself, and well integrated in the social life of its area, the individuals in it can expand to the best of their ability. The family itself bears a relationship to society rather like the child to the mother and cannot function properly without acceptance and support.[1]

The effective device of the family for the security and physical and mental health of the child was dislocated up and down the country by the second world war. The war also exposed on a wide scale conditions of failure of many families whose standards were far below those to which the general public had attained. The mass evacuation of children from towns vulnerable to enemy attack revealed conditions of neglect and incompetence within the slum home of which many people had never dreamed and which disturbed the public conscience. Although many condemned the homes and parentage from which the children came, there were others who believed these conditions of dirt, squalor, laziness and ignorance had been aggravated by the lack of support and understanding given to the family, and, particularly the mother, by social services whose policies were still based on a change of environment rather than personal insight into the needs and inabilities which lay behind the failure. Concern was expressed for a more imaginative and constructive approach to the problem of the neglectful mother and her family.[2]

There was also, in the course of the war, a great number of children requiring to be taken into public care because of disrupted family life, and this imposed a severe strain on the administration and on the various voluntary children's homes and public assistance institutions. In a letter to *The Times* of the 15th July, 1944[3], Lady Allen of Hurtwood drew attention to the fact that the quality of care given to homeless children was generations out of date. She pointed out the nature of the administration, the central control divided between three

[1] See Innes H. Pearce and Lucy H. Crocker, *The Peckham Experiment*. George Allen and Unwin, 1943. This theory needs to be considered when the question of segregating or integrating 'problem' families arises.

[2] See *Our Towns. A Close Up*. A study made by the Women's Group on Public Welfare during 1939–42. Oxford University Press, 1943.

[3] See Appendix VI, p. 230.

different government departments, the inadequate nature of standards and inspection, and the lack of trained personnel in all fields. There was considerable concern shown by the public, expressed vividly in further correspondence in *The Times*, calling for a Government inquiry. Lady Allen followed up her letter with a pamphlet *Whose Children?*[1] intended to inform public opinion about the conditions under which deprived children lived, and to stir the government and people into action. Its importance cannot be over-estimated. The pamphlet incorporated evidence from individuals, who had been brought up or worked in children's homes, and contained complaints so similar, and so appalling, that they could not be disregarded. Yet, as she herself had warned, the pace of improvement was too slow. In the end it was the children who had suffered who had to be their own advocates. The public care of children was drawing to a crisis which was tragically precipitated by a series of administrative weaknesses culminating in the violent death of one who had been taken from a neglectful home and committed by the court for care to the local authority.

In November 1939 a seven year old boy, Dennis O'Neill, and his two younger brothers and sister were removed from their home to a place of safety by an inspector of the National Society for the Prevention of Cruelty to Children, while informations were laid against both their parents for offences of cruelty. Sixteen years earlier the father had been convicted and sentenced for neglecting one of his children, his wife being dismissed with a caution, and over this long period the inspector had paid more than two hundred visits to the family. This time the magistrates hearing the case took sterner measures. The parents were ordered to pay a fine or go to prison for one month in default, while the three boys were committed to the care of the local authority as being in need of care or protection, and the girl to the care of her maternal grandmother.

The local authority had now a statutory duty to make arrangements for the boys committed to its care to be boarded out,[2] and as soon as possible, in fact from September 1940,

[1] Published by the Favil Press Ltd., 1945.
[2] Under Section 84 of the Children and Young Persons Act, 1933.

the boys were boarded out in the area of another authority in successive foster homes, and Dennis, at the end of June, 1944, was moved to a country farmhouse to which, one week later, his younger brother was brought. Here the foster parents neglected and ill-used Dennis so much that he died, in January 1945, as a result of their treatment. The coroner's jury returned a verdict that his death was due to acute cardiac failure following violence applied to the front of the chest and back, while in a state of undernourishment due to neglect. They added a rider that there had been a serious lack of supervision by the local authority.

The public disquiet was profound. That a child, removed from his own home because of its bad conditions and entrusted, for his greater good, to the public care, should yet experience even worse neglect and cruelty leading directly to his death, caused such concern that the Government requested Sir Walter Monckton to conduct a public and independent legal inquiry into the circumstances leading to the boarding-out in this particular foster home and to the supervision given there to the children's welfare.[1]

The inquiry immediately threw into startling relief the lack of trained and skilled social workers and the confusion and defects of the administrative machinery provided for the care of children removed from their own homes and committed to the care of the local authority. The record of it also remains as a lesson to any administrator; a story unfolds in the report of small carelessnesses, pressures of other work, difficulties of staffing and human procrastinations and failure to co-operate, by which few workers, if they are honest, have not at times been tempted from their standards, but which collectively resulted in individual tragedy and public scandal. The report stated that there was need for the administrative machinery to be improved and informed by a more anxious and responsible spirit, and indicated where it was thought such improvement was needed. This, however, was not enough. The failure of the machinery and the patent and urgent need for overhaul so

[1] See the *Report by Sir Walter Monckton, K.C.M.G., K.C.V.O., M.C., K.C. on the circumstances which led to the boarding-out of Dennis and Terence O'Neill at Bank Farm, Minsterly and the steps taken to supervise their welfare.* Published May 1945 by H.M.S.O. Cmd. 6636.

tragically disclosed had already led the Government to appoint in March, 1945, under the Chairmanship of Miss Myra Curtis (as she then was), the principal of Newnham, an inter-departmental committee of inquiry on the Care of Children. The duties of the Committee were 'to inquire into existing methods of providing for children who from loss of parents or from any cause whatever are deprived of a normal home life with their own parents or relatives; and to consider what further measures should be taken to ensure that these children are brought up under conditions best calculated to compensate them for the lack of parental care.'[1]

A similar inter-departmental Committee was appointed to study the problem in Scotland, under the Chairmanship of Mr. J. L. Clyde, K.C. The Clyde Committee, however, was not so wide in its terms of reference, for already in Scotland an advisory committee was inquiring into conditions in remand homes and approved schools. The number of homeless children in Scotland, too, was only about one-seventh of the number in England and Wales. The Clyde report did not have the breadth of the Curtis inquiry. However, the Clyde Committee made important recommendations which, with those of the Curtis Committee, became incorporated in the legislation.[2]

The two Committees spent up to seventeen months examining witnesses, visiting institutions and foster homes and interviewing officials and members of local authorities, and in the late summer of 1946 produced the first reports of inquiry ever undertaken into the care of the several different groups of deprived children.

The recommendations of the two separate committees of inquiry were striking in their similarity. At once the existing statutory and administrative arrangements disclosed an almost unbelievably complicated position, summed up in the Curtis report. 'Responsibility for providing or supervising the substitute home for the deprived child may be taken by the State,

[1] Warrant of appointment of the Care of Children Committee (familiarly known as the Curtis Committee). The report was published in September 1946. See Cmd. 6922.

[2] E.g. it was the Clyde Committee which recommended that children should remain in care up to the age of 18, so helping them to weather under protection the difficult storm of adolescence.

by local authorities, by voluntary organisations or by private persons. The State through the Ministry of Health supervises the work of local authorities in caring for destitute children under the Poor Law. Such children, may however, be accepted by voluntary Homes independently of any public authority, in which case, if the voluntary organisations concerned receive subscriptions from the public, the State, through the Home Office, brings them under inspection; or it may do so through the Ministry of Health if that Department "certifies" the Homes as suitable for Poor Law children or if Poor Law children are received in them. If the voluntary organisations receive no public subscriptions, and do not take in Poor Law children their Homes may, if they take children under 9 years of age "for reward", be visited by the welfare authority's child protection visitors; otherwise, they may come under no public supervision at all. Children under 9 years of age "fostered" for reward, or placed by private persons (not the parents or guardians) for adoption, are supervised by local authorities under the direction of the Minister of Health through the child life protection service. Those over 9 received for reward and those for whose maintenance no reward is given are not the care of any public authority. Children removed from their homes by order of a juvenile Court may, if "Committed to" and accepted by the local authority as a "fit person", be entitled to full parental care and guardianship from the authority; normally this responsibility is exercised by boarding the child out under rules laid down by the Home Office, but if there is difficulty in finding a foster home, the child may be left in a public assistance institution, in which case the Ministry of Health is concerned. Other children removed from their homes by Court order may be in approved schools for remedial training or in remand homes awaiting a decision of the Court, in which case, though the local authority (or a voluntary organisation) may provide the institution, the Home Office is directly and closely concerned with its regulation and management.'

It was indeed possible for different members of one family, according to the circumstances in which they were found, to be cared for by three different departments of the local authority and inspected by two different Government departments or by none at all.[1] The situation may be described as Gilbertian, but to the child too often it brought disaster or unhappiness.

Nor were the Committee satisfied with the general impressions they formed of the ways in which the children were cared for in nurseries, residential homes and foster homes. They were concerned about the quality of care provided at the immediate moment of the child becoming deprived. The lack of understanding of his needs which was then shown and the poor facilities for caring and planning for him at a time of acute tension and misery caused them to stress the importance of special reception facilities.

Their observations were candid and they pulled no punches. In long term provision they noted the influence of the growth of imaginative and scientific thought on the care of young children reflected in the arrangement and equipment of the most progressive nurseries,[2] but found a wide variety of standards particularly in the residential Homes for older children and in the foster homes. '. . . in many Homes was a lack of personal interest in and affection for the children which one found shocking. The child in these Homes was not recognised as an individual with his own rights and possessions, his own life to live and his own contribution to offer. He was merely one of a large crowd, eating, playing and sleeping with the rest, without any place or possession of his own or any quiet room to which he could retreat. Still more important, he was without the feeling that there was anyone to whom he could turn who was vitally interested in his welfare or who cared for him as a person. The effect of this on the smaller children was reflected in their behaviour towards visitors, which took the form of an almost pathological clamouring for attention and petting. In the older children the effect appeared more in slowness,

[1] (a) The health department (child fostered for reward); (b) the public assistance department (child homeless and destitute); (c) the education department (child found in need of care or protection). (a) and (b) under the central control of the Ministry of Health, (c) under the Home Office. If a child were placed privately by a well wisher in an endowed voluntary home not dependent on public subscriptions no local authority worker or Government department inspector saw him.

[2] Among the non-progressives, however, it was a Nursery which of all the Institutions they visited, had sunk to the lowest level of child care to come to their notice. See para 144.

backwardness and lack of response, and in habits of destructiveness and want of concentration. Where individual love and care had been given, the behaviour of the children was quite different. They showed no undue interest in visitors and were easily and happily employed in their own occupations and games '.[1]

Everywhere the Committee stressed the immense power for good or evil which lay with the individual carrying authority in the Home. Too often their portraits of the behaviour of the children they saw show how deeply the lack of a loving inheritance had marked the institutional child. Widespread was a deplorable shortage of the right kind of staff, personally qualified and trained to provide the child with a substitute home background. So urgent and acute was this need felt to be that an interim report was published by the inter-departmental Committee in March 1946, recommending the formation of a Central Training Council in child care, and the provision of special courses of training to provide for the recruitment of staff of better quality who would bring improved status into the work.[2]

The Committee was convinced that the divided responsibility at local and central levels was bedevilling the administration and called for a sureness and clarity of direction and insight impossible within the muddled framework of the legislation. Their final recommendations in the field of administration and care were therefore radical; they looked for a service both comprehensive and unified.[3] They thus aimed at recasting the whole machinery of legislation and care.

At the central government level the relevant powers under the Poor Law Act, Children and Young Persons Act, Public Health Acts, and Adoption of Children Act were to be concentrated in one department which would be responsible for the care of the deprived children, defining and maintaining standards by direction, advice and inspection and acting as a clearing house for progressive ideas; the actual provision for the deprived child should lie with the voluntary organisations and

[1] *Curtis report* para. 418.

[2] *Training in Child Care.* Interim Report of the Care of Children Committee. Cmd. 6760.

[3] Though radical this concept was not original, it had been broached by the Maclean Committee in 1913. See ante p. 120.

the local authority aided by exchequer grants; the local authority having immediate responsibility and working through a
single *ad hoc* committee with specialist executives to be known
as Children's Officers. Many detailed recommendations
were made about the quality and methods of care based on a
more informed, scientific and imaginative understanding of the
needs of children separated from their homes and families.
Adoption was described as the most completely satisfactory
way of providing a substitute home, if it could be used, but
closer supervision of present adoption procedure was recommended.

The Committee then emphasized the value of boarding-out
for suitable children and recommended that local authorities
should make vigorous efforts to extend this form of care.
Institutional care they wanted to see modelled to a far greater
extent on the family group system while still emphasising the
importance of sound education and co-operation in the life
of the neighbourhood. Small mixed family group homes of a
maximum of eight boys and girls were considered the ideal
form of institutional care. Concern had been expressed about
the care given to the child at the receiving stage and a recommendation was made that reception centres should be set up
which should serve partly to provide observation and more informed understanding of the child in order to plan for his
appropriate placing, and also partly to help prepare the
child to come to terms with his present and his future. The
after-care of boys and girls leaving the Homes was a matter
of deep concern. The Committee stressed the need for support
and understanding to be given to the adolescent at this time,
the need for co-operation with the Juvenile Employment
service, and for the provision of hostel accommodation,
and for adolescents going into employment in strange places
to be aware of someone to whom they could turn for help if
necessary

The Committee was not asked to deal with the treatment of
delinquent children, but, as children in need of care or protection are dealt with by the Juvenile Courts under the Children
and Young Persons Act 1933, and as many thereby find their
way into Remand Homes and Approved Schools, certain
recommendations were made in this field also. While it was

hoped that committals of children for care or protection to the local authority would increase as a result of their recommendations the Committee still wished the Approved Schools to be available for children likely to benefit from their special kind of social training. They also emphasised the need for remand homes to be used much more as places of short-stay observation and not for purposes of punishment.

When the Curtis Committee recommended that the central responsibility for deprived children should be vested in a single government department, they did not suggest which one this should be. Though previously the care of different specialised ministries, the factors in common which all deprived children shared were their homelessness and need of a relationship, and to provide these was not the special province of any of the government departments. Once the child's main needs of deprivation were met, he was to share, like other children, the provisions of all the social services provided for them and their families. The ultimate choice of which central department should be legally answerable was of less importance to the Committee than the achievement of a single responsibility for the care of the child.

The choice for the Government, between the Ministries of Health and Education or the Home Office, was not a simple one, but, in due course the Home Office, with its historically progressive traditions in the care of homeless children, was regarded as the most appropriate for the responsibility.

The legislation was passed in a fresh and hopeful atmosphere. The end of the second world war brought about opportunities for the revolution of social policy towards which the people had been striving for a hundred and fifty years, but until this time never had the climate of thought or conditions of experience been so favourable to consummation. Six years of common sharing, both of danger and the means of life, had created patterns based not upon opportunity or privilege, but on fulfilment of the individual's need. This ideal had first been expressed, before the war itself had ended, when the Education Act of 1944 secured the principle of equality of educational opportunity for everyone. By 1948 the old paternalistic pattern of the poor law was brought to an end, and services which the individual could claim as a right were substituted.[1] The report of Sir William Beveridge, *Social Insurance and Allied Services*, published in 1942, crystallized and symbolized the long historical struggle which he imaginatively described as an attack on the five giants of want, disease, squalor, ignorance and idleness. The welfare state was brought into existence to maintain this attack and to provide an enabling environment for its people.

The plan for social security—insurance benefits based upon adequate subsistence and covering dependants; the introduction of family allowances to relate income to family size; a health service for all members of the community, workers and dependents, without charge and based on prevention as well as cure ; and above all the raising of the level of wages among the lowest paid workers, a government policy of full employment and redistribution of income through taxation—strengthened not only the individual, enabling him to stand as a responsible and independent member of the community, but strengthened also, as never before, the position of the family. By this supportive policy and legislation the family was released from its former economic subjection and enabled more easily to concentrate on the work it alone can do. This change of status had important repercussions on the service for the care of children deprived of family life.

---

[1] The poor law was brought to an end by the National Assistance Act of 1948. The services which replaced and substituted its provisions derived their authority from :
    (1) The Family Allowances Act 1945.
    (2) The National Insurance Act 1946.
    (3) The National Insurance (Industrial Injuries Act) 1946.
    (4) The National Health Service Act 1946.
    (5) The Children Act 1948.
    (6) The National Assistance Act 1948.

CHAPTER NINE

THE UNDERLYING CONCEPTS OF POST-WAR LEGISLATION

THE social security legislation of the immediate post-war period, which brought to an end the existing poor law, enabled the care of deprived children to be transferred to a comprehensive administration. By 1948 the laws of England contained a fairly wide code of protection for children which had been built up over the last hundred years.[1] The legislation of 1933 covered their protection from harmful conditions of employment, from cruelty and moral corruption and regulated their treatment before courts of law and when in the care of public authorities or voluntary bodies. The child life protection provisions had been finally incorporated in the public health measures by the Public Health Act of 1936, which ensured that the child taken for reward would have the protection of a health visitor trained in infant and child care and his foster-mother the skilled guidance and advice she would so often need. There had also been developments in the adoption field. The very popularity of adoption since it became legal in 1926 had led to an increase in the number of adoption societies and an extension of their activities, as well as an increase in the numbers of private individuals who arranged the placing of babies. Adoption work was entirely unsupervised and uncontrolled and the standard was naturally extremely variable and sometimes haphazard. Some attention was needed now to the methods employed and the quality of work undertaken in the responsible task of placing children for

[1] See W. Clarke Hall *The Queen's Reign for Children*. T. Fisher Unwin, 1897. Between Queen Victoria's accession in 1837 and her Diamond Jubilee over a hundred Acts for the welfare of children had been placed on the statute book of England.

permanent adoption. A committee of inquiry was set up in January 1936 under the chairmanship of Miss Florence Horsburgh, M.P. whose recommendations were embodied in the Adoption of Children (Regulation) Act 1939. This legislation empowered the Secretary of State to make regulations about the way in which adoption societies conducted their work,[1] and also laid certain duties with regard to them on the local authorities. Adoption societies must be registered as approved by the local authorities before they could place children for adoption[2]; and the local authority was required to be notified seven days in advance of all children placed by private persons acting as third parties for adoption, and to supervise these placings until the adoption came to the court. The legislation thus brought protection to the child by ensuring that more skill and knowledge would be applied to placings by all adoption societies and by providing for supervision where the work was undertaken by unskilled and inexperienced private persons.[3]

The Children Act of 1948 (which applies to England and Wales, and, with some adaptations to Scotland) attempted to bring together under one responsibility the care of all homeless children. Local authorities now had an inescapable duty to receive into care as a voluntary measure children whose parents were temporarily or permanently unfit or unable to care for them, and to carry out the duties laid on the local authority by earlier child protection measures which were not repealed, that is, to supervise, under child life protection provisions, children maintained for reward; to register adoption societies and supervise direct third party placings for adoption; to provide the magistrates with information about the background of children appearing before the courts, and to be responsible for the care of children sent to remand homes or committed by the Courts to the local authorities as fit persons,

---

[1] I.e. about the necessity for case committees, for paying visits to the homes of prospective adopters, and about inquiring into the health of the child.

[2] However in some places, before the setting up of children's committees, this registration was undertaken by the Treasurer's department after scrutiny of the balance sheet.

[3] Owing to the outbreak of war the legislation was not brought into force until 1943.

or to approved schools.[1] The duty to receive deprived children into care, as a voluntary arrangement with the child's guardians, replaced the old poor law provisions, and is complementary to the duty of undertaking compulsorily the care of a child committed for care or protection by the Courts under the Children and Young Persons Act 1933.[2]

The age up to which children were to be received into care by the local authority was to be seventeen years, instead of sixteen years of age as in the old poor law regulations, and they could remain in care up to the age of eighteen, instead of sixteen as previously. The age groups of the children received into care and those committed by the Courts were thus the same, but the widening of the age group for the received children meant an immediate greater increase of adolescents in care. The duties of the local authorities under the Public Health Act 1936 to supervise children maintained apart from their parents for reward, and under the Adoption of Children (Regulations) Act 1939 to supervise children placed for adoption by third parties, were extended to apply to children up to school leaving age instead of up to the age of nine years, and in certain circumstances supervision of a child maintained for reward could now continue till he attained eighteen. Guardians' allowances paid under the National Insurance Act 1946 and family allowances paid under the Family Allowances Act 1945 to persons other than parents, legal guardians or relatives, brought the children under supervision of the local authority as children maintained for reward.[3] The central responsibility for the public care of children deprived of a normal home life was now vested in the Home Office and local authorities were now required to carry out their work

[1] See Children Act 1948, section 39. The relevant earlier legislation is: (a) the provisions relating to child life protection of Part VII of the Public Health Act 1936, the provisions of Part XIII of the Public Health (London) Act, 1936, or the provisions of Part I of the Children and Young Persons (Scotland) Act 1937 as the case may be; (b) the Adoption of Children (Regulation) Act, 1939; (c) Parts III and IV of the Children and Young Persons Act, 1933, or, as the case may be, Parts IV and V of the Children and Young Persons (Scotland) Act, 1937.

[2] The local authority could no longer decline to undertake the duty if the Court wished to make a committal order, unless there was already in existence, or the Court proposed to make in addition, a probation or supervision order. The court can, however, permit the local authority to make representations about the order provided no undue delay will be caused (Section 5, Children Act 1948).

[3] Sections 35, 36 and 37.

through a specially appointed children's committee (which could co-opt private persons with special qualifications for the work) and with a children's officer as executive, working under the general guidance of the Secretary of State.[1]

In this development the unified central control was of great importance. The Home Office, through the specialised understanding made available by the work of the Advisory Council and Central Training Council,[2] and the accumulation of field experience of its inspectors over the whole country, was able to promote an interchange of experience and dissemination of knowledge among the local authorities and the voluntary organisations, and encourage the whole service to work together towards a nationally accepted standard. The powers of inspection of the Secretary of State now covered the whole field of care of deprived children, with the exception of adoption work, and he had wide powers of registration, regulation and guidance, controlling developments by the giving or withholding of exchequer grants.

The Act made substantial changes in the financial arrangements between the local authorities and the exchequer.[3] The principle behind the arrangement was that the cost over the whole field of care for deprived children should be shared between them. The local authorities were to receive individually a grant of up to fifty per cent of their total expenditure, but to contribute collectively up to fifty per cent of the Secretary of State's expenditure on grants for training and for the improvement of voluntary homes. In the financial provisions of the Act, therefore, the unity and interdependence of the parts of the service one with another are underlined.[4]

[1] Section 42 (1).
[2] The Central Training Council in Child Care, recommended by the Curtis Committee, had been appointed as a matter of urgency by the Secretary of State in July 1947 to encourage the organising of training courses for child care residential and field staff by universities and other educational bodies. In October 1947 the first training courses for boarding-out officers were started with the co-operation of the London School of Economics and the Universities of Leeds, Liverpool and Cardiff. Under the Children Act (section 43) Advisory Councils on Child Care were to be set up for England and Wales, and for Scotland. The Training and Advisory Councils were amalgamated in 1953.
[3] Section 47.
[4] This was changed by the Local Government Act of 1958, by which block grants based on an aggregate amount fixed annually took the place of percentage grants.

At the immediate level of impact with the child the responsibility for reception and care was laid squarely on the local authorities, the councils of counties and county boroughs with their specially constituted Children's Committees and specialist Children's Officers. The Curtis Committee stressed in its recommendations that the Children's Officer should be an officer of high standing and qualifications, a specialist in the needs and care of the deprived child, just as the Medical Officers of Health and Chief Education Officers are specialists in their own different fields.[1] The Act embodied a further recommendation that the appointment of Children's Officer shall not be made without prior consultation with the central government department.[2] This enabled the Home Office to begin to ensure that administrative officers with similar standards and field experience and academic background would be appointed up and down the country. For the first time in our history, men and women with theoretical qualifications in social science and practical experience in social casework were appointed, as a national policy, to key positions in the social services.

Now for the first time also the voluntary organisations became properly integrated in the field of child care.[3] Every voluntary home had now to be registered at the Home Office and a new and stricter control was imposed. The Secretary of State was empowered to make regulations governing the conduct of voluntary homes and the care given to children in them.[4] and to make regulations governing their methods of boarding-out and emigration. For the first time grants could be made by the Home Secretary towards making improvements in the premises or equipment of voluntary homes, and to assist with the provision of better qualified staff. Local authorities too, with the consent of the Secretary of State were

[1] Curtis report, paras. 441–446.
[2] Children Act 1948—sect. 41(2).
[3] Sections 29, 31, 33 and 46.
[4] By section 31 the Secretary of State is empowered to see that the accommodation and equipment provided is adequate; that the children are not dressed in an undesirable, distinguishing fashion; that there are satisfactory arrangements for safeguarding the children's health and preventing overcrowding, for allowing parents and guardians to visit and write to their children, for requiring consultation with the Home Office about the appointment of persons in charge and notification of changes, for ensuring that children receive a religious upbringing appropriate to their own religious denomination.

enabled to make contributions to any voluntary organisation whose object is to promote the welfare of children. In the pattern of child care the voluntary organisation was given its distinctive and integrated place. Working under the same central control and subject in planning and minimum standards to the central government department, which could now assist them financially, the voluntary organisations still maintained their salient characteristic, to speak for the needs of a minority. When, as here, a service is provided for a group so inarticulate as the deprived child, who passes only a mute judgement on the service provided for him, it is all the more essential that in searching for standards and methods of care there should be some scrutiny and challenge of ideas. This is provided in the voluntary bodies, historically critical of the state, who, unlike the statutory authorities, have the power, based on their private income, to go beyond the statutory legal provisions, and, where they find a need unsatisfied, to devise a means of care.[1]

The various ways in which the local authorities could provide for the children in their care are set out in Part II of the Act. The crux of them lay in the arrangements to be made for the individual care and study of each child at the period of intake, and to meet this specially appointed reception centres were to be provided.[2] Special emphasis was laid on the primary duty of the local authority to board the children out in foster homes as being the nearest approach to providing a normal home life for the child. In doing so religious belief was to be carefully safeguarded.[3] There were also important new provisions

[1] e.g. supplementary services, such as mother and baby homes, family aid units, adoption societies, colleges for training residential workers, are provided and specialised services such as homes for maladjusted deprived children needing special training and care, and also schools for unusually young delinquent children, etc.

[2] Section 15 (2), legislative requirement for this was based on evidence of need received by the Curtis Committee and on the results of a pilot experiment—see the interim report 1948 of the Children's Reception Centre, Mersham, Kent, published by the Caldecott Community, March 1949. The development of the work of this Reception Centre, under the Children Act 1948, is described by its psychiatrist, Dr. Hilda Lewis in ' *Deprived Children*'. *A Social and Clinical Study*. Oxford University Press, 1954.

[3] Religious care was the subject of a reservation and a note which was appended by certain members of the Curtis Committee to the full report. See p. 183 of the *Curtis Report*.

covering the care of the adolescent after he had left school. A local authority had the duty to advise and befriend any child up to the age of eighteen and living in their area who had left the care of a local authority or voluntary organisation since leaving school. Hostels could also now be provided for adolescents right up to the age of twenty one, and other young people who had come from normal homes could live in them too. This was to help the gradual integration of the adolescent into life in the normal community. It also became possible now to assist children in care to complete their higher education right up to maturity. Grants could be made by the local authority, for the education of children for whom they have cared, up to the age of twenty-one, or even later.

An important concept in the Children Act 1948, the emphasis on the strength and formative power of the natural family, was influenced by the great change which had taken place in the status of the family in recent years. The Act was revolutionary in laying on the local authorities a duty to restore those received into care to their own natural home.[1] This concept was entirely new and had not been found even in the temporary nature of the care given by the old public assistance committees. Children, under the old poor law, as under the new legislation, were received into care in situations of crisis, of loss or abandonment, incapacity or illness or domestic tragedy of the parents. Most usually skilled help was needed if the crisis was to be resolved and it is here that the lack of case workers had been apparent. Children too often remained in the care of the public assistance authorities because no casework service existed to treat the actual problem which had precipitated the reception into care. The new duty to restore the child emphasised the casework aspect of the new service, and was only made possible by the supportive legislation

---

[1] See section 1 (3) of the Children Act 1948. 'Nothing in this section shall authorise a local authority to keep a child in their care under this section if any parent or guardian desires to take over the care of the child, and the local authority shall, in all cases where it appears to them consistent with the welfare of the child so to do, endeavour to secure that the care of the child is taken over either—

(*a*) by a parent or guardian of his, or

(*b*) by a relative or friend of his, being, where possible a person of the same religious persuasion.

which ensured for each family basic minimum material standards on which to build. Casework was no longer concentrated on removing the individual from his environment of poverty and overcrowding with their attendant evils. In so far as these environments were tackled by comprehensive social policies the caseworker was set free to examine the unsatisfied personality needs and the processes which lay behind the problem, and to guide and enable the individual to solve his problem in his own way, increasing his sense of worth and enabling him to gain control over his own environment.

This development of casework made it possible to consider working with the problem parents with a view to eventual restoration of the child to the family, instead of regarding the reception into care as a final break after which a permanent substitute home must be found. The contact of the child with his own family must not, therefore, be broken completely, and continuity was required by the legislation. Local authorities were authorised in the Act to pay the fares of parents, when necessary, to help them to make visits to the child placed some distance away, while parents had a duty to maintain contact with the local authority and keep them informed of their address.[1] The integrity and responsibilities of the natural family were also reinforced by the new duty to inform parents of their entitlement to appeal against the assumption of their parental rights by the local authority and to have their objection heard in a court of law.[2] One important provision of the old administration had been deliberately excluded from the Children Act. The legislation from 1824[3] had made the leaving of a child chargeable to the local authority a punishable offence in the hope of deterring the parent who abandons the child and refuses to take over his care again. No such deterrent now existed unless neglect or cruelty could be proved.[4] The aim of the new legislation was not to punish bad parents but to act in the

---

[1] See Children Act 1948, Sections 22 and 10 respectively.

[2] The court is, however, the juvenile court. No provision is made, therefore, for the parents to receive legal aid. The power to assume parental rights was new in Scotland.

[3] 5 Geo. IV, c. 83, Section 4. Act for the Punishment of Idle and Disorderly Persons.

[4] As in the Children and Young Persons Act, 1933, Section 1.

interests of the child, and to force him back on an unwilling parent, or to discourage by punishment the parent who might later want to claim him again, was thought detrimental to the child's welfare.[1] From this changed approach, building on and preserving what is good in the family, however weak and unsatisfactory, it became possible to see the problem of the deprived child and the failing parents as an interrelated whole.

Finally, in a clause, perhaps unmatched for its humanity in all our legislation, the Act defines the general duty of the local authority towards the child in care, " Where a child is in the care of a local authority it shall be the duty of that authority to exercise their powers with respect to him so as to further his best interests, and to afford him opportunity for the proper development of his character and abilities."[2] The measure of the long road the reformers have travelled can best be seen by placing beside this clause the definition of the duty of the poor law to such children as it still remained until its dissolution in 1948, modelled on the words of the Elizabethan statute " To set to work or put out as apprentices all children whose parents are not, in the opinion of the Council, able to keep them ".

Yet in ensuring the paramount importance of individual care for the child, his integration with the community, and not his segregation, was stressed. " In providing for a child in their care, a local authority shall make such use of facilities and services available for children in the care of their own parents as appears to the local authority reasonable in his case".[3] The vision of the purpose of the legislation is based on the social, psychological, material and spiritual needs of the child as a citizen with rights, unique, but sharing in the community.

At the same time, the emphasis was thrown upon the child's need for a relationship of affection and support in which he could be helped to grow and understand what happens to him, and upon finding the type of relationship and form of care most suited to him individually. Thus he could be fostered,

---

[1] It was, however, possible for non-compliance with Section 10—the duty of the parent to keep the local authority of his address—to be used in a punitive way.

[2] Children Act 1948, Section 12(1).

[3] Section 12(2).

placed in a home provided by the local authority, in a voluntary home, a residential special school, or he could be placed for adoption or helped to emigrate. None of these was a new method of care, but the working of the new Act with its emphasis on community participation, on restoration to the family and on the individual fulfilling of the child's best interests, profoundly altered their character and precedence.

CHAPTER TEN

METHODS OF POST WAR CARE

THE new Children Act of 1948 provided a framework based on principles of administrative unity, individual need and the value of the natural family which were new in the legislation for deprived children. These principles themselves, and the insight of the new administrators, stimulated a development in the service which led very quickly to change, to awareness of the best form of treatment for the child and later to an emphasis on the conditions leading to deprivation, and the prevention of them.

At first however, the administrative problems were acute. Almost immediately following the implementation of the Act, and the appointment of Children's Committees and Children's Officers, the numbers of children in care noticeably increased. The fact that reception into the care of the local authority was now made on a judgement of need rather than a test of destitution meant that many more children were brought within the interpretation of the Act, while the Courts now began to make increasing use of their extended powers to commit both young offenders and children neglected or beyond control to the local authority. In two years the number of committed offenders doubled while the number of committed non-offenders rose by one in twenty.[1] Whereas in 1946 the Curtis

[1] Not all, but the majority of, those committed were committed to the local authority. The figures are :
OFFENDERS—
    1947 of 57,562 offenders found guilty 307 or .5% were committed to fit persons.
    1950 of 69,085 offenders found guilty 620 or .9% were committed to fit persons.
    1953 of 63,191 offenders found guilty 666 or 1% were committed to fit persons.
NON-OFFENDERS—
    1947 of 4,182 non-offenders 1,809 or 43% were committed to fit persons.
    1950 of 4,531 non-offenders 2,200 or 48.5% were committted to fit persons.
    1953 of 5,249 non-offenders 2,156 or 41% were committed to fit persons.

Committee had estimated the numbers of deprived children in the care of local authorities as about 46,000, by November 1949 the numbers had risen to 55,255 and by 1953 had reached a peak figure of 65,309. These heavily increasing numbers of children in care threw a great strain on the new administrative departments and on the available accommodation for children. Nor was this generally of the right kind or quality in which to carry out the principles of care represented by the new service. The Children's Committees inherited the poor law residential nurseries, usually in the grounds of the public assistance workhouse or hospital, the grouped cottage homes, the large district school type of home and the all purpose receiving homes, which now had to meet the needs of a much more heterogenous group of children in an individual way, taking into account the sort of family situation which had brought each one into care. Many more children were now received in conditions of temporary breakdown of the family, where for example illness or hospital treatment of the mother made this necessary, as well as in the pathological situation of abandonment or committal by the courts. The first group which represented the majority (colloquially they became known as short-stay children) required generally short term care during which the continuity of their own family life need be only superficially broken, the second group (the long-stay children) required long term treatment and often a permanent substitute home. The immediate provision of shelter and care became an overriding anxiety, accentuated by the lack of staff. In this situation local authorities turned their attention, not to the providing of field staff (for the service was new and its development to be watched carefully) but to the provision of the right kind of residential care and the improvement in its quality. In this, it is now evident, they were mistaken, but the tradition of institutional child care was a long one, administratively convenient and largely understood. In a new service the children's homes provided immediate evidence of the quality of the work ; the buildings, staff and children could be seen in reaction together by the committees whose heavy responsibility it was to operate the new legislation. In this they were supported by the Inspectorate of the Home Office who saw as the most pressing need the raising of the standard of institutional care.[1] The Committees, therefore, first concentrated on closing down the unsuitable premises they had inherited and in moving the children into newly built or newly adapted homes more suited to the need of the child in care. The old poor law residential nurseries and the large children's homes were the first to go, and new residential nurseries, reception homes, small children's homes scattered and integrated in the new estates, and hostels for the adolescents were opened. The Children Act, in order to raise the very low standards of nursery care which prevailed, expressly required the consent of the Secretary of State for the continued use of the old poor law institutional nurseries and it was here that the first improvements were made.[2] One hundred and forty six institutional nurseries were in use when the Act came into force. By 1951 they had been reduced to seventy four, and one hundred and seventy four residential nurseries were provided by voluntary organizations and by local authorities in new or adapted buildings.[3] Administration of such nurseries was not easy, they had to provide stability, a home and an affectionate relationship for both long stay and short stay children, to consider the individual needs and future placing of each child, and at the same time guard against the very real dangers of cross infection where such vulnerable groups of babies and young children were cared for together. Professional staff had therefore to be employed who would combine experience in the care and training of healthy children with skill in nursing and the prevention of sickness and who

---

[1] It is easy to judge after the urgency of events has faded, but it seems a pity now that pressure was not brought on local authorities to appoint more field staff with the right training, who could extend the amount of boarding-out, and help foster parents to understand its changing nature. The Children Act 1948 did convey such powers. Section 41(5) laid down: 'A local authority shall secure the provision of adequate staff for assisting the Children's Officer in the exercise of his functions', and section 13(1) laid on the local authority a primary duty to board out the children in care. Doubtless the difficulty of persuading local authorities to accept the need for staff was accentuated by the lack of available candidates qualified for the work and so the emphasis was laid on the immediate and easier provision of residential shelter and care.

[2] See section 13 of the Children Act and the comments in the Home Office Circular No. 160/48 issued to the Councils of Counties and County Boroughs in England and Wales on 8th July, 1948, on the Children Act, printed on Page 99 of the Sixth Report on the Work of the Children's Department, Home Office. H.M.S.O. 1951.

[3] ibid. p. 19.

could make of a strangely artificial structure a place of warmth, understanding and satisfaction for the youngest homeless child.

The setting up of the nurseries in the early days of the development of the service, with its lack of staff available for boarding out and casework, was a most necessary step ; the pressure on local authorities was in just this age grouping, nearly two-thirds of the children coming into care were below compulsory school age and frequently showed signs of minor or major neglect requiring attention.[1] Boarding out such children required not only intensive propaganda but assurance of a highly disseminated knowledge of child care in the population, good co-operation with health department staffs and some awareness on the part of the child care worker of the principles governing child health and the dangers of disease as well as skilled supportive casework to enable the foster-mother to give confident, hopeful mothering to a baby disturbed and anxious. Deprivation in children is first and foremost a problem of emotional conditions and the staff skilled enough to cope with both physical and emotional aspects of the work did not exist thickly enough upon the ground, or, where they did, were too absorbed by the sheer weight of the increasing numbers to be able to give the intensive care and support that the boarding out of nursery age children would require. So the nurseries went up, places vastly different from before[2]

[1] This was the writer's personal experience borne out by colleagues. The age groupings of children on coming into care were later tabulated by the Home Office :

	Nov. 1952	Nov. 1953	Nov. 1954	Mar. 1956
Year Ending				
Aged under two years	9,766	10,204	10,107	9,782
Aged two but not of compulsory school age..	12,107	11,983	11,961	11,373
Of compulsory school age	15,209	16,299	16,520	16,109
Over school leaving age	895	814	910	856
Total	37,977	39,300	39,498	38,120

[2] See the illustrations facing p. 22 in the *Home Office Sixth Report of the Children's Department*, and facing p. 8 and p. 24 in the *Home Office Seventh Report*.

and the Committees next began to concentrate on the setting up of reception centres and the separating of long-stay and short-stay children with their different needs, and finding appropriate means of care for them.

The provision of proper reception facilities has been regarded from the beginning as the keystone of an authority's child care arrangement, whether a statutory or voluntary body, and as early as July, 1949 the Home Office issued a memorandum giving guidance on the provision to be made at the time of the reception of children into care.[1] The aim of the reception centre is stated clearly in the memorandum. ' When a child is received into care by a local authority under section 1 of the Children Act, 1948, or is committed to their care as a fit person, the best method of providing him with a substitute home can not be decided without a close study of his needs as an individual. The children will differ widely and will come from a great variety of homes, and it is essential that there should be opportunity for preliminary investigation, and for obtaining accurate and co-ordinated information about each of them. A right decision about placing, taken at the outset, will reduce the risk of subsequent changes and the disturbing effect on the child of breaking his relationships by transferring him to new surroundings. In order to obtain the fullest possible knowledge and understanding of a child's health, personality, conduct, intellectual capacity, emotional state and social history, provision must be made for his reception and temporary accommodation in a place where facilities are available for enquiry into these matters and for observation by a skilled staff.'

The child's time spent in the reception centre was intended to be for assessment only, generally of long -stay children, and to be kept as short as possible. Because of the nature of the centres in combining assessment with homely care they required a high proportion of professional and lay staff as well as proper accommodation for children of a wide age teaching group (boys 2–12 years, girls 2–16 years) with facilities for and skilled observation on the premises. Both were difficult to find, and expensive to provide, and as

[1] See Appendix III, p. 116 of the *Home Office Sixth Report*.

their urgency was less apparent their provision was a much slower business than in the case of residential nurseries. By 1951 only fifteen reception centres had been provided in the country.[1]

But by 1950 the movement had begun towards establishing more and smaller scattered homes in which the children could live as nearly as possible as a normal family unit. By November, 1950 we find the Children's Officer for Ipswich is describing their first Home built on a new housing estate. " It accommodates 10 children and 2 Housemothers in a building barely distinguishable from a pair of semi-detached Council Houses,"[2] and a visible attempt is being made again to integrate the child within the living community of the new estate in many local authorities.

Two factors of major importance now became operative in influencing the path of development of this new service. In the first place the costs of the service had risen rapidly since 1948. More children were received into care each year by the local authorities, the majority of whom were provided for in local authority homes, while large sums were now being spent by the central government department in grants to voluntary Homes to enable them to make improvements to their accommodation for children.

The exchequer costs were examined by the Select Committee appointed by the House of Commons to examine the various Estimates presented to Parliament, and tribute was paid to the great and satisfactory advances which had been made in the child care services since the Act of 1948.[3] The Committee recognised the fact that much leeway had to be made up by those administering the new service but at the same time it laid stress upon two recommendations by which it appeared that the interests of the child and the interests of economy would alike be served—the possibility that the number of children coming into care might be reduced " if more attention were directed towards the means whereby situations that end in domestic upheaval and disaster might be dealt with and

---

[1] See p. 22 *Sixth Report of the Home Office Children's Department.*
[2] See *Bulletin No. 7 of the Children's Officer's Association* dated 9.11.50.
[3] See *Sixth Report from the Select Committee on Estimates, Session 1951–52 Child Care.* Published by H.M.S.O. July 1952.

remedied before the actual break-up of the home occurs."—
and the insistence that boarding out, with due safeguards,
should be the primary objective. The high costs of residential
care itself emphasized for the Committee the view that boarding
out still remained the best, as it was the cheapest, form of
public child care.

But in another sphere, among the child care specialists
themselves, doubts had begun to grow about the effectiveness
of much residential care, particularly at the nursery stages,
and were crystallized in the historic exposition of John Bowlby
on the relationship between maternal care and mental health.[1]
His work published by the World Health Organisation in
March, 1951 was of great importance, for it was the first
accessible study to stress the conclusion, based upon observable
data, that mother love in infancy and childhood is as important
for mental health as are vitamins and protein for the physical
health of the child. He emphasized how essential it was in the
development of mental health for the infant and young child
to experience " a warm, intimate and continuous relationship
with his mother (or mother substitute) in which both find
satisfaction and enjoyment " ; and showed that the proper
care of deprived children is not merely an act of common
humanity but is essential for the mental and social welfare of
a community. Inadequate care, or care based on the satisfaction of material rather than emotional needs, meant that
children so deprived were more likely to grow up to reproduce
themselves as neglectful parents unable to make the necessary
warm relationship with their children, or to fill the prisons
and mental wards of hospitals and so produce another
generation of neglected or delinquent and maladjusted boys
and girls.

This argument was substantiated by the findings of the
Children's Officers themselves in dealing with the adolescents,
with institutional backgrounds often lasting from infancy, who
were now frequently unable to make the relationships required
in the new forms of more personalised care provided in smaller
homes and in the fostering situation.

---

[1] *Maternal Care and Mental Health*, by John Bowlby : World Health Organisation, 1951, and later published in an abridged form in the Pelican series under the
title *Child Care and the Growth of Love*, and edited by Margery Fry.

These two factors, the one based primarily on economy, the other on the basic need of the child, together influenced the work of the administration and of the caseworkers in the field, and confirmed the development of the service. Already there had been agitation to try to secure the prevention of conditions of neglect which should lead to the breakup of the family and separation of the child from his home, culminating in a Government circular in 1950 encouraging all departments concerned with the welfare of children to try to co-ordinate their work to this end.[1] As staffs were effectively built up social workers set about seeing if deprivation could be prevented by helping the family to solve, by other means than public care, the problem which they had brought to the Children's Department. This they were enabled to do by one of the aspects of the Children Act which emphasized the preservation of the family—that the local authority shall not intervene to receive the child into their care unless it is necessary in the interests of his welfare.[2] They were therefore able, sometimes, to help the family to make arrangements in their crisis or difficulty which would in the long run be more satisfactory than the immediate solution of separating the child. Where, however, the child was received into care, there was developed a greater emphasis on the warmer, closer relationship which is present in the foster-home, and even where children were received into care for temporary periods foster-parents were sought for them. Less use was made of the large home and even of the new residential nurseries. There was also now a continuous emphasis on the restoration of the child to his family[3] after he had been received into care, which required the worker to support and help and enable the parents to become capable of alleviating or coming to terms with their own sources of difficulty. This emphasis on restoring the received children to their own homes after a period of work with the parents proved so successful that the workers were encouraged to apply on a large scale this principle of restoration to the children committed by the Courts, and this was a

[1] See *Post*, p. 177.

[2] Section 1. (1) (c).

[3] Section 1 (3). See page 156 ante. and Section 3 (3). There was no similar provision for committed children.

new policy.[1] Before 1948 children committed by the Courts to the local authority were generally regarded as having made a final break with their family and the duty laid on the authority to board them out was in order to provide them with a new home in which they could grow up in happiness and satisfaction to take their place in the world. The new extension and emphasis on restoration, which found its justification in the actual framework of the Act and in the working out of the service and the early realisation by the child care workers of the importance of the bonds of relationship within the natural family, changed the whole nature of the service. The child's period in care—whether he was committed by the Court or received voluntarily by the local authority—was no longer necessarily a break with his own family, and all the forms of care which the local authority provided in substitution for the

[1] The principle by which the fit person is free to send the child home on trial to his natural parents had never been decided in a court of law. A judicial opinion of persuasive value was given in 1943 by Sir Rayner Goddard, then a Lord Justice of Appeal, later Lord Chief Justice of England, in the report of a Tribunal established to inquire into certain proceedings before the Hereford Juvenile Court: 'I think it is desirable to say a few words with regard to the effect of the Order placing them in the care of the Education Authority. The Order commits them to the care of the Authority till they are 18 years of age. This is what the Statute requires. Section 75 (3) is explicit that the Order shall remain in force till the child attains the age of 18. If the Justices are of opinion that it is a proper case for making an Order of this character they have no power to make it for any less period. The Order can be revoked or varied at any time and on the application of any person. (Section 84 (6)). There appears to be no reason why the Education Authority should not, in its discretion, allow the child to go back home, if satisfied that it can safely do so, though it would still retain the control of the child and could again remove him if his conduct or the home was unsatisfactory, and it is hardly necessary to say that the Secretary of State can always discharge the Order if he sees fit.' pp. 14–15 *Hereford Juvenile Court Inquiry. Report of the Tribunal Appointed under the Tribunals of Inquiry (Evidence) Act, 1921.* Cmd. 6485. The practice of sending children home on trial was recognised by the Home Office Circular 15/20 of the 1st February, 1950. Paragraph 12 states 'a child committed by the Court to the care of a Local Authority as a fit person will, of course, not be placed by the Authority with his parent or parents except on trial when the home conditions have improved and there is a prospect of an early application to the Court for revocation of the Order.' In individual communications to local authorities the Home Office has drawn attention to the importance of consulting the magistrates before sending a committed child home on trial. See the report issued by the Association of Children's Officers on *The Law Relating to Children Committed to the Care of a Local Authority as a Fit Person who are allowed Home on Trial.* (Later the Family Allowances and National Insurance Act, 1956 (s. 5) recognized the practice of local authorities and other fit persons who were increasingly restoring committed children to their parents. But following the death of a child returned to her home the practice is under criticism.

natural family now had to be considered in the light of the eventual restoration. His care was also a form of treatment which would enable him to take his place as a member of a family, either his own natural one or a new one which he built up for himself as his own home.

In the meantime, therefore, the emphasis was laid upon a form of care which would satisfy the needs of the child or adolescent, both individually and as a vital and valued member of the community. The day-to-day experience of the child care workers and the growth of skilled assessment and observation in the reception homes[1] stressed the importance of a relationship as the vital factor in treatment of the deprived child. It is indeed significant that reference began to be made no longer to the deprived child but to the child " in care ". This relationship had been found pre-eminently in the foster home, or in the small family group home on the new estate, in size, appearance and in spirit indistinguishable from the normal council house. Both these forms of care emphasize the close relationship between the child and substitute parent by which he is helped to grow emotionally and physically and eventually to come to terms with himself and his environment.

The development is clearly shown in the increase in the number of children boarded-out between the years 1949 and 1956. In spite of the rise in the number of children in care during the first five years of the working of the Act the numbers of children for whom foster homes were found increased also and reflected a considerable concentration and emphasis here:

Year ending	Number of children in the care of local authorities	Number of children in the care of local authorities who are boarded-out	
		Actual	Percentage
November 1949	55,255	19,271	35%
November 1950	58,987	21,710	37%
November 1951	62,691	24,319	39%
November 1952	64,682	26,277	41%
November 1953	65,309	27,536	42%
November 1954	64,560	28,710	44%
March 1956[2]	62,347	27,098	45%

[1] By the end of 1952 38 authorities had established reception homes and a further 13 were about to be set up. See answers to Parliamentary question on 13.11.52.
[2] Corrected for those in lodgings and residential employment.

A new and rather remarkable development has been the extension of short-stay fostering. Two-thirds of the admissions of children into care come as short-stay cases, but an attempt was made to give to them the same quality of relationship. This meant a change in the nature of the fostering situation itself and a need for greater skill in handling it on the part of the child care worker. In the past fostering had a permanency about it which helped the relationship between child and foster-parent to grow in a way which would absorb the child more completely into his substitute family. The new policy of extending fostering to children in care for limited periods and with the prospect of return eventually to their own homes has brought a complication into the relationship and changed the nature of much of the fostering work. Nevertheless the emphasis on close and warm contact as the therapeutic measure is there between the foster mother and the child, and the important integration of the child within the community sharing in its normal experiences, which is foster-home life, is present and secondary to it.

Again the emphasis on relationship was seen in the increasing number of small family group Homes on the housing estates, a new twentieth century form of child care developed most extensively in the north west of England, a great urban area whose problems had not been particularly well solved before the Children Act and which were now becoming acute. These Homes seem to have arisen from the need to reconcile care to be provided by local authorities for the increased numbers of deprived children for whom there are no foster-homes, with the need to ensure for them a relationship which would both console and heal. They are mostly to be found on post-war housing estates and they are indistinguishable in appearance from the rest of the houses there. They accommodate eight or less children who are in the care of a married house-mother paid by the local authority and whose husband goes out daily to his employment as a father normally does.[1] In

[1] The first of such Homes appears to have been opened in Bolton on 19.6.50. See *Annual Report of the Children's Officer for 1953-54.*
" The Local Authority has 7 mixed family group homes. Each home is in the charge of a housemother, whose husband follows his normal occupation. The housemother is a full-time employee of the Local Authority, but her husband only receives free board and lodgings in return for taking a fatherly interest in the

the beginning they were used to accommodate as a unit the several large families of children who often were committed altogether by the Courts for care or protection after neglect, and who previously had either to be placed in the large children's homes or separated and boarded out. The family group home enabled the brothers and sisters of one family to be kept together under the care of a husband and wife through whom, perhaps for the first time, they learnt the true meaning of family life. Later, however, they were used for the placing of children who for various reasons could not be fostered, and a family group is made artificially of unrelated children. These small Homes still have the advantage of providing care which is very similar to that given in the foster-home— close feeling with the parent substitutes, closer attention to the personal difficulties of the children, and more consistent handling of them than can be provided in the larger Children's Homes. This very close relationship does, however, bring difficulties, too, which the child care service has yet to solve.[2]

While these two forms of care, fostering and the provision of small family group Homes, illustrate the change in emphasis in the service, this change was underlined by the very remarkable decline in the numbers of children in care who were helped to emigrate. The Children Act 1948 continued the earlier poor

children. Each home has a part time domestic assistant. Three of the homes have 6 children in each, and four homes have 4 children in each. The homes cannot be distinguished from other houses in the district. The children attend local schools and mix freely with other children in the neighbourhood. They attend local churches and youth organisations. Each housemother receives a weekly cash allowance, based on the boarding-out scale of allowances for household expenses, including food, and a quarterly cash allowance for clothing. The house, and the furniture and equipment, are provided by the Local Authority, and additional grants are made for holidays and Christmas. These small homes are no more costly than large children's homes, and they provide the nearest approach to a normal family life that any children's home can offer. Results so far are encouraging. The first four were opened in 1950, and there have only been two changes of staff. Two handicapped children with severe speech defects have shown much improvement since being placed in a smaller home, and one boy who did badly in a larger children's home, has become much steadier and has gained the respect and confidence of his employer.'

[2] The damaging effect on the child if the housemother and her husband leave is the paramount difficulty, and the fact that children selected for the family group homes tend now to be the more 'awkward' children, who have been proved or thought to be unsuccessful in foster homes, means that the staff need both skilled support and excellent working conditions, in addition to training, if they are not to find the work a severe strain.

law arrangements which empowered local authorities to arrange for the emigration of children in their care provided that suitable arrangements for safeguarding the child's welfare were observed,[1] but how far this was a measure based upon the nineteenth century policy of re-education in a new environment, and a complete break with the old way of life and home, is seen by the change of emphasis. The boards of guardians since 1850 had been provided with powers for the emigration of orphan or deserted children in their care[2] and though these powers were considered to be used to a far less degree than was desirable we find that about 7,000 children had been emigrated by the end of the nineteenth century. The number of children from unions throughout England and Wales who emigrated to Canada during the year 1894 for instance was 299 and Dr. Barnardo had been emigrating children at the rate of about 280 a year since 1873.[3] The safeguards and precautions were, however, liable to break down, and in the changing balance of population a cogent argument developed against emigration because it tended to be used for the healthiest and fittest children who were eligible. Figures on the emigration of children since the operation of the Children Act are only available since 1952 :

	During the year ended					
	Nov. *1952*	*Nov.* *1953*	*Nov.* *1954*	*Nov.* *1956*	*Mar.* *1957*	*Mar.* *1958*
Children in the care of local authorities in England and Wales who emigrated ..	20	41	28	24	16	14

The subject of child migration had been considered both by the voluntary bodies and by Her Majesty's Government.[4] An investigation made in 1952 held that for many children in

---

[1] Section 17 Children Act 1948.

[2] 13 and 14. Vict. c.101. S.4. Poor Law Amendment Act. The child, who could not be over sixteen, was required to give his consent. The guardians generally used one of the voluntary societies as their agent.

[3] *Report of* the Mundella Committee on *Poor Law Schools Committee*, pp. 131–138. See also the Macnamara report *Children under the Poor Law*, op. cit. 1908.

[4] Report by John Moss, C.B.E., on *Child Migration to Australia* published as an independent impression for the Home Office by H.M.S.O., 1953, and the *Official Report of a Fact-Finding Mission on Child Migration to Australia* presented by the Secretary of State for Commonwealth Relations in August, 1956. Cmd. 9832.

children's homes in the United Kingdom there were much better prospects in Australia provided the children were carefully selected for examination and were of suitable age. But, though some 2,000 children had been emigrated from Britain since the war to Australia, the interest of the local authorities in emigration had declined. It is now practically non-existent.

In 1956 more cautious recommendations were made and the need was stressed to provide a more personal relationship for migrant children when they reached their new country of adoption.[1]

The majority of children for whom emigration is chosen are among those few in care, who are also usually eligible to be placed for adoption. A comparison of the figures of children emigrated and those placed in the close relationship of adoption is also significant :—

	Year ending					
	Nov.	*Nov.*	*Nov.*	*Mar.*	*Mar.*	*Mar.*
	1952	*1953*	*1954*	*1956*	*1957*	*1958*
Children emigrated	20	41	28	24	16	14
Children adopted ..	977	1,008	982	1,118	1,094	1,136

The policy reflected in legislation for adoption has itself shown a significant development over recent years. It has moved on from providing legal *status*, for those who lacked this, to providing a legal *relationship* between adopted child and adopters as similar as possible to that which exists between a child and his natural parents. This principle was expressed in the Adoption of Children Act, 1949, introduced as a private members' bill by Sir Basil Nield. The Act took great care to see, particularly by the safeguarding of consents, that the divestment of the natural family, and particularly the mother, should not be lightly undertaken, but that, where it was, the integration of the child with his new family should be complete

---

[1] It is perhaps significant that of the record of 113 local authority children emigrated between 1952 and 1956 thirty four (30%) have been emigrated by the Children's Committee of the County of Cornwall, whose Children's Officer before the war worked for a time with the Fairbridge Society, a society responsible for arranging the emigration of boys and girls to Australia and Canada. The emigration here was therefore based on some personal knowledge of the places and schools and even the people with whom the children came in contact and was not so governed by fear of the unknown people to whom the children were sent which understandably complicated emigration policies for children's committees.

and natural.[1] The law relating to adoption was again examined and recommendations for change were made in 1954 in
order to ensure that the policy behind adoption and the
object at which it aims should be the welfare of the child, first
and paramount.[2]

In all the care which is given to the deprived child at this time
the nature of the emotional relationship he requires to meet his
needs is emphasized over and over again. His care is not only
a casework process or a process of education, but provides a
quality of relationship through which alone both are possible. It
is in providing this, with all its extensive need for insight and
understanding, that the skill of the child care worker lies.

So by the nineteen fifties we find the development of ideas of
care for the deprived child can be gradually but clearly traced.
The Elizabethan policy, re-emphasized after 1834, was to root
out the destitution which lay behind deprivation and neglect by
providing the deprived child with education, education for
employment which again characterised nineteenth century
care. Some children, in their need for compensation for an all
too loveless life, were able to accept and use this. The majority,
it is clear from contemporary reports, especially of the girls,
were not.[3] It was the twentieth century scientific knowledge
of the needs and development of the child and the examination
of the effects on him of separation such as was experienced on
such a wide scale during the second world war which led to an
emergence of emphasis on the family and a change from a policy

[1] This was seen in the now compulsory provision of three months supervision by
the welfare authority of the placing immediately before the adoption order is
made; by the fact that adopter and adopted child are now deemed to be within the
prohibited degrees of consanguinity; that an adopted child can inherit as a member
of his adoptive family and not of his natural family in the case of intestacy (except
in Scotland); and that application for an adoption order can now be made without
the natural parents knowing the adopters' identity; and that citizens of the United
Kingdom may now adopt a foreign child who thus becomes himself a citizen
of the United Kingdom. The various adoption acts were consolidated in the 14
Geo. VI. c. 26. Adoption Act 1950.

[2] See the Report of the Departmental Committee on the Adoption of Children
(Hurst Committee) published for the Home Office and Scottish Home Department by H.M.S.O. September, 1954. Cmd. 9248.

[3] One of the great values of the care given by the voluntary organisations,
however, was the emphasis and encouragement they gave to the child's religious
upbringing by which he could make a relationship with God, a consistently loving
Father to his children, who never deserts or fails them. On the reality of this
experience and belief the child was able to grow and change.

of treatment through education to treatment through a relationship such as that provided by fostering or in the small family group home. And this relationship is not isolated but is given within the community. In a sense the wheel has come full circle, though it has travelled far as well. In the earliest records of the middle ages we have evidence that the care of the deprived child was undertaken largely within the community as part of the obligation of people one to another. But the decay of the old manorial community, and of the family in later times of industrial development, led to the delegation of the care of the deprived child out of the community to the institution, whether administered by the poor law or a voluntary philanthropic society. It has been the development of social philosophy during the last hundred and fifty years, towards the achievement of collective responsibility for conditions of adequate living and a finer quality of life, which has enabled responsibility for the care of the child to move away from the institution and back to the community again. And in the providing of foster-home care, of care in the small Home within the community of the parish or the new estate, is found the relationship so vital to the child, not in isolation, not delegated, but given as the living corporate service of a society whose citizens are members one of another.

CHAPTER ELEVEN

THE GROWTH OF PREVENTIVE AND ENABLING ASPECTS OF THE SERVICE

WHILE the child care service was developing and clarifying the work for the deprived child public attention began to turn towards the causes of deprivation, and the conditions of neglect and ill treatment which so often precipitated it. On the 22nd July, 1949 a debate was initiated in the House of Commons by the late Mrs. Ayrton Gould, during which it was pointed out how difficult it actually was, in default of legal powers, to take action to remedy home conditions before positive and sometimes permanent harm had been done, and the Minister was asked if he could devise some administrative means to forestall the neglect of children. The problems of those whose task it was to administer the new services are reflected in the reply of the Under Secretary of State who pointed out that local authorities were strained to the utmost, and could not at the time carry any additional burdens. " We have to tackle the problem in stages," he said, " partly because of its administrative burden and partly because of lack of trained personnel." He promised to initiate consultations between the Home Office, Ministry of Health and Ministry of Education to see if, by co-ordination, it might be possible to come nearer to a solution.

However, on the 12th December, 1949 Mrs. Ayrton Gould again raised the matter in Parliament and the Home Secretary, in reply to the debate, said that a working party had been set up inside the Home Office to investigate and report on the problem. On the 20th July 1950 when making a further statement he stressed, not the need for new powers, but for co-ordination in the use of those which exist, and which were already very wide. The right use of these powers at an early stage, and in co-ordination with the different departments whose responsibility they were, was felt to be the answer.

The Government view was based on conditions as they were, and represented a realist attempt to get to grips with the conditions of neglect in the home which so frequently led to the appearance of the child before the court in need of care or protection, and his subsequent removal from his family. It did not take into account—if indeed this was largely understood—the unevenness of standards between the different groups of social workers and their different approaches and methods of work. Nevertheless the statement and the action which followed were historic in linking the prevention of neglect and ill treatment with the prevention of removal of children from their homes and committal of them to public care. On the 31st July, 1950 a circular was issued jointly by the Home Office (No. 157/50), the Ministry of Health (No. 78/50) and the Ministry of Education (No. 225/50) to the Councils of Counties and County Boroughs for action. The circular pointed up the need for skilled action to prevent the conditions leading to deprivation " It is apparent that, while in some cases prosecution and removal of the child from home may be the only possible course, in many it will be possible to remove or mitigate the causes of neglect by social action . . . . If the right help is not given in time children who might otherwise have remained with their parents may have to be removed from home because deterioration has gone too far." The circular suggested the designation by the Council of an officer whose responsibility would be to secure co-operation between all the local statutory and voluntary services concerned with the welfare of children in their own homes, and who should hold regular meetings, attended by representatives of these services. The authorities were recommended " to arrange for significant cases of child neglect, and all cases of ill treatment coming to the notice of any statutory or voluntary service in the area, to be reported to the designated officer, who would arrange for such cases to be brought before the meeting so that, after considering the needs of the family as a whole, agreement might be reached as to how the local services could best be applied to meet those needs ". The value of preventive work as an economic measure is underlined by the provision for the administrative expenses of co-ordination to be charged to the service in which the designated officer is already employed, and for such expenses to attract any Exchequer grant applicable to that service.

In the past the major part of the work aimed at preventing neglect and cruelty had consisted in removal of the child to a better environment. This was a natural solution in the conditions of pre-war society, the poverty, bad housing, and lower standards of child health and child care. But in work with neglectful parents our increasingly organised knowledge of the patterns of human behaviour and studies of their social and psychological motivation was now of vital importance. With this knowledge, incomplete and imperfect as it is, it begins to be possible for the case worker to accept the historic challenge thrown down by the new approach, to change the psychological and social environment of the neglected child, but by working with the family, supporting them and enabling them to procure better resources for parenthood. It thus becomes possible for the first time to see the prevention of neglect as the prevention of deprivation too.

The importance of preventing deprivation, even where this was not due to neglect or cruelty in the home, was also emphasised by the study of Bowlby in 1951 and by the recommendations made by the Select Committee on Estimates in 1952. The child care workers were now looking not only towards the prevention of children coming into care—on grounds of emotional need and necessary economy—but towards the prevention of those conditions which led either to requests for reception into care or to the child's appearance before the Court. In 1952 had been passed the Children and Young Persons (Amendment) Act which specifically laid upon the local authorities (i.e. the Children's Committees) the duty of making inquiries into the position of any child or young person about whom they might receive information suggesting he was in need of care or protection.[1] The duty of the State as

---

[1] The Children and Young Persons (Amendment) Act of 1952 goes further than the 1933 Act in specifically imposing upon local authorities the duty of making an investigation upon receiving information that a child or young person may be in need of care or protection, unless the local authority is satisfied that such inquiries are unnecessary (e.g. if someone else is making them.) This section avoids delay caused by more than one authority being involved and the possibility of each thinking that it is the duty of the other to investigate. The Children and Young Persons (Amendment) Act further defines a child or young person as being in need of care or protection where the neglect is not wilful, i.e. it covers cases of neglect through ignorance where no criminal offence can be proved.

the primary protector of the child was thus laid down and child care workers with sufficient casework skills could treat the acute distress which they found in two ways depending upon their assessment of the total situation; they could prevent the development of harm caused by neglect by removing the child from those conditions, or by appropriate help within the family enable the causes leading to the acute problem to be understood and overcome.[1] It is therefore in the worker's casework skill, insight and specialised knowledge that the work of prevention is found, although the basic social services of health and housing are obviously among the primary sources of prevention in that they provide the groundwork for family life.[2]

The general experience of co-ordinating committees however appeared to be that they were gradually left with an irreducible group of families who did not respond to the assistance the committee could give, while the problem of trying to prevent the personal and social conditions which were themselves the cause of symptoms leading to the family breakdown was not being tackled. Concern was therefore being expressed because there was no one social service department whose *primary* legal duty it was to give advice and help with the emotional and social difficulties which, if they remained unresolved, would lead to family break and separation and deprivation of the child, though several departments undertook this work as part of a wider field.[3] It was this, and their experience of the results of actual deprivation, which led the Children's Officers themselves to press for wider powers to undertake " preventive " work. Preventive work should mean not only providing skilled help which will prevent the immediate separation of the parents and children, and enable the family as a unit to solve the material and emotional problems satisfactorily within themselves, but also the prevention of those conditions of personal and

[1] These ways are not mutually exclusive. Removal of the child is often necessary to enable the parent to be helped.

[2] This is not to say that the child care officer should be the only, or even the primary, worker aiming at preventing the break-up of family life.

[3] For example probation officers can give guidance on matrimonial problems, and health visitors are encouraged to give special attention to the risk of psychological disturbance and retarded mental development to which neglected children are exposed, and to aim at recognition ' of the early signs of failure in the family which may lead to the disruption of normal home life' see Ministry of Health circular 27/54 issued on 30.11.54 to County Councils and County Borough Councils.

social failure which leave the family with no alternative but to make applications to children's departments for reception of the children in care or which eventually call for intervention by the Court. This second, and deeper and more fundamental, definition of what preventive work really means raises other questions of training and co-operation at common levels of understanding among the many other social workers in touch with families at a stage when the child care service has no concern with them. These important questions were only now beginning to be fully explored, and are dealt with in the following chapter.[1] What is significant here is the way in which the child care service was moving to become an enabling family service, rather than a depriving one.

The pressure now to widen the scope of the local authority so that the children's department could develop more enabling aspects of their work through case work skills grew more insistent. The pressure of public opinion calling for the prevention of neglect to children in their own homes had not been answered by the setting up of co-ordinating committees, and on the 21st June, 1956 the Government announced in Parliament the setting up of a Committee of Inquiry under the chairmanship of Lord Ingleby to consider whether new powers and duties for preventive work should be given to local authorities.[2] The question, too, of revision of the law, which applies equally in the Courts to juvenile offenders and to those who have committed no offence but are in need of care, was also to be examined. If preventive work was to be encouraged, and rehabilitative work extended, it became necessary to consider whether there was any possibility of separating the punitive stigma from the Courts before which the juveniles appear, offenders and non-offenders alike, and whether the practice of

---

[1] A study of the work done in Manchester and Salford by various social services for 118 families whose children eventually came into public care was made by D. V. Donnison and published in *The Neglected Child and the Social Services*. Manchester University Press. 1954. See also the pamphlets *The Child and the Social Services*, by D. V. Donnison and Mary Stewart, Fabian Society, 1958, and *Families with Problems. A new approach*, presented by the Council for Children's Welfare and the Fisher Group. 1958.

[2] The duties of the Ingleby Committee were:—

'to inquire into and make recommendations on (*a*) the working of the law, in England and Wales, relating to :—

(i) proceedings, and the powers of the courts, in respect of juveniles brought

committal should be altered in such a way that greater facilities may be made available for treatment.

This development towards what is called " preventive " work in a service previously only protective is an illustration of the trends in policies which have governed generally the development of the social services. It arose from the very nature of the specialisation of the service, the complex nature of deprivation, the increasing knowledge about it, the resources to be used in its solution, and the need for a positive approach in thinking about the family. Preventive work implies not only a recognition of the child's needs and birthright, but also implies that the community places value on the parents, and, instead of condemning them, aims to support them while it makes them able, and underlines the assumption that family life is good. Looking back we see how greatly the character of the child care service has changed ; from an administration which was palliative, whose methods aimed to deter, if not even to punish, the socially inadequate, it moved on towards becoming a service enabling to all the individuals concerned, and preventive of the problem itself. The enabling aspect of the service is already seen in the support which is given by the worker to the parents, to the child, and to the foster-parent or housemother who is the means by which the child's hurts are made whole again. The service provided by the Children Act is an expression of the authoritarian requirements of society that parents shall fulfil certain definite standards, which, if they fail, the service must intervene to supply. But it also expresses the benign attitude of the community, replacing for the underprivileged child the relationship which he has lost, either by supplying a substitute home or by

before the court as delinquents or as being in need of care or protection or beyond control ;
(ii) the constitution, jurisdiction and procedure of juvenile courts ;
(iii) the remand home, approved school and approved probation home systems ;
(iv) the prevention of cruelty to, and exposure to moral and physical danger of juveniles, *and*
(*b*) whether local authorities responsible for child care under the Children Act 1948, in England and Wales, should, taking into account action by voluntary organisations and the responsibilities of existing statutory services, be given new powers and duties to prevent or forestall the suffering of children through neglect in their own homes.'

helping to rebuild the home which he has left, and enabling the parents to relate to the child again.[1]

The idea of treatment by relationship and the concept of restoration and prevention are fundamental developments in the service. The caseworker was now using skill to evaluate the nature of the family problem, and to assess the respective needs of child and parents and their capacity to relate to one another at different stages of help. Sometimes this adjustment, and the fulfilment of standards required, cannot be made, and the service must then provide for the child a permanent substitute home where new family bonds of vitality and warmth can be forged. In an enabling service the worker seeks first to understand, and then to help to grow. So, in the child care service after 1948, the community defined and accepted again the obligations which it bears towards its defenceless and ineffective members, helping the child, by a needed relationship, and the parent, by an understanding which promotes the will to change, to grow to achieve a place of worth in an enabling society.

[1] For fostering see Dorothy Hutchinson *In Quest of Foster-Parents. A Point of View on Home-finding*. Colombia University Press. 1943, and Draza Kline and Helen Mary Overstreet *Casework with Foster Parents*. Published by the Child Welfare League of America 1956. See also the article by Clare Britton 'Casework Techniques in the Child Care Services,' *Case Conference* January, 1955, and Vic George *Foster Care. Theory and Practice*. Routledge & Kegan Paul. 1970, Robert Tod. *Social Work in Foster Care*. Longman. 1971, Olive Stevenson. *Someone Else's Child*. Routledge & Kegan Paul. 1965, R. Dinnage and M. L. Kellmer Pringle. *Foster Home Care: Facts and Fallacies*, Longman/National Children's Bureau. 1973, R. A. Parker. *Decision in Child Care*, Allen & Unwin, 1966.

For casework see Jean Kastell, *Casework in Child Care*, Routledge & Kegan Paul, 1962, and Noel Timms, *Casework in the Child Care Service*, Butterworth, 1962. See also the article by Clare Winnicott, 'Face to Face with children,' in *New Thinking for Changing Needs*, published by the Association of Social Workers, 1963, Elizabeth Pugh. *Social Work in Child Care*, Routledge & Kegan Paul, 1968, Eileen Holgate. *Communicating with Children*, Longman, 1972.

CHAPTER TWELVE

CHILD CARE AND SOCIAL CHANGE

B Y the sixties of the twentieth century some assessment could be attempted of the developments and trends in a co-ordinated child-care service. The preceding ten years had been mainly years of consolidation, confirming the value of the provisions of 1948 and calling for no decisive changes of policy, even in the relevant legislation which was passed during this period.[1]

1958 saw the passing of two Acts which confirmed the now general child-care policy of providing a service both child-centred and family-centred. The Children Act of 1958 highlights the significant trends. It dealt with the child-life protection provisions and with children about to be adopted, and was an attempt to tidy up the scattered legislation which existed to cover these two groups, as well as put into effect the recommendations of the recent departmental committee which had reported on adoption.[2] The Act was therefore in two parts, Part I dealing with child-life protection, and Part II dealing with adoption. Part II was later repealed and an Adoption Act to consolidate all adoption legislation was brought into force later in the same year. The effect of Part I of the Children Act, 1958, was to repeal all the current child-life protection legislation,[3] to make a comprehensive code for what is now termed child protection and to remedy weaknesses which had been exposed since 1947.[4]

[1] e.g. Children and Young Persons (Amendment) Act, 1952, Children Act, 1958, Adoption Act, 1958.

[2] *Hurst Report*, Cmd. 9248, 1953 4.

[3] i.e. in the Public Health and Public Health (London) Acts of 1936, the Children and Young Persons (Scotland) Act of 1947 and the Children Act of 1948.

[4] i.e. the Wallbridge v. Dorset County Council case in 1954, where a decision was made that children in independent boarding schools were not 'apart from their parents' and so did not come under child-life protection provisions. The new Act brought such children under the child-life protection provisions if they stayed at the school for a month or more during vacation periods.

The greater confidence in widespread public understanding of child care and child health is reflected in the now minimal regulational demands which were made for protecting children. This was itself a silent tribute to the great reforms consolidated by the education and public health movements.[1] The local authority could no longer fix the maximum number of children to be taken for reward and was empowered only to make requirements at all about accommodation or medical care if the persons were keeping children taken for reward in premises which were used wholly or mainly for that purpose. Such persons could now appeal to a juvenile court against the local authority's decision. This provision reflects the growing emphasis on the social-work aspect of the child-care service, its ability in an improved, more enabling society, with better all-round standards, to concentrate on individual welfare rather than health aspects, which are more appropriately the concern of public health departments. So the phrases 'health and well-being' and 'nursing and maintenance' become restricted to 'well-being and maintenance', and the term 'child-life protection' becomes now 'child protection'.

The changes in Part II of the Act relating to adoption become embodied in the Adoption Act of 1958. The changes here are interesting. They circumscribe more than ever before the rights of natural parents in a way which is intended to facilitate the process of adoption, and they tidy up some restrictions which made difficulties for adopting-parents. The powers to dispense with parental consents, for example, are widened, so that parents who fail, without reasonable cause, to fulfil their obligations are no longer able to hold up adoption procedures by withholding their consents. Their consents may be dispensed with and the adoption go forward without them.

Other changes modify the restrictions which formerly applied when applicants for adoption were not resident in this country. A major change enabled local authorities to act as adoption societies even if the children concerned were not in statutory care, since it was hoped that by creating more bona fide agencies the number of unsatisfactory third-party placings would be reduced. Three stages of development can now be

[1] Particularly the spread of knowledge about child health disseminated through the work of health visitors and school nurses.

traced in the adoption legislation, which reflect not only the growth of a personalised concern for the child to be adopted, but also the rise of a professionalised class of social workers with a recognized ethical code and a body of knowledge about the assessment of social and personal problems. The first stage is exemplified by the Act of 1926 concerned with the legality of adoption itself, while the second stage, concerned with regulating the conduct of persons and societies arranging or supervising adoptions is seen in the Adoption of Children (Regulations) Act of 1939. The third stage follows the historical changes of 1948 and is concerned with the personal welfare of the child and ensuring his complete integration with his new family. So in the Adoption of Children Act of 1949 provision is made for protecting the identity of adopters, ensuring the child's right to inheritance in his new family and equating his relations in the family to consanguinity.[1]

But the third stage is most clearly seen in some of the changes in the Adoption Act of 1958 which at first seemed to cut across the emphasis of the child-care service on the strengthening of natural family life, for they make it easier for adoption to take place. In fact, however, they can be said to show the confidence of the public in its social workers, for only a service which had proved its intention to re-build and support the natural family could be trusted with the wider powers the new legislation gives.

This confidence in the new service in the fifties was also reflected in further legislation by which judges and magistrates hearing divorce or separation cases in their respective courts were enabled to commit children to children's departments if no better arrangements could be made for them on the break-up of the family unit.[2] About this time the Legitimacy Act of 1959[3] further emphasized the state's attempt to integrate the child within a family setting and to remove barriers to this end. This Act legitimates automatically the children of a void marriage, and those illegitimate children whose father or mother was married to a third person at the time of birth were now

---

[1] These Acts were all repealed and consolidated in the Adoption Act of 1950.

[2] Matrimonial Proceedings (Children's) Act, 1948, Section 5 (1), and Matrimonial Proceedings (Magistrates' Courts) Act, 1960, Section 2 (1).

[3] 7 & 8 Eliz. II, c. 73, Legitimacy Act, 1959.

automatically legitimated on the subsequent marriage of the parents; while the custody and guardianship of infants protected by legislation since 1886[1] was now extended to illegitimate children, and the putative father entitled to ask the courts for custody and access to his illegitimate child.

The growth of professional training encouraged by the Central Training Council in Child Care became marked in the middle fifties and, growing ever since at an accelerating rate, has had very considerable repercussions upon the techniques employed by the child-care service. The emphasis on fostering which had been paramount since the inauguration of the Children Act[2] was developed with greater discrimination and social and psychological research was undertaken into some of its aspects.[3] Special rates began to be paid on a wider scale to foster parents taking children with special physical handicaps or emotional problems and an attempt by some authorities was made to recruit as foster mothers women who, besides being able to give good mothering, had received some form of professional training before marriage, for example, as caseworkers, teachers or children's nurses.[4]

The limitations of fostering as a method of treatment were clearer to the trained child-care workers than to their lay committees and developments later in the sixties showed a

[1] 49 and 50 Vict. c. 27, Guardianship of Infants Act, 1886, Cmd. 18 and 19, Geo. V, c. 26, Administration of Justice Act, 1928.

[2] This had received the accolade of the Select Committee on Estimates in 1952, essentially as a lay approach, trying to combine in a lay way both financial expediency and the findings revealed by Dr. John Bowlby in his study on maternal deprivation.

[3] Gordon Trasler, *In Place of Parents: A Story of Foster Care*, Routledge and Kegan Paul, 1960; P. G. Gray and Elizabeth A. Parr, *Children in Care and the Recruitment of Foster Parents: An Enquiry made for the Home Office*, Central Office of Information, 1957; Rachel Jenkins, '*The Fostering of Coloured Children*', *Case Conference*, October, 1963; Jessie M. Williams, 'Children who break down in Foster Homes: A psychological study of patterns of personality growth in grossly deprived children', *Journal of Child Psychology and Psychiatry*, Vo. 2, No. 1, 1961; Seymour I. Gross, 'Critique: Children who break down in Foster Homes', *Journal of Child Psychology and Psychiatry*, Vol. 4, No. 1, 1963.

[4] Some unpublished research at Manchester University, however, showed that fostering tends to be unsuccessful unless the worker can assess and help the needs and problems of foster parents, and that fostering is almost invariably undertaken as an attempt to meet various needs and problems which foster parents have. The caseworkers must therefore understand as much the needs of the foster parents as the needs of the child, if the interaction between them is to be mutually satisfying.

renewed awareness of the value of the children's home as a form of treatment for special kinds of problems.[1] Differentiated treatment based on the skilled appraisal of the worker rather than on the policy of the lay committee became the future trend.

Fostering itself in the sixties and seventies has been undergoing re-appraisal. More time given to really skilled preventive casework with deprived parents might well lessen the present drift of children into unplanned long-term care. Fostering is seen as a means to the eventual rehabilitation of the child with his natural parents after they have enjoyed the right to a casework service themselves. Therefore, contact between the child and natural parents is essential both to make possible the aim of rehabilitation and to enable the child to maintain his own identity and continuous development. Research into fostering supports the view that foster children are happier and less upset if they are helped to know as much as they need and want to know about their natural parents, and can then make their own choice about whether they go back home. The children themselves want to get to know their parents again before they can make up their minds about going to live with them or staying with their foster parents. However, the children are much too scared to say this, and they feel that their social workers and foster parents do not help them in this respect. Most foster parents see themselves as parent substitutes and do not want the natural parents to have contact with the child. The social workers are trying to cope with the very difficult and complex task of helping the foster child to maintain and improve his loyalty and affection for his own parents when he

---

[1] This awareness was developed only after a dramatic improvement in the training of houseparents for work in children's homes has been encouraged and extended by the Home Office Central Training Council in Child Care. The use of the children's home for differentiated treatment is only possible when it can be staffed by skilled people. Developments in the United States led the way. See Bruno Bettelheim, *Love is not enough*, Glencoe, 1950; Suzanne Schulze, *Creative Group Living in Children's Institutions*, New York, 1951; Fritz Redl, *Children who Hate*, Glencoe, 1951; Gisella Konopka, *Group Work in the Institution*, New York, 1954; Eva Burmeister, *Forty-five in the Family*, New York. In 1954 the Child Welfare League of America published a descriptive study entitled *Residential Treatment of Emotionally Disturbed Children*, by Joseph H. Reid and Helen R. Hagan. In Britain this sort of work is being integrated into the child-care service. See Additional Bibliography.

lives with and is cared for by another family. Foster parents who need to care possessively for the child, as all good parents do, are expected to be involved and understandingly sympathetic to the natural parents and their problems. The social worker here has perhaps one of the most difficult tasks in all social work.[1]

The spread of casework in the service and the application of trained knowledge and the accommodation of this to the lay thinking of the policy-making committee with its public accountability was one of the major developments of the sixties. In 1960 the Ingleby Committee reported, and its view accurately represented the informed lay opinion of the day. The field of inquiry was a very wide one and was an attempt to meet the interests of two pressure groups: firstly, the Magistrates' Association concerned with the principles and procedure of the Juvenile Court; and, secondly, some independent but similarly oriented groups—the professional associations of those working in the child-care field, and the associations of their committees of elected representatives, and a group of influential private individuals led by Mrs. Fisher, wife of Dr. Geoffrey Fisher, at the time Archbishop of Canterbury.[2]

[1] See Vic George, *Foster Care, Theory and Practice*, Routledge & Kegan Paul,. 1970, and the research article by Rosamund Thorpe on the situation of the long-term foster child and his natural parents entitled (unhappily!) 'Mum and Mrs So and So' in *Social Work Today*, vol. 4, no. 22, 7 February 1974, and the two articles in *Concern*, nos 14 and 15, published by the National Children's Bureau, autumn and winter 1974. The Children Act of 1975 has not helped here. In giving powers of custodianship in certain circumstances to foster parents, the relationship between the social worker and natural parents is made more difficult, and natural parents will be reluctant to allow their children to be placed in foster homes if custodianship is used widely.

[2] After 50 years of accumulated experience of Juvenile Court procedure, the time was ripe for re-consideration of its workings in the light of the social changes which had taken place. Various bodies were presenting recommendations in this field while the Ingleby Committee was sitting; i.e. in 1957 the Advisory Council on the Treatment of Offenders made certain recommendations about the detention of and after-care of young offenders. In 1960 the Durand Committee of Enquiry into the Disturbances at Carlton Approved School suggested an extension of individual classification of offenders sent to approved schools and more effective means of dealing with what might arise there. In 1958 the fifth International Congress for Social Defence held at Stockholm took as its subject the comparative study of the experience of juvenile courts and of administrative Committees or Boards as contrasting methods of dealing with 'socially maladjusted juveniles'.

The Ingleby recommendations concerned with the juvenile courts were affected by the changes which had taken place in the social structure making the family more sufficient, as well as by increased general knowledge and public interest about the psychology of child development, but they retained the empirical democratic approach so characteristic of earlier legislation. Fundamental in their recommendations was the basic principle that, before any action to deal with a juvenile can be taken, the allegations against him should be specifically defined in a court of law. He should not be dealt with by a welfare tribunal whose findings cannot be challenged in law. They, therefore, recommended that the juvenile court be retained, but the minimum age of criminal responsibility should be raised from 8 to 12 years and, in dealing with younger children and with children whose main need is for care or protection, the juvenile court should move still further away from its origin as a criminal court, along lines which would enable it to deal more effectively with younger 'offenders' and children needing care or protection, ensuring that the child's parents are closely associated with the proceedings. Such children should be brought to court as 'being in need of protection or discipline' and parents should be summoned to attend and bring the child with them.[1] In all the recommendations dealing with the juvenile court procedure and the methods of punishment and treatment available to it, the Committee was concerned to extend and use more profitably the methods of care which had been developed on more individual lines over the past 30 years and to underline the bonds between parent and child. It was influenced very much by feelings and fears about family responsibility and the need to emphasize this. All this is seen most clearly in the Committee's dealing with the problem of preventing duplication of action and their attitude to what members felt was a striking lack of co-operation in the social services.[2] The Committee saw the removal of children from home as something destructive in its nature and were concerned to promote machinery for its greater prevention mainly

[1] For a critical assessment of the Committee's recommendation see W. E. Cavanagh, 'Reflections on the Ingleby Report', *Case Conference*, Vol. 8, No.3, July, 1961.

[2] i.e. evidence of what seemed to be a competition for the child in trouble between health visitors, education welfare officers, child-care officers and others.

through the more efficient detection of families at risk. They therefore recommended that a *duty* should be laid on local authorities to prevent or forestall the sufferings of children through neglect in their own homes. Consultation and co-ordination between relevant departments had been taking place regularly up and down the country since the issue of the joint circular in July, 1950, but co-ordination was not felt to be enough and local children's departments had felt the need for express statutory authority to meet the expenditure involved in casework with families at risk. There was no statutory power of responsibility for ensuring that action could be taken quickly to give help in situations which might otherwise deteriorate into family break-up. The growth of skills in casework within the children's departments had made the workers sensitive to the possibility of effective preventive work, and they had pressed for this through their professional organizations, while, at the same time, many workers were aware that methods of care for deprived children were not yet skilled or effective enough to make the reception of children in care a satisfactory answer to the emotional and material problems of the families they dealt with.[1] Here they were caught in a dilemma, for they needed all their skill to perfect their methods of care, while public feeling and their own knowledge about separation led them to place the emphasis on preventive work.

• The Children and Young Persons Act, 1963, which followed the Ingleby Committee's report, was again a piece of consolidating,[2] as well as inaugurating, legislation. Its fundamental object was to protect families at risk and to amend the law relating to the jurisdiction, constitution, powers and procedure of juvenile courts, to emphasize still further their constructive social purpose. It also amended the law dealing with the

[1] The awareness of a need to co-ordinate and examine specialized knowledge about problems connected with deprived children lay behind the Foundation of the National Bureau for Co-operation in Child Care, which originated with the suggestion of Miss Joan Cooper, Children's Officer for East Sussex, in her address as President at the Annual Conference of Children's Officers in 1954. The Bureau's first Director, a clinical psychologist, was appointed in 1963.

[2] For example, its provisions are based not only on the report of the Ingleby Committee (Children and Young Persons Committee Cmd. 1191) but on those of the Departmental Committee on the Employment of Children as Film Actors, in Theatrical Work and in Ballet (Cmd. 8005), which had reported in 1950.

treatment of children and young persons after they had been subject to orders of the courts, and dealt with the employment of children in entertainment. In range, therefore, and in originality it was comparable to the great Children's Act of 1908 passed more than half a century ago. But the absence of resources to deal effectively with primary sources of deprivation robbed it of effectiveness.

The Act extended the powers of the local authorities to 'promote the welfare of children' and the wording of the Act here is important, for it marks a new attitude, a final moving-away from the paternalistic, protective child-centred attitude to positive and skilled family-centred work. Case-work treatment in the home in itself now becomes a justifiable service and the removal of children from home is a form of differentiated treatment for a child to be used only when he requires the particular kind of care and help which the children's department could give him by placing him elsewhere.[1]

'It shall be the duty of every local authority to make available such advice, guidance and assistance as may promote the welfare of children by diminishing the need to receive children into or keep them in care under the Children's Act, 1948, the principal Act (i.e. the Children and Young Persons Act, 1933) or the principal Scottish Act (Children and Young Persons (Scotland) Act, 1937) or to bring children before a juvenile court.'[2] This new duty did not affect the existing powers and duties of other departments in local authorities to promote the welfare of children who were not at risk or to fulfil their statutory obligations to those who are,[3] but it gave force and authority to the children's departments to work in this newly centred way. This inevitably meant an increasing deployment and development of casework skills and an examina-

---

[1] On analogy with illness, removal from home having to take place as a result of the doctor's skilled assessment in the light of his treatment given in the home and the treatment facilities which can be provided in the hospital.

[2] Section I (1) Eliz. II, 1963, 37, Children and Young Persons Act, 1963, Section I (1).

[3] The great importance of the work done by Health Visitors in their educative role should be more widely acknowledged. As their training comes more and more in line with modern psychological findings their potential for disseminating knowledge about the emotional needs of children at their different development stages could be a major tool of social reform.

tion of results, and the Act empowers local authorities as well as the Home Office to involve expenditure on research into matters connected with deprived children.[1]

Those sections in the Children and Young Persons Act of 1933 were repealed which dealt with the definition of 'care or protection' and an amended definition of care, protection or control was substituted to include not only children who are in danger and whose parents are not exercising guardianship, but those children who are also beyond the control of their parents and need to be brought before the Court. This amendment invested in the local authority powers of earlier enactments in which the parents could bring their children before the court as being beyond control. Their parents' rights to do so were now repealed, since such a public act of rejection was felt to strike at the root of family stability; though parents could still request the local authority to act in this way for them.[2]

The Act in its protective measures also dealt with grounds for assuming parental rights and extended them to cover cases where the parent has disappeared for over a year, or is suffering from some mental illness that renders him unfit to undertake the care of the child, or has persistently failed without reasonable cause to discharge the obligations of a parent.[3]

The age of criminal responsibility was raised from eight to 10, and all findings of guilt recorded before the age of 14 must be disregarded in the case of a person again convicted after 21. Certain changes of procedure were introduced in the juvenile court in order to lessen the child's ordeal, to make what is happening more meaningful to him, and to ensure that the magistrates are as well equipped as possible to deal with young offenders.

In the case of children sent to Approved Schools the Act tried to ensure that better use was made of improved selection techniques and increasing specialization at the schools. Steps were taken to ensure the maintenance of links between child and parents, or between child and children's department if he should already be in care. Local authorities were now required

---

[1] Section 45 (2). See, as a result of this power, *Financial Help in Social Work* by Jean S. Heywood and Barbara K. Allen. Manchester University Press. 1971.

[2] If the local authority refuses, the parents may then apply to the court for an order directing it to do so.

[3] There are echoes here of the most recent adoption legislation.

to undertake the after-care of a boy or girl released from an approved school, if the managers so requested.[1] This important provision underlies the development of work in the delinquency field which was now coming to the children's committees. More of them were setting up approved schools, and the new Act enabled local authorities to designate remand homes as classifying centres.[2] In 1964 the Home Office issued a circular asking the police to consult local children's authorities before any action was taken in the juvenile court against children between 10 and 12 years of age, unless there were good reasons for not doing so. The connection between unhappy childhood and delinquency has been stressed by both the Curtis and Ingleby reports, and this legislation was an attempt to bring co-ordinated skill to bear on these two aspects of what was felt to be a single problem.

Finally the Act tightened up regulations about the employment of children in new as well as old forms of entertainment, protecting them against financial exploitation, bad living conditions and excessive hours of work.

In the developments embodied in this legislation there has been an interplay of knowledge between the workers with individual children and parents, and the committee members and magistrates responsible for policy and jurisdiction. This interplay is an important and vital element in the child-care service. An examination of the position disclosed by statistics reveals the dependence of the child-care service on community participation and understanding and the repercussions on it of the social changes taking place, as well as of the efficacy or failure of other social services.[3] On 31st March, 1972, there were 90,586 children in the care of local authorities in England and Wales, or 5.9 per thousand of all children under the age of 18.[4] Within this figure there was, and continues to be, a very big movement of children in and out of care. For example, during the same year 53,365 children had to leave their homes and were admitted to local authority

[1] Paragraph 26 of Schedule 3 of the Children and Young Persons Act, 1963.

[2] Section 11, Children and Young Persons Act, 1963.

[3] See Eighth Report on the work of the Children's Department, Home Office, 1961, H.M.S.O.

[4] See *Children in Care in England and Wales*, March, 1972, Cmnd. 5434. These figures are still slowly rising. Figures are published under the same title in a white paper each year.

care, and 50,486 were discharged from care. Moreover, the children coming into care represent only about half the members for whom care is sought; about half of the families applying are helped by social workers in children's departments to avoid separation by the use of other community resources, such as home helps, school meals, day nurseries, nursery schools and help from relatives or friends.[1]

The causes precipitating the separation of children from parents and home are analysed yearly in relation to the total figures and are of important social significance. The 53,365 deprived in 1972 came into care on the following grounds:

1. No parent or guardian 250
2. Abandoned or lost.. 809
3. Death of mother, father unable to care 730
4. Deserted by mother, father unable to care .. 4,984
5. Confinement of mother 4,413
6. Short-term illness of parent or guardian .. 15,624
7. Long-term illness of parent or guardian .. 1,095
8. Child illegitimate and mother unable to provide a home 2,046
9. Parent or guardian in prison or remanded in custody 925
10. Family homeless because of eviction 1,155
11. Family homeless through a cause other than eviction 1,833
12. Unsatisfactory home conditions 3,522
13. Care order under the Children and Young Persons Act 1969 9,559
14. Under section 36 (1) of the Matrimonial Causes Act 163
15. Under section 2 (1) of the Matrimonial Proceedings (Magistrates Court) Act, 1960[2] 72
16. Order under section 7 (2) of the Family Law Reform Act, 1969 24
17. Other circumstances 6,161

These figures seem to reflect the difficulties, failure perhaps, experienced by a highly industrialised society functioning as a

[1] See Eighth Report of the Children's Branch of the Home Office, op. cit.

[2] Under these two acts magistrates and judges hearing a divorce or separation case have power to commit children to children's departments if no better arrangements can be made for them.

neighbourhood community. In situations of crisis some families find themselves alone and unable to cope and have to turn to the local authority for help. A big social problem is revealed of housing and family care.

There has been a wide variation in the numbers of children in care in the different areas of the country, for which there is no explanation, but the difference appears to have been related to the amount of social need in a local area and the demand made on the children's departments rather than on other basic social services, such as those concerned with health, housing or supplementary educational provisions. The social conditions which tend to produce the need for children to be received into care in an area have been defined[1] and point the way to primary prevention; they are: a rapid inflow of population from both inside and outside the country; heavy pressure on housing; a high illegitimacy rate; many inhabitants without the support of relatives living nearby; a large amount of mental illness and marital breakdown; the district is often also industrially depressed, contains a high proportion of unskilled workers and has a high rate of unemployment. Even so, the *demand* for care, and the actual *intake* of children are not correlated with need. Demand and intake were found to be affected by many factors such as the policy decisions of the local authority, and the effectiveness of other personal social services and voluntary organisations in the area. The rationalisation of the personal social services was clearly a necessary move.

The rationalisation of the social services under the influence of the Seebohm recommendations has been directly influenced by the child care movement; and, in the end, history may see this as its most enlightened and important contribution.[2] The story behind this development reflects the great social changes of the 1960s, a period which has been a watershed, and which has produced two major pieces of legislation, the Children and Young Persons Act of 1969 and the Local Authority Social Services Act of 1970, which brought the specialised children's departments to an end, and set up a comprehensive social service for the needs and welfare of families and individuals.

[1] See Jean Packman *Child Care Needs and Numbers*. Allen & Unwin. 1968, and Mia Kellmer Pringle, *Investment in Children*, Longman, 1966.

[2] See Appendix VIII.

The sixties produced profound misgivings about the nature of society and about its so-called progress after the setting up of the welfare state. Young men looked back in anger as sociologists revealed the extent of poverty, and the growing number of very poor families on low wages; the bulldozer began to symbolise contemporary life in which old communities were broken up and families callously left homeless or rehoused by bureaucracy without any coherent attempts to rebuild old neighbourhoods; on television and in entertainment and in the daily news there was an open and constant display of brutality and violence which could not fail to impress itself upon the mind. Allied to this was a growing concern about world toleration of the powerful destructive devices in the hands of governments and armies; the price exacted by technology and economics was clear for all to see at Aberfan, in the collapse of the Ronan Point flats, the pollution of the coast by the *Torrey Canyon*, and callous indifference to life marked by the public toleration of very serious driving offences. The new phenomenon of drug abuse among young people, and the growing crimes of violence, compounded by the unjust hanging of Timothy Evans, led to concern about the whole nature and efficacy of deterrence and to fresh thinking about the nature of crime.

In the child care field there were internal pressures from the workers themselves which were providing a climate for change and a more radical approach to tackling their problems. Homelessness in London caused over three and a half thousand children to be received into care, more newly trained workers in the field meant more understanding of the psychology of children and their emotional problems, which gave grounds for discontent with the state of society permitting such suffering, and led to ideological pressure for change. Influential children's officers had worked hard to demonstrate the correlation between delinquency and deprivation and had discouraged magistrates from committing juveniles to approved schools and pleaded for their committal to local authority care instead.[1]

[1] In particular, see the report by Mrs Barbara Kahan, Children's Officer for Oxfordshire County Council, *The Work of the Children's Committee and the Children Department. October 1969.*

'[Preventive] work, combined with the responsibility in the early fifties for most of the home surroundings reports for juvenile courts, enabled the children's

About the same time the Labour Party published in June 1964 an important pamphlet, *Crime, A Challenge to Us All*, expressing their concern at the correlation of delinquency with social and emotional deprivation, the consequent anachronism of the courts as machinery for dealing with the delinquency of working-class children, and their belief that a new approach to social work should be based on a comprehensive social service which would aim to meet the needs of all families, and that preventing delinquency would be part of the help given. They therefore recommended the appointment of a committee of inquiry into the administrative structure of the social services, and this was set up in 1965, after the Labour Party had come to power, under the chairmanship of Frederick Seebohm.

In 1965 the new Government issued a White Paper, *The Child, the Family, and the Young Offender* (Cmnd 2742), based upon the earlier pamphlet, proposing the abolition of juvenile courts and the setting up of Family Councils where social workers and other experts would reach agreement with parents about the treatment appropriate for all children under 16 instead of bringing the matter before the juvenile court. If agreement could not be reached, special magistrates' courts, to be known as family courts, would then decide treatment. Such courts would also sit as young offenders' courts exercising criminal jurisdiction over persons between the ages of 16 and

committees and their staff to observe at first hand how artificial were the distinction between the children who were referred for neglect, the ones who were received into care, and the ones who appeared before the juvenile courts as offenders. Child care officers carrying out their normal duties in the juvenile courts were able to suggest ways in which magistrates could help these children and young people through the social services for children which were now additional resources to the existing ones of probation and approved schools. Courts began to commit young offenders to care when they needed to leave home for a time and, although there was no obligation to do so, the children's department offered to report back on the progress they made while in care. Two developments grew out of these early beginnings. The first was that there was a steady drop in the number of approved school committals from courts, until a point was reached in 1964 when only one child from the whole county was in an approved school . . . The second development was that six-monthly Magistrate/Children's Officer Liaison Committees were started in most of the courts in the county at which the child care staff meet and discuss with the juvenile court magistrates all the boys and girls committed to care, approved schools or on supervision orders, and in addition are able to help the magistrates with information and suggestions about the services available for children and how they are administered.'

21. These suggestions about the legal machinery proved too radical for public opinion at the time and were modified in a second White Paper, *Children in Trouble* (Cmnd 3601), issued in April 1968, dealing more specifically with the treatment of delinquent juveniles in the light of the knowledge—now widely accepted—about their deprived social conditions, which had been corroborated by the Plowden Report in the educational field and its then novel concept of positive discrimination for the deprived areas.

The vision and flexibility of approach still inherent in the second White Paper was characteristic of the traditions of child care reform. While retaining the juvenile court it envisaged radical change in its powers to deal with offenders, making their treatment much more a matter of professional expertise by the child care workers, who were to concentrate on the family deprivation rather than the delinquency. The powers of the courts were therefore to be changed in three ways. The approved school order was to be brought to an end; instead of committal to an approved school for an offence, children were to be committed to the care of the local authority and then only if they had committed an offence *and* the parents were not fulfilling their roles. To help to combat social deprivation a new concept of 'intermediate' treatment was introduced which allows the child to remain at home but be brought into contact with a new and enriching environment, sometimes, but not always, for short residential periods. Supervision orders, which replaced some probation orders, were now to be the responsibility of the children's department for all children under 14, and for young people between 14 and 17 at the discretion of the courts. The Paper thus attempted effectively to destroy the stigma of delinquency and replace it with a concept of care for the deprived.

These changes were embodied in the Children and Young Persons Act, 1969, which received the Royal Assent on 22 October 1969. In introducing the bill in the House of Commons, the Home Secretary defined its purpose: 'to prevent the deprived and delinquent children of today from becoming the deprived, inadequate, unstable or criminal citizens of tomorrow.' It was to effect this purpose by two main methods, first by providing support through the social services to the parents of deprived or delinquent children in order to keep the children out of court (a consolidation of the measures in the 1963 Children and Young Persons Act), and second by ensuring that the juvenile courts could provide a wider range of provision after sentence, which would be much more flexible and more realistically tailored to the individual needs. This was in fact the social work concept of 'treatment' to be given only after an individualized assessment, and shows the influence of social work training as it had developed over the last twenty years of new legislation.[1] The Act confirms the intention of giving more responsibility to the social workers for helping children and less responsibility to the courts, and has thereby laid upon the child care social workers a heavy additional burden of diagnosis and assessment, from which they had previously been protected, such decisions having been made by the juvenile bench. Such a change has forced the new profession of social workers to consider more carefully the quality and ethics of the decisions for which they alone are responsible, and has placed such decisions where they should be, in the public eye, for it is to the public that social workers are accountable and public knowledge and understanding of social problems which they have to increase.

The Act is to come into effect by stages, since it is recognised that resources of manpower and public opinion cannot yet cope with all its ramifications. Children between the ages of 10 and 14 will gradually cease to appear charged with offences before the juvenile court and will appear instead for care proceedings. Criminal prosecutions are possible only for young persons aged 14–17. But the bringing of care proceedings is subject to consultation with the social workers of the local authority, the police or the N.S.P.C.C., for example; and any person authorised to bring proceedings, before doing so, must notify the local authority which then has a duty to inquire into the case, and 'provide the court before which the proceedings are heard with such information relating to the home surroundings, school record, health and character of the person in

[1] For a study of the influence of thinking and developments in the child care field upon other personal social services and finally upon the provision of an integrated social service for families as envisaged by the Seebohm Committee, and ratified in the Local Authority Social Services Act 1970, see the table in Appendix VIII.

respect of whom the proceedings are brought as appear to the authority likely to assist the court'.[1] Like the 1933 Children and Young Persons Act,[2] the 1969 Act requires a double test to be proved before a care order can be made, the *need* for care must be demonstrated and also the fact that, as things are, the child is in need of care or control which he is unlikely to receive unless the court makes an order.[3] The case therefore will not be brought to court unless everyone is satisfied that nothing less than a care order of the court will ensure that the child is cared for, and this emphasises the necessity of casework first with the family.

There are somewhat similar conditions laid down in dealing with young people from 14 to 17 who are to be prosecuted. The authorised person bringing the prosecution must first be satisfied 'that it would not be adequate for the case to be dealt with by a parent, teacher or other person by means of a caution from a constable or through the exercise of the powers of a local authority or other body not involving court proceedings'. Consultation is therefore required between the police, social workers and teachers before the case ever comes to court, as a result of which prevention and supportive work with the family may be started, and periodic discussions between agencies are to take place.

When eventually it is felt necessary to bring a case to the juvenile court, the child may now be dealt with in a great variety of ways: if he is brought as being in need of care or control, there are five kinds of order which can be made: (a) an order requiring the parent or guardian to enter into

[1] Section 9.

[2] See page 127.

[3] Section 1 (2) the following conditions must be satisfied in respect of the child:
  - (a) his proper development is being avoidably prevented or neglected or his health is being avoidably impaired or neglected or he is being ill-treated; or
  - (b) the court or another court found that that condition is or was satisfied in the case of another child or young person who is or was a member of the household to which he belongs; or
  - (c) he is exposed to moral danger; or
  - (d) he is beyond the control of his parents or guardian; or
  - (e) he is of compulsory school age and is not receiving efficient full-time education suitable to his age, ability or aptitude; or
  - (f) he is guilty of an offence, excluding homicide and also that he is in need of care or control which he is unlikely to receive unless the court makes an order under this section in respect of him.

recognisance to take proper care of a child or young person and exercise proper control over him; or (b) a supervision order (here the child normally remains at home, except for certain short periods which may be arranged away); or (c) a care order similar to the former committal to care, whereby the child is in the care of the local authority who decide what to do with him; or (d) a hospital order, which must be supported by the certificate of two doctors, as laid down in the Mental Health Act, 1959; or (e) a guardianship order, which must be similarly supported.

When there is a prosecution for an *offence* of a young person between 14 and 17, the same orders can be made as in the care or control proceedings, though here, in addition, there may be an absolute or conditional discharge, or there may be a fine of up to £50; payment of damages may be ordered, or compensation, or an order made for the juvenile to attend a detention or an attendance centre, although both of these will be abolished as soon as alternative treatment—to be known as intermediate treatment—is widely available.

In this way the courts no longer specify in detail through their sentence the kind of treatment the child or young person will receive. The approved school order is abolished and such schools now change their name and function and become part of the new structure for residential care which is based upon meeting the needs of children within their own local region. The social workers will themselves decide the form of care, residential or otherwise, most appropriate to the needs of the child.

Because an understanding of the child's needs and family deprivation is so basic to the legislation, provision had to be made for organising resources, to ensure that proper assessment could be made of the child's problem, and appropriate care planned for him. Each region of the country is therefore required by the Act to look at the children's homes, ex-approved schools, reception centres, boys' and girls' hostels, and every form of statutory and voluntary residential care, in a rational way, making sure that there is enough provision within each region to meet the needs of all the children within it, and to plan its homes—now to be known as community homes—so that there is less overlapping and more tailoring to local regional needs, by local authorities and voluntary organisations in each region acting together. As in 1948 stress is laid on the importance of careful assessment for the child's needs which the larger number of well-trained workers in the service now made a more likely possibility.

The Act therefore re-stated the contemporary emphasis on care within the family, but for the first time stressed the importance of the *quality* of residential care where this had to be provided. This piece of legislative reform has again laid very heavy burdens upon the children's sections of local authority departments. The casework was greatly increased in 1963 by the duty to work with some of the most difficult and deviant families, and the more flexible and imaginative planning of residential care in 1969 now posed many new problems in the adaptation of staff as well as buildings. Since 1948 residential care had been regarded as second-best, and only gradually as a result of trying to cope with children who showed severe emotional and behavioural difficulties, had the departments begun to use residential care as treatment-centred, rather than custodial or sheltering, provision. This requires much clearer definitions of the aim and purposes of each community home, and recognition of the skills required in helping children in them.

Finally, the Act strengthened the protective measures always present in child care legislation, by dealing with the supervision of that always vulnerable group, children who are privately fostered.[1] Included in supervision for the first time were children whose fostering is undertaken without reward, including those long-term arrangements which amount to *de facto* adoptions.

There is no doubt that while the emphasis from the fifties onwards has been upon the work with families, the emphasis on the protective side of child care has been allowed to decline. This is not because the social workers have given undue importance to the 'blood tie'. Their psychological theory since Bowlby had emphasised for them the importance of a relationship which was warm, intimate and continuous, and this they are very well aware may be provided by a parent substitute.

[1] For a recent account of this vulnerability see Robert Holman *Trading in Children*. Routledge & Kegan Paul. 1973.

Rather they felt compelled out of social justice to work with the underprivileged parents to enable and support them, and in this it may well be they have taken on an unrealistic burden for themselves. They know only too well that the real problems to be tackled are education, poverty and housing, and mental health and until these are dealt with no one can say whether bad parenthood is a matter of social and economic deprivation or lies in personality difficulties which would still be there even in privileged parents.

In attempting to deal with the roots of delinquency, every study and committee led back to the conditions in which children were brought up. Knowledge of the socially deprived backgrounds of families of young delinquents led the Government to set up the Seebohm Committee concerned with the personal social services. This Committee sat during the time when social work training, principally developed in the child care field, was concerned with casework skills and methods and when, in order to develop expertise in working with individuals with severe behaviour difficulties, less emphasis was being placed on the British social work traditions of social reform directed against the great social evils of our time such as the re-emergence of poverty and homelessness.[1] The Seebohm Report therefore, when it came, tended to reflect the views of social work as a profession, rather than as a movement for social reform, but, in any case, it had been asked to advise only upon the organisation and responsibilities of the local authority personal social services, and to consider what changes in them would be desirable to secure an effective family service. Its proposals for rationalisation led to the Local Authority Social Services Act 1970, one of the last of the major social reforms passed by the Labour Government as it went out of office. It represents the fulfilment of the principle to which social work has committed itself from the beginning, namely that it should meet the needs of the under-privileged with respect for the individual within his family.

While family casework remains the basis of the approach to

[1] The effects of Bowlby's work in 1952, while very necessary, had tended to confirm social workers in their emphasis on individual relationships, and it was not until 1965 that two sociologists, Peter Townsend and Brian Abel-Smith, published their 'discovery' of poverty in the welfare state, *The Poor and the Poorest* (G. Bell).

work in the child care field, recent developments have led to some re-emphasis on the protection of children and of their rights. This re-emphasis is seen most clearly in the discussion of parental rights and relinquishment, following the recommendations of the Houghton Committee on adoption, and following much publicity given to a case of ill-treatment and death of a child who had been returned by the local authority from a foster home to her natural parents' home at the request of the natural parents.[1]

The Departmental Committee on the Adoption of Children was appointed on 21 July 1969 under the chairmanship of Sir William Houghton[2] to consider the law, policy and procedure on the adoption of children and what changes were desirable. The Committee was asked to interpret its terms of reference fairly broadly, considering the alternatives of guardianship and adoption, and the position of long-term foster parents who wish to keep a child permanently, by adoption or otherwise, against the will of the natural parent. Their work was thoroughly done and included commissioning of a considerable amount of research and study. It reported in October 1972, in unanimous agreement, underlining the principle that the long-term welfare of the child, rather than parents, should be the first and paramount consideration in considering the nature and extent of adoption services, and in resolving conflicts.[3]

The Report therefore marks a final break with the old legal concept of children as chattels of their parents, and the presumption that parents are the most appropriate people to

[1] See the *Report of the Committee of Inquiry into the Care and Supervision provided in relation to Maria Colwell*, 1974. This report—not unlike the O'Neill case at the end of the Second World War—reflects the pressures and overwork of the post-Seebohm re-organisation of social work services. But it reveals also, perhaps, a too uncritical acceptance by workers of the emphasis on the natural family, which had been seen as so important an innovation in 1948. The protective nature of child care must always be its priority.

[2] Sir William Houghton, a distinguished educationist, and concerned for the welfare of children, died on 16 November 1971 and was succeeded by Judge F. A. Stockdale. The main principles behind adoption have been outlined earlier in chapter 9—see pages 150-3. The history of adoption in this country up to 1954 was given in some detail in the report of the Hurst Committee (Cmd 9248, London 1954). It is briefly recapitulated in the Houghton Report. For a good bibliography of adoption publications see M. L. Kellmer Pringle, *Adoption in Brief: An Annotated Bibliography, 1966-1972*. National Foundation for Education Research (London). 1972.

[3] *Report of the Departmental Committee on the Adoption of Children*, Cmd 5107, 1972.

represent their children's interests is recognised as a presumption not always related to the facts. The thinking of the report reflects the complex background in society of altering values, rapid sociological change, growing psychological insight. The Committee recommended various ways in which central and local government can support and extend provisions for the adoption of children and for the refining of adoption procedure and practice, and considered carefully the alternative rights of guardianship, the position of foster children held in a 'tug-of-war', and the important procedure of consent in adoption by the parents and the dispensing of their consent.

A year after the publication of the Houghton Report, public opinion was severely shocked by the tragic death of an eight-year-child who had been committed to the local authority, placed in a foster home and then returned to her natural mother and step-father, where she was so severely assaulted and beaten that she died.[1] Recognition of the syndrome known as 'battered babies' was slowly growing, but generally this recognition had not been applied to older children. As a result of the public disquiet, Dr. David Owen, Member of Parliament for Sutton, Plymouth, in 1974 put forward a private member's bill intended to carry out the main recommendations of the Houghton Report and to broaden its scope to include the forestalling of child battering and to deal more effectively with the custody of children in divorce and separation of their parents. His bill disappeared with the dissolution of the Conservative Government in February 1974, but on the return of the Labour Government was reintroduced as a Government bill.

The clear intention of the subsequent Act—the Children Act 1975—is to make the welfare of the child paramount in all proceedings concerning children, in contrast to the family-centred nature of earlier legislation. This is perhaps a sad reflection on the difficulties which social workers have experienced in the seventies in attempting to cope with a greatly expanded social service following on the Seebohm re-organisation. The Act has tried to give effect to the recommendations of the Houghton Committee, as well as matters arising from the report of the Maria Colwell inquiry. A new welfare principle is laid down in relation both to adoption and to

[1] See Report on Maria Colwell, quoted earlier.

children in care. In making *any* decision relating to adoption,
courts and adoption agencies must have regard to all the
circumstances of the child and his parents, but, where there is
a conflict of interests, first consideration must be given to the
child and his wishes and feelings, bearing in mind his age and
understanding. A similar duty is required when decisions are
made about a child in care. New procedures laid down in the
Act to free a child for adoption and restrict the removal of
foster children were influenced by a survey requested by the
Houghton Committee in 1970. It was found that 3,465 children
had been fostered in the same home for two to five years. A
study, *Children Who Wait* by Jane Rowe and Lydia Lambert
(Association of British Adoption Services, 1973), examined
more than 2,000 children in care in institutions and found that
60 per cent were expected by their social workers to remain in
care until the age of eighteen; 40 per cent had no contact at all
with either living parent; and 23 per cent saw one or both their
parents as often as once a month. It was estimated that there
were about 6,000 children in the country who could be released
to the permanent care of foster or adoptive parents. A duty is
now laid on every local authority to establish an adoption
service in conjunction with its other social services, and parents
may consent to their parental rights and duties being transferred to the adoption service or agency, thereby freeing their
child for adoption before a specific couple is selected.

Adopted persons over 18 now have the right to information
about their birth records, and a duty is laid on local authorities
and adoption societies to provide counselling for them should
they need an outsider's help.

As an alternative to adoption, relatives and other people,
such as foster parents who are looking after children on a
long-term basis, can now obtain the legal custody of their
children on application to the courts. The bonds established
between children and substitute parents may thus be legally
safeguarded. In all these cases the over-riding principle of the
Act is relevant—that first consideration shall be given to the
need to safeguard and promote the welfare of the child
throughout his childhood. This innovation is also a sad and a
somewhat retrogressive step, emphasising the need of the child
over and against that of his parents, and represents, perhaps,

in the light of experience a more realistic assessment of the serious and sometimes intractable family problems with which the child care service has to deal, and a less optimistic view about their solution than prevailed in 1948 or 1963. The rights and welfare of the child are not seen as so complementary and, indeed, provision is made in the Act for the child to be separately and independently represented in court hearings.

Third-party placings are finally to be brought to an end by the provision that parents who want their child adopted must give the child to an adoption society unless it is a relative who is adopting. The courts may dispense with the parents' consent where the child has been seriously mistreated, even on an isolated occasion, and if the court is satisfied that rehabilitation of the child with his family is unlikely. Parents giving up children for adoption can no longer bind the adoptive parents to bring the child up in a specific religious faith, but instead they can place their child with a denominational adoption society.

All these proposals emphasise the welfare rights of the child in distinction to the rights of parental authority.

We have seen the way in which the child care service has led the way and been a major influence in the professionalisation of other services concerned with the elderly, the handicapped and the homeless.[1] Thus specialisation in the problems of the deprived, and the priority given to them by a specialised department which was the *raison d'être* for the child care service in 1948, has been more than justified. Since 1970 it seems doubtful whether the knowledge and understanding which has come from specialisation in the problems of deprived children will have much opportunity to grow while the demands of neglected services for adult deprived groups require so much attention to bring them up to even comparable standard. The loss to child care must be the gain to them, and for the next few years it is expected that the quality of residential care in children's homes will see the most concentration in the child care field.

The great discrepancy in the quality of care in deprived groups of the elderly and handicapped has laid an almost impossible burden upon those social workers trained within the child care service in trying to assert their own accepted

[1] This is set out in Appendix VIII to illustrate the cross-fertilisation of ideas.

standards. It is salutary to reflect what a long period of trial and error, crisis and experience, and what slowly accumulated knowledge and public education, lie behind the great achievements in child care between 1948 and 1970. It seems unlikely that the service can now be given the priority it once enjoyed while there is so much to be done elsewhere. The history of the child care service clearly shows that in building up knowledge and understanding, and in sensitising the public, specialisation is an essential element, at any rate for a time.

APPENDIX I

ACCOUNT OF THE FIRST ADMISSION AT THE FOUNDLING HOSPITAL

WEDNESDAY THE 25TH MARCH, 1741

Minutes of the daily Committee of the Hospital for exposed and deserted young Children :—

' HAVING according to the Resolution of the General Committee with all possible diligence put this Hospital into a Condition proper for the Reception of Children This Committee met at seven o'clock in the Evening. They found a great number of People crowding about the door, many with Children and other's for Curiosity, the Committee were informed tha Several Persons had offered Children but had been refused admittance The Order of the Gen¹ Committee being that the House shoᵈ not be open'd till Eight o'Clock at Night. AND this Committee were resolved to give no Preference to any person whatsoever—The Committee were immediately attended by the Peace Officers of the Parish and Two Watchmen of theirs were ordered to assist the Watchman of the Hospital. He had orders to prevent any Childs being laid down at our Door and to give a Signal to the Parish Watchman in Case any Child was refused to be admitted into the Hospital, who thereupon was to take Care that it was not Dropt in the Parish.

' At Eight o'Clock the Lights in the Entry were Extinguished, the outward Door was opened by the Porter, who was forced to attend at that Door all night to keep out the Crowd immediately the Bell rung and a Woman brought in a Child the Messenger let her into the Room on the Right hand, and carried the Child into the Stewards Room where the proper Officers together with Dr. Nesbitt and some other Govʳˢ were constantly attending to inspect the Child according to the

Directions of the Plan. The Child being inspected was received Number'd, and the Billet of its Discription enter'd by three different Persons for greater Certainty. The Woman who brought the Child was then dismissed without being seen by any of the Gov^rs or asked any Questions w^tsoever. Imeadiately another Child was brought and so continually till 30 Children were admitted 18 of whom were Boys and 12 Girls being the Number the House is capable of containing. Two Children were refused, One being too Old and the other appearing to have the Itch.

' About Twelve O'Clock, the House being full the Porter was Order'd to give Notice of it to the Crowd who were without, who thereupon being a little troublesom One of the Gov^rs went out and told them that as many Children were already taken in as Coud be made Room for in the House and that Notice should be given by a publick Advertisement as soon as any more Could possibly be admitted, And the Gov^rs observing Seven or Eight Women with Children at the Door and more amongst the Crowd desired them that they would not Drop any of their Children in the Streets where they most probably must Perish but to take care of them till they could have an opportunity of putting them into the Hospital which was hoped would very soon be and that every Body imediately leave the Hospital without making any Disturbance which was immediately complyed with with great Decency, so that in two minutes there was not any Person to be seen in the Street except the Watch.

' On this Occasion the Expressions of Grief of the Women whose Children could not be admitted were Scarcely more observable than those of some of the Women who parted with their Children so that a more moving Scene can't well be imagined.

' All the Children who were received (Except Three) were dressed very clean from whence and other Circumstances they appeared not to have been under the care of the Parish Officers, nevertheless many of them appeared as of Stupifyed with some Opiate, and some of them almost Starved, One as in the Agonies of Death thro' want of Food, too weak to Suck, or to receive Nourishment and notwithstanding the greatest care appeared as dying when the Gov^rs left the Hospital which was not til they had given proper Order's and seen all necessary Care taken of the Children.

March 26th

' The Gov^rs found the Child we apprehended dying yet alive, tho in a very bad Condition, and to have so offensive a Smell that the Nurse could Scarce bear to attend it which shewed them the necessity of imediately fitting up the Infirmary, and the Gov^rs present were of opinion that two Nurses shou'd be taken into the Hospital with proper salaries to attend on the Sick Children.

' The Gov^rs were informed that no Children had been Dropt in the Parish the last night.

' This day many Charitable Persons of Fassion visited the Hospital, and whatever share Curiosity might have in inducing any of them to Come, none went away without shewing most Sensible Marks of Compassion for the helpless objects of this Charity and few (if any) without contributing something for their Relief.

27th of March

' We found that in the night a Child (No. 14) dyed it is imagined to have dyed of an Inflammation in the Bowells we imagine this to be one of the Children who we observed Stupify'd with Opiates and after it came to itself it never left complaining. We found two other's Ill one wanting the assistance of Surgeon from some Hurt on its arm. Mr. Sainthill was sent for and Capt Coram was desired to ask Dr. Mead to visit the Hospital this afternoon to direct what was proper for the Safety of the Sick Children.

' In the afternoon Dr. Mead visited the Hospital it was his opinion that 6£ p Ann. was the proper wages to be allowed for the Nurses who are to attend the Infirmary. The Child No. 26 who appeared dying when we took it in was alive when the Committee left the Hospital, the rest of the Children were well.

March 28th, 1741

' This morning the Box was opened and £7 11s. taken out we found the Children in a good Condition except the Child No. 26 who was this day christened according to the Order of the Genl Committee being thought in Danger of Death. The Chief Nurse was also discharged for incapacity. We put the

Books of the Hospital in Order according to the Plan, we found some Confusion in our accounts by having money paid by the Secretary as well as the Steward who ought to take Receipts in the Book.

March 29th

' This day the Gov^{rs} mentioned were present at the Christening 28 of the Children taken into the Hospital the 25th and named the Boys as the Dutchess of Richmond Lady Caroline Lenox Countess of Pembroke and other Ladies of Fashion did the Girls. The Children were baptiz'd by Mr. Smith, there was collected on this occasion 35£ 8s. and 5£ 5s.—of which being given by Mr. Thos Osborne was entered into the Register Book.

' Sarah Clarke one of the Nurses was Discharged for Disobedience and Sawciness to the Chief Nurse.'[1]

(Extract from *The History of the Foundling Hospital* by R. H. Nichols and F. A. Wray, O.U.P. 1935, pp. 38 ff.   )

APPENDIX II

EARLIEST INDENTURE OF APPRENTICESHIP FOUND AT STYAL

THIS Indenture, made the 14th day of September in the twenty-fifth year of the Reign of our Sovereign Lord, George the Third, by the Grace of God, of Great Britain, France and Ireland, King, Defender of the Faith, and so forth ; and in the year of our Lord one thousand seven hundred and eighty five, witnesseth that Thomas Payne, Church warden of the parish and Borough of Newcastle-under-Lyme in the county of Stafford, and Thomas Barratt, overseer of the said parish, by and with the consent of His Majesty's justice of the Peace for the said Borough whose names are hereunto subscribed, have put and placed and by these presents do put and place John Drakeford a poor child of the said parish, apprenticed to Samual Greg of Manchester, in the county of Lancaster, Esquire and cotton manufacturer with him to dwell and serve from the day of these presents until the said apprentice shall accomplish his full age of twenty-one years according to the Statute in that case made and provided, DURING all which term the said apprentice his said Master faithfully shall serve in all lawful business, according to his power, wit and ability ; and honestly, orderly and obediently in all things demean and behave himself towards his said Master and all his during the said term, AND the said Samual Greg, for himself, his executors and administrators, doth covenent and grant to and with the said Church wardens and overseers, and each of them, their and each of their executors and administrators, and their and each of their successors for the time being, by these presents that the said Samual Greg the said apprentice in the art and business of cotton manufacturing which he now useth and followed shall and will teach, instruct, or cause to be taught and instructed in the best way and manner that he can in consequence of the faithful service of the said apprentice. And shall and will during all the term aforesaid, find, provide and allow unto the said apprentice meet, competent and sufficient meat, drink and apparel, lodging, washing, and all other things necessary and fit for an apprentice, AND also shall and will to provide for the said apprentice that he be not in any way, a charge to the Borough of Newcastle under Lyme as aforesaid, or parishioners of the same ; but of and from all charge shall and save the said Parish and parishioners harmless and indemnified during the said term.

IN WITNESS whereof, the parties above said to these present indentures, interchangeably have put their hands and seals, the day and year above written. Sealed and delivered in the presence of (the several interlineations being first made and deserved by)
James Davies
Mathew Fawkner witness to Saml. Greg and John Drakeford.

We whose names are subscribed, justices of the Peace of the Borough aforesaid (one of us being of the Quorum) do consent to the putting forth of the above said John Drakeford apprentice, according to the intent and meaning of the above indenture.

THOS. KINNERSLEY   (*Mayor*)
JNL. TILSTONE
(*Quarry Bank MSS*)

After the passing of the Health and Morals of Apprentices Act in 1802, which required the factory master to attend to the children's religious intruction, the indentures begin to contain a new clause :

' . . . . . . shall and will permit, suffer, promote and encourage the said apprentice to attend divine service at one of the Established Churches of this Kingdom, at least twice in each and every Sunday, and shall and will find and provide a suitable sitting in such church for that purpose.'
(*Quarry Bank MSS*)

APPENDIX III

MEMOIR OF KITTY WILKINSON OF LIVERPOOL
1786-1860

THESE notes on the life of Kitty Wilkinson are taken from a memoir written about her in 1835, and republished in 1927. It is not known who was the author. The manuscript was found among papers left by Mrs. William Rathbone, who visited Mrs. Wilkinson each week. The internal evidence of the memoir makes it clear that while Mrs. Rathbone was not the writer, the manuscript is compiled from her notes of talks with Kitty which are often copied word for word. The memoir ends with the year 1835, but was edited and continued with additional information by Herbert R. Rathbone and published by Henry Young and Sons Ltd., of Liverpool in 1927.

In Liverpool Kitty Wilkinson is chiefly remembered as the originator of baths and wash-houses for the poor, during the great cholera epidemic of 1832, but she deserves to be better known for the work she performed so humbly and charitably as foster-mother to many orphaned and deprived children of Liverpool. Her epitaph describes her as the widow's friend, the support of the orphan, and the fearless and unwearied nurse of the sick ; and she is represented in the Lady Chapel windows of Liverpool cathedral, which commemorate the lives of great and good women.

Catherine or Kitty Seward was born in Londonderry in 1786. Her mother was Irish, her father an English soldier. Mr. Seward died while Kitty was still a child and her mother, after a severe attack of brain fever, became a permanent invalid and lost her sight. Kitty's home life in England was spent in poverty. She continued to live with her mother but went out daily to help the servants of a Mrs. Lightbody, a woman of means who was both blind and lame but an active worker for the poor of the Liverpool district. Here Kitty was taught to read and accompanied her mistress on her visits to the poor. Mrs. Lightbody's lameness made it impossible for her to walk or to ride in a carriage, so she used a sedan chair and Kitty (to quote her own words from the memoir) " used to take a little basket and walk by her side ; then she would say to me ' Kitty, go into that cellar and see how the poor woman is to-day. Is there any fire in the grate ? Has she any coals ? ' Then she would send me back to get what was wanted, and when I came back, if it was wet she would say, ' Now go and put your feet to the fire and tell me what you thought of so and so,' and then she would say ' Kitty, poverty will probably be your portion through life, but you will have one talent to exercise ; you may be able to read for half an hour to a sick neighbour, or to run an errand for those who have no one else to go for them. Promise me, child, that you will try to do what you can for others, and then we may meet again in another world, where I shall be thankful to see you above me.' "

In 1797, when Kitty was eleven, her mother had to enter the Infirmary and on her discharge went over to Ireland to be with her own friends. The two children, Kitty and a young brother, were left behind in England. Kitty was not strong and Mrs. Lightbody thought she would be better in the country, and the children were therefore sent as apprentices to a cotton mill at Caton, near Lancaster.

Mrs. Lightbody died during Kitty's apprenticeship at the mill. She left a very deep impression on the child who recalled her influence many years later, " I never saw her after I went to Caton ; but every word she said is precious, and is graven deep in my heart."

Kitty remained at Caton from the age of eleven to eighteen when her apprenticeship ended. She was happy there and has described her life at the apprentice house in these words " If ever there was a heaven upon earth it was that apprentice house where we were brought up in such ignorance of evil ". Kitty's whole life shows that this ignorance of evil was no sheltered environment which unfitted the children for making their own way in the world, but a preparation for a life of courage and hard work and a sense of belonging to a community. In 1804, when her apprenticeship ended, Kitty left the apprentice house and lodged with a woman in the neighbourhood of Caton until in the same year she received news that her mother had returned to Liverpool. Although her master, the workpeople at the mill and the woman with whom she lodged all tried to persuade Kitty to stay in Caton she decided to leave to try to make a home for her mother in Liverpool.

In Liverpool Kitty found lodgings for her mother and went into service to maintain her. After three years her mother's health became so bad that Kitty left her job, hiring a large room in which she opened a small school to maintain them and in which she and her mother could sleep at night. Five years later, in 1812, she married John de Monte or Demounto, a sailor of French extraction, and in 1815 her first son was born ; but Kitty's life with her sailor husband was brief, shortly before the second son was born John de Monte was drowned at sea.

Kitty now had to maintain herself, her two small sons and her invalid mother who began to have periods of insanity in which their food, fuel and clothes and bedding were burnt or destroyed. After a few years of working as a charwoman or on agricultural work in the fields round Liverpool Kitty remarried in 1823. Her second husband Thomas Wilkinson, had been an apprentice with her in the Caton Mill and was now working as a porter in Mr. Rathbone's cotton ware-house in Liverpool. One day here he overheard Kitty singing the words of the old Lancashire songs she had learned as a village child, and which found a responding music in his heart. Their family now consisted of Kitty's two children, her blind and deranged mother and a deaf blind destitute woman who had been taken into Kitty's own home five years previously. This large household was soon to be increased by the addition of foster children.

Shortly after her marriage Kitty nursed a sick neighbour in a severe and fatal illness which left the woman's four children orphaned and without a home. Mr. Wilkinson immediately agreed with Kitty to take them into his home, saying, according to the Memoir, " Let us take the children and I will work early and late and live upon two meals a day if it is necessary."

Shortly after this they took in two more orphans, delicate ricketty twins, who were eventually apprenticed by Kitty to a sea Captain on whom she could rely to give them both protection and care.

A year or two after their marriage, when the Wilkinsons

had saved a little, they were persuaded by a respectable widower to rent a small house. The widower had three children he was anxious to place under Mrs. Wilkinson's care and he agreed to pay 24s. weekly for board and lodging for himself and his family. This arrangement continued until seven years later he died but Mrs. Wilkinson, without any financial help, continued the care of the children. The younger boy she educated in the Bluecoat School, then fitted him out for sea, giving him a home between voyages. The girl she kept with her for two or three years until she found her a good place. The elder boy after being apprenticed had several periods of unemployment following his master's failure in business, during which time Kitty continued to give him a home. She also took in another apprentice named MacAllister, with whom her foster-son worked, whose father said he could not afford to keep him on his wage of four shillings a week. Rather than see this boy have to give up his apprenticeship Mrs. Wilkinson, whom training and poverty had made an excellent manager, took him into her own home and kept him on his wage.

In 1828 Mrs. Wilkinson's mother had to be removed to the workhouse for her own safety and that of others, and soon afterwards her second son died of tuberculosis.

In 1832 an epidemic of cholera broke out in Liverpool. There were few homes in the poorer quarters of the city which remained immune. Many children, whose parents were dead or dying, were running about the streets neglected. Kitty was asked to nurse a poor woman, who died, leaving a feckless husband and five young children. Kitty, told the man that if he would go to sea and earn something to maintain his children, she would take charge of them while he was away. The children had been very neglected and caused her a good deal of worry and anxiety but by the time their father returned from sea both their health and behaviour had improved and she had arranged to provide decent clothing for all of them. The work, however, had been a severe trial and Kitty asked the father to find a relative to take over the children, who were then removed to the care of a sister.

Soon afterwards Mr. Wilkinson was passing along the street in which these children lived. When they saw him they ran after him asking if he would take them back. All their good clothes were gone and they looked in a very poor state. The Wilkinsons took them back along with their father who was now unemployed. After a time the father went to sea again, leaving twenty shillings a month for the children. Kitty had considerable trouble with this family, however. The father was frequently unemployed and unable to pay anything for his children's maintenance, and his drunkenness and swearing were so disturbing that eventually he was not taken back into the family. The eldest girl proved very difficult and was described as a great mischief maker, and seems to have been unable to accept the security and affection Kitty tried to give her.

During 1834 a man came one day to Kitty asking her to take in a fourteen year old orphan boy who had got into bad ways for want of someone to care for him. Kitty agreed to do this, but in the Spring of 1835 she had a breakdown, precipitated no doubt by the work she had been doing and the strain involved by the size of her present household, which consisted of fourteen in all.

About this time we have a record of Kitty's weekly budget for a family of fourteen, consisting of five men, two women, two boys and five girls.

EXPENSES

Flour (at 8lbs. for 1 /–)	12s.	
Meat	4s.	
Potatoes, 14 pecks	4s.	2d.
Oatmeal	1s.	
Herbs and seasoning		6d.
Coffee (1lb.)	2s.	
Sugar (4lbs.)	2s.	2d.
Butter 5lbs. at 8d.)	3s.	4d.
Milk	1s.	9d.
Buttermilk	1s.	
Soap and soda	1s.	4d.
Coals and Candles		9d.
Rent and water	10s.	6d.
£2	4s.	6d.

The income was derived from Mr. Wilkinson's wages of 2s. 6d. a day ; Kitty's own wage for cleaning, 2s. 6d. a week ; from the rent of the cellar, 2s. 6d. a week. The boys and a lodger contributed to the general fund and paid the rent each week. No contribution was apparently made on behalf of the girls and the elderly woman. In addition Kitty earned between three and six shillings a week for taking charge of a washing establishment, but this money was paid to her quarterly and not paid into the weekly housekeeping but kept for emergencies.

The memoir ends in 1835 just following Kitty's recovery, and describes how on her return from a period of convalescence she took in two sick babies for care and nursing.

Two things of interest in the child care field stand out from this memoir. First the paternalism of some of the well-to-do toward deprived children, and the willingness, affection and practical help shown by a poor working family towards children in need as a concrete and literal expression of their duty towards their neighbour, help to which the community turned in preference to, as well as in default of, the poor law ; secondly, the difficulties and dangers which the social conditions of the time imposed on the self-help of the poor. Kitty Wilkinson is of the calibre of saints, and her work was surely blessed, but in her nineteenth century small and overcrowded home, as in many others of the time, the deprived children taken for care ran the direct risk of infection by tubercle bacillus and, perhaps, injury by an insane relative, while the strain of working in these conditions overtaxed the health of a more than willing foster-parent.

Kitty was a good manager and able to make her small amount of money, fulfil the needs of her large family, but unscrupulous women could, and did, use the same opportunities to exploit a child because of the inadequacy of allowance, or else make profit from a more adequate one. It was these conditions of danger both to health, to life, and to the personality of the child, which caused the parish overseers, and later the boards of guardians, to approach so cautiously and even reluctantly the system of boarding out, and to adopt it only under a highly regulated form.

The epitaph on her grave reads :

" Indefatigable and self-denying she was the widow's friend,
The support of the orphan,
The fearless and unwearied nurse of the sick,
The originator of Baths and Wash-houses for the poor.
'For all they did cast in of their abundance; she of her want
did cast in all that she had, even all her living.' "

Mark xii. 44.

APPENDIX IV

" THE GIRL FROM THE WORKHOUSE "

From *All the Year Round*[1], October, 1862.

" Among the witnesses upon this subject (the immorality of the workhouse girls) we have the Revd. J. Armitstead vicar of Sandbach, Cheshire, who has been long in his parish, where he has rebuilt one large Church, built two new Churches and established several schools. During the whole life time of the new poor law this gentleman has been a guardian, attentive to the needs of the poor in a well managed union. But in all his experience he has never known of a girl, passing out of the workhouse school to service in a gentleman's family. The stigma of the workhouse stands in the girl's way. Mr. Armitstead offered himself as a witness for the compatability of the principle of Charity with the principle of poor law administration for he has seen the misery of profligacy into which girls, with starved undisciplined affections fall after quitting either the workhouse or the district school, for want of help from anything that has the aspect of home. He is not deluded by the fallacies of returns that report all well with those who are out of sight, and lead to pen and ink conclusions contradicted by the commonest experiences of common life. Mr. Armitstead thinks that with dealing with destitute children, orphans and others, towards whom it stands in place of a parent, the State should make the nearest practicable approach to the fulfilment of a parent's duty. For the last nine years and with the greatest possible success the system has been tried in his own parish of seven thousand people, of taking orphan paupers by two or three at a time, and placing them with respectable dames in their own districts : the dames being under the superintendence of the clergyman, the Guardians and the relieving officers. The orphan children are thus placed in homes with childless couples and others, who with small pay for their maintenance are glad of their service and companionship. Experience has proved that strong domestic attachments arose out of

[1] *All the Year Round. A Weekly Journal* conducted by Charles Dickens and published by Chapman & Hall in weekly numbers and in monthly parts.

such relations. The well-selected household guardian usually becomes a lasting friend. The child dressed in no workhouse clothes, and its relation to the workhouse almost unknown to itself, goes to the national school, in due time goes out to work, with a fair chance of getting good situations and when out of work the orphan girl knows where to find a chimney corner where she may look for a welcome. Upon some such system Mr. Armitstead believes that radical defect in poor law administration as applied to the young, may in all country, and in some town districts be greatly softened."

APPENDIX V

ORDERS AND REGULATIONS OF THE POOR LAW BOARD FOR THE BOARDING OUT OF PAUPER CHILDREN

To the Guardians of the Poor of the several Unions and Parishes named in the Schedules (C) and (D) hereunto annexed :—

To the Clerk or Clerks to the Justices of the Petty Sessions held for the Division or Divisions in which the said several Unions and Parishes are respectively situate :—

And to all others whom it may concern :

We, the Poor Law Board, in pursuance of the authorities vested in us by an Act passed in the fifth year of the reign of his late Majesty King William the Fourth, intituled, " An Act for the Amendment and better Administration of the Laws relating to the Poor in England and Wales," and by all Acts amending the same, do hereby order, direct, and declare, with respect to each and every of the unions and parishes named in the Schedules (C) and (D) hereunto annexed, as follows :—

ARTICLE I.—Notwithstanding any provisions contained in any Orders issued by the Poor Law Commissioners or the Poor Law Board relating to the administration of relief to paupers not residing within the union or parish in which they are settled, the guardians of any union or parish named in the Schedules (C) and (D) hereunto annexed, may board out pauper children from such union or parish in homes beyond the limits of such union or parish : Provided that they have entered into arrangements approved of by the Poor Law Board, with two or more persons, hereinafter called the Boarding-Out Committee, for the purpose of finding and superintending such homes.

ARTICLE II.—No such arrangements shall be made with any such boarding out committee unless each member of the committee have signed an undertaking, truly and faithfully to observe all regulations in this Order prescribed, or which may from time to time be prescribed by the Poor Law Board, with respect to the boarding-out of pauper children, and unless the committee have obtained the written authority of the Poor Law Board to make such arrangements.

ARTICLE III.—Any person deriving any pecuniary or personal profit from the boarding out of any child shall thereby be disqualified from becoming or continuing to be a member of any such committee.

ARTICLE IV.—The guardians of any union or parish from which any child is sent to be boarded out in any home so found, may at any time withdraw such child from said home, notice of their intention to do so being given at least one week beforehand to the boarding-out committee.

ARTICLE V.—The regulations to be observed by the guardians with respect to the boarding out of pauper children shall be as follows :—

No. 1. No child shall be so boarded out unless such child is an orphan, or being illegitimate, deserted by the mother, or being legitimate, deserted by both parents or deserted by one parent, the other parent being dead or under sentence of penal servitude, or suffering permanently from mental disease, or out of England.

No. 2. No child shall be first boarded out at an earlier age than two, or at a later age than ten years.

No. 3. No child shall be boarded out without a certificate, signed by the medical officer of the union or parish from which it is sent, stating the particulars of its health ; such certificate to be forwarded by the guardians to the boarding-out committee.

No. 4. No more than two children, save only in the case of brothers and sisters, shall be boarded out in the same home at the same time, and in no case shall the number of children boarded out in the same house exceed four.

No. 5. In no case shall a child be boarded out with foster-parents of a different religious persuasion from that to which the child belongs.

No. 6. Before receiving any child to be boarded out with them, the foster-parent shall sign an undertaking in duplicate, which shall, in addition to any other matter which may be agreed upon, contain an engagement on the part of the foster-parents that, in consideration of their receiving a certain sum per week, they will bring up the child as one of their own children, and provide it with proper food, lodging and washing, and endeavour to train it in habits of truthfulness, obedience, personal cleanliness, and industry, as well as in suitable domestic and out-door work ; that they will take care that the child shall attend duly at church or chapel, according to the religion to which the child belongs, and shall, while boarded-out between the ages of four and 12 years, attend a school, unless prevented by sickness or other urgent cause, during all the usual hours for instruction thereat ; that they will provide for the proper repair and renewal of the child's clothing, where an allowance is made by the guardians for that purpose ; and that in case of the child's illness, they will report it to the guardians, and also to the boarding-out committee ; and that they will at all times permit the child to be visited by any member of the boarding-out committee, and by any person specially appointed for that purpose by the guardians or by the Poor Law Board.

The Guardians shall cause one copy of this undertaking to be forwarded to the Poor Law Board.

No. 7.   On the delivery of the child to the foster-parents or foster-parent, an acknowledgement shall be given in the form set out in Schedule (A) hereto annexed, or to the like effect.

No. 8.   In no case shall the weekly sum to be paid by the guardians to the foster-parents for the maintenance of a child, inclusive of lodging, but exclusive of clothing, school pence, and fees for medical attendance, exceed 4s.

No. 9.   No child shall be boarded out in a home distant more than a mile and a half from a school, the schoolmaster of which is willing to undertake to send to the guardians a written report upon the child in the Form contained in the Schedule (B) hereto annexed, at least once a quarter.

No. 10.   The guardians may allow an extra school-fee, not exceeding 1d. per week, to be paid to the schoolmaster of the school at which such boarded-out child attends, the same to be a remuneration to him for drawing up and sending the quarterly report upon such boarded-out child prescribed in the regulation last preceding.

No. 11. No child shall be boarded out in any home which is distant more than five miles by the nearest road of access from the residence of some member of the committee.

ARTICLE VI.—Every boarded-out child shall be visited not less often than once in every six weeks at the home of the foster-parents by a member of the committee, and the visitor shall thereupon make a report in writing to the committee stating the apparent bodily condition and the behaviour of such child, and all reasonable complaints made by or concerning the child, against or by the foster-parents.

These reports shall be forwarded by the committee to the guardians not less often than quarterly.

And if in the case of any boarded out child, no such report shall be received by the guardians for the space of four consecutive months, the guardians shall either provide for the visiting of such child at the home of its foster-parents by an officer of the guardians at intervals of six weeks, or shall withdraw the child from the home with all reasonable expedition.

ARTICLE VII.—If the Poor Law Board shall withdraw from any boarding out committee the authority required by Article II, the guardians who have made arrangements for the boarding out of pauper children with the said committee shall, on receiving notice of such withdrawal, take back, with all reasonable expedition, all children boarded out in homes found by such committee ; nevertheless, it shall be lawful for the guardians, subject to the approval of the Poor Law Board, to continue to board out the children then being in such homes, provided that they cause the children to be visited by one of their own officers at intervals of six weeks.

ARTICLE VIII.—It shall be lawful for the guardians, notwithstanding any provision contained in the General Order of the Poor Law Board bearing the date the 14th day of December in the year 1852, or in any order containing the same provisions since issued to any union or parish where children are boarded out in conformity with the previous articles of this Order, to pay out of the funds in their hands the reasonable expenses incurred by them in conveying the child to and from the home in which it is boarded out, and, in the case of a union, to charge the same to the common fund.

ARTICLE IX.—Whenever in this Order the word importing the singular number or the masculine gender only is used, it shall be taken to include and apply to several persons as well as one, and to females as well as males, unless there be something in the subject or context repugnant to such construction.

ARTICLE X.—The word " Guardians " in this Order shall be taken to include any governor, director, manager, acting guardian, or other officer in a parish or township appointed or entitled to act as a manager of the poor, and in the distribution of the relief to the poor from the poor rate, under any general or local Act of Parliament.

ARTICLE XI.—Whenever the word " Union " is used in this Order, it shall be taken to include not only a union of parishes formed under the " Poor Law Amendment Act, 1834," but also any union of parishes incorporated or united for the relief or maintenance of the poor under any local Act of Parliament.

ARTICLE XII.—Whenever the word " Parish " is used in this Order, it shall be taken to signify any place for which a separate overseer is or can be appointed.

Schedule A.

I, A.B., of . . . . . . hereby acknowledge that I have this day received C.D., aged . . . . . . years, from the guardians of the poor of the . . . . . . union or parish, on the terms and conditions contained in the annexed undertaking ; and that I have also received for the use of the said C.D. the articles of clothing set out in the list appended hereto.

Dated this . . . . .day of . . . . . .

(*Signed*)
(*Witness*)

LIST OF CLOTHING
(*Here set out the Articles in detail*)

Schedule B.

School				Report for the Quarter ending			
Name of Child	Age	Names and Address of Foster-Parents	Days absent from School during the Quarter	Alleged Causes of Absence and Progress of Child	Observations as to appearance, Conduct during the Quarter	Books and Stationery Supplied	School Fees and Cost of Books and Stationery

APPENDIX VI

WHOSE CHILDREN?

WARDS OF STATE OR CHARITY

To the Editor of *The Times*

Sir,

Thoughtful consideration is being given to many fundamental problems, but in reconstruction plans one section of
the community has, so far, been entirely forgotten.

I write of those children who, because of their family
misfortune, find themselves under the guardianship of a
Government Department or one of the many charitable
organisations. The public are, for the most part, unaware that
many thousands of these children are being brought up under
repressive conditions that are generations out of date and are
unworthy of our traditional care for children. Many who are
orphaned, destitute, or neglected, still live under the chilly
stigma of " charity " ; too often they form groups isolated
from the main stream of life and education, and few of them
know the comfort and security of individual affection. A letter
does not allow space for detailed evidence.

In many ' Homes ', both charitable and public, the willing
staff are, for the most part, overworked, underpaid, and
untrained ; indeed, there is no recognised system of training.
Inspection, for which the Ministry of Health, the Home
Office, or the Board of Education may be nominally responsible, is totally inadequate, and few standards are established or expected. Because no one Government Department
is fully responsible, the problem is the more difficult to tackle.

A public inquiry, with full Government support, is urgently
needed to explore this largely uncivilised territory. Its
mandate should be to ascertain whether the public and
charitable organisations are, in fact, enabling these children

to lead full and happy lives, and to make recommendations how the community can compensate them for the family life they have lost. In particular, the inquiry should investigate what arrangements can be made (by regional reception centres or in other ways) for the careful consideration of the individual children before they are finally placed with foster-parents or otherwise provided for ; how the use of large residential homes can be avoided ; how staff can be appropriately trained and ensured adequate salaries and suitable conditions of work, and how central administrative responsibility can best be secured so that standards can be set and can be maintained by adequate inspection.

The social upheaval caused by the war has not only increased this army of unhappy children, but presents the opportunity for transforming their conditions. The Education Bill and the White Paper on the Health Services have alike ignored the problem and the opportunity.

Yours sincerely,

Marjory Allen of Hurtwood.

Hurtwood House, Albury, Guildford.

July 15th, 1944.

APPENDIX VII

BOARDING-OUT AND THE WORDSWORTHS

A Nineteenth Century Tale of Prudence and Charity

(With acknowledgement to the Trustees of Dove Cottage Library)

In the lovely wild valley of Easedale there is an isolated cottage of grey mountain stone, once sheltered by a magnificent yew, whose decayed, silver trunk now bleaches by the door, with a garden sloping down to the brawling Blind Tarn ghyll, with huge stones and rocks scattered on every side. It was from here that eight children in 1808 were orphaned and made the responsibility of community care in a small village, an example of voluntary effort before the standards of the State for deprived children were properly developed.[1]

On a cold, snowy Saturday, the 19th March, 1808, George and Sarah Green, who lived in this cottage, having sold their horse for some ready money, went over on foot from Easedale to Langdale to spend a few hours at a country sale and at the same time to see if they could find à fresh place for Mrs. Green's illegitimate daughter, Mary, who was in service there, in a public house. After unsuccessfully trying to get Mary a fresh job as a servant through the acquaintances they met at the sale, they set off home about five o'clock, intending to cross the fells and drop down just upon their cottage. They were

[1] The story has already been told, though not from this angle, by Professor de Selincourt in a beautiful and definitive piece of work in which he has edited and prefaced the original 'Narrative Concerning George and Sarah Green of the Parish of Grasmere', by Dorothy Wordsworth. It was written as a record 'of human sympathies and moral sentiments' and was not to be published, said Dorothy, while there was any chance of the children becoming by it 'objects of curiosity'. It was not published until 1936, when Professor de Selincourt added much material given to him by Wordsworth's grandson. It is now alas! out of print and I acknowledge here my debt to it. See George and Sarah Green. A narrative by Dorothy Wordsworth edited from the original manuscript with a preface by E. de Selincourt, Oxford. At the Clarendon Press, 1936. The story had moved de Quincey when he heard it, and, 31 years later, in 1839, he wrote an inaccurate and rather fanciful account of it for *Tait's Magazine*, entitling it 'Early Memories of Grasmere'. It is published in his collected works.

never seen alive again. The woman's body was later discovered upon some rough ground above Mill Beck and Dungeon Ghyll waterfall, and her husband, terribly injured from a fall, was found at the foot of a precipice close by. Cries had been heard by some people in Langdale about 10 o'clock that night, but little attention was paid to them, they were thought to be the drunken noise of revellers returning from the sale. It is thought that husband and wife became lost in a mist which came down over the mountain in the late afternoon, and that, after wandering about in the dark in an exhausted condition, George Green was killed instantly by a fall, and his wife, injured in going to help him, probably died from exposure.

The Greens had left a daughter Jane, aged 11, at home in charge of five small children, the youngest, Hannah, being an infant at the breast, and the remaining four all boys, George, John, Thomas and William. The Wordsworth's knew the family, though not very well, for an elder sister, Sally, was in their employment as a not very satisfactory nursemaid-help to Mrs. Wordsworth at Dove Cottage, and Dorothy remembered her brother's description of Jane as she had crossed the valley one day in early winter, 'This same little girl, Jane, had been noticed by my brother and sister some months ago, when they chanced to meet her in Easedale, at first not knowing who she was. They were struck, at a distance, with her beautiful figure and her dress as she was tripping over the wooden bridge at the entrance to the valley; and when she drew nearer the sweetness of her countenance, her blooming cheeks, her modest, wild and artless appearance quite enchanted them. My brother could talk of nothing else when he came home, and he minutely described her dress, a pink petticoat peeping under a long dark blue cloak, which on one side gracefully elbowed out, or distended as with a blast of wind, by her carrying a basket on her arm; and a pink bonnet tied with a blue ribband, the lively colours harmonizing most happily with her blooming complexion.'[1]

During the night of the tragedy, the children sat up waiting for their parents until 11 o'clock and then went to bed, thinking they had decided to stay all night in Langdale because of the weather. All Sunday they waited, while Jane milked the cow

[1] Dorothy Wordsworth. Narrative Concerning George and Sarah Green.

night and morning, wound up the clock, nursed the baby, and took good care that the fire should not go out as they had no tinder box with which to light another. At mid-day on Monday she became anxious and one of the boys crossed the Easedale valley to Lancrigg farm to borrow a cloak so that she could go to look for their parents. The alarm was immediately spread throughout the neighbourhood, and about 50 or 60 men set off at once up the snow-covered hills to search for the Greens, while two or three women went to the cottage to comfort the children. They found no money in the house,[1] or food beyond two boilings of potatoes, a very little meal, a little bread, and three or four legs of lean dried mutton, and all the children were crying except the baby, who lay sleeping peacefully in her cradle, 'a delicate creature,' says Dorothy, 'the image of Sara Coleridge'.[2]

The family was very poor and was in the habit of bartering anything that could be spared from the house or stable for potatoes or meal. They had an old cow, which did not give a quart of milk a day, but they could not afford to buy another. George Green, who had been married once before, was now 65 and his land was deeply mortgaged; besides the scanty living he eked out from it he earned a little by selling peat and doing odd jobs for his neighbours. But though they were so poor the Greens had never been known to complain; they were always cheerful, and decently dressed and few people had realized how great their poverty was.[3] The children, though very ragged, were clean and healthy and seemed happy. The mother, Sarah Green, who was at the time of her death 45 years of age, had been a parish apprentice 'and therefore', says Dorothy, 'probably a neglected child', but she had always seemed a happy person. Dorothy remembered her cheerful face and described seeing her often, a typical mother, 'two or three little ones about her, and their youngest brother or sister, an infant, in her arms'. Her only pleasure was to go to

[1] The Greens, when their bodies were found, had no more than 3d. each in their pockets.

[2] Letter to William (who was in London with Coleridge) dated 23rd March, 1808.

[3] Though one or other of the little girls, five or six years before, used to come the two miles to the Wordsworth's house to fetch away the used tea leaves to make a drink at home.

auction sales and country fairs, where, for a few hours she could meet and mix with the jolly crowds of people and join in the liveliness without any need to spend money.[1]

The bodies of George and Sarah Green were brought down from the hills to their cottage on Wednesday, and on Friday afternoon they were buried in Grasmere churchyard.[2] After the funeral the older children returned home, there was a sale of their furniture on the following Thursday, and the next day the house was left empty and silent.

There were orphaned altogether eight children under 16 years of age. Mary, the eldest, who was in service in a public house in Langdale,[3] and Sally, who was with the Wordsworths, had begun to earn their keep, and one of the boys, George, was taken by his half brother, James, the eldest son of George Green by his former marriage. There remained, therefore, five children to be provided for by the parish, for after the estate had been sold and the mortgage paid off, there was nothing left for the family.

Legislation had been passed in 1782 to provide for poor children, left orphaned and destitute in this way, by boarding them out,[4] 'And be it further enacted, that all infant children of tender years, and who, from accident or misfortune, shall become chargeable to the parish or place to which they belong, may either be sent to such poorhouse as aforesaid, or be placed, by the guardian or guardians of the poor, with the approbation of the Visitor,[5] with some reputable person or persons in or near the parish, township or place to which they belong, at

---

[1] de Quincey in *Early Memories of Grasmere* describes these Westmorland auction sales and what they meant to the poor, and says that the main secret of their attraction to country folk was the social rendezvous among people often separated from each other by mountains 3,000 feet high. The pleasure was heightened by the prospect of excellent ale (for the men) and excellent tea (for the women) being provided on the hospitality of the house where the sale was to take place.

[2] William Wordsworth wrote a poem about this, but it is a bad one.

[3] A better place was found for Mary a year later with the Wordsworth's friend, Miss Weir, who kept a small school at Appleby, later attended by little Dora Wordsworth.

[4] Gilbert's Act. 22. Geo. III C. 83. See Section 30.

[5] The Visitor of the poorhouse, 'a person respectable in character and fortune,' was a separate appointment nominated by the guardians to superintend the poorhouse, see to the accounts and settle questions of admission, and the Governor of the poorhouse, guardians and treasurer were to obey the Visitor's directions.

such weekly allowance as shall be agreed upon between the parish officers and such person or persons, with the approbation of the Visitor, until such child or children shall be of sufficient age to be put into service or bound apprentice to husbandry or some trade or occupation; and a list of the names of every child so placed out, and by whom and where kept, shall be given to the Visitor, who shall see that they are properly treated, or cause them to be removed, and placed under the care of some other person or persons, if he finds just cause so to do; and when every such child shall attain such age he or she shall be so placed out, at the expense of the parish, township or place to which he or she shall belong according to the law in being; provided, nevertheless, that if the parent and relations of any poor child sent to such House, and so placed out as aforesaid, or any other responsible person, shall desire to receive and provide for any such poor child or children, and signify the same to the guardians at their monthly meeting, the guardians shall, and are hereby required to, dismiss or cause to be dismissed such child or children from the poorhouse, or from the care of such person or persons as aforesaid, and deliver him, her or them, to the parent, relation or other person so applying as aforesaid;[1] provided also that nothing herein contained shall give any power to separate any child or children, under the age of seven years, from his, her or their parent or parents, without the consent of such parent or parents.'

Gilbert's Act, therefore, not only encouraged boarding-out, but encouraged responsible people to come forward and offer a home as an alternative to those which the parish could provide, as a piece of voluntary service. But, writing in 1808, Dorothy Wordsworth drew a rather grim description of boarding-out as it had developed during the last 20 years or so. 'It is the custom at Grasmere, and I believe, in many other places, to *let*, as they call it, those children who depend wholly upon the parish to the lowest bidder, that is, to board them out with those persons who will take them at the cheapest rate; and such as are the least able to provide for them properly are often the readiest bidders, for the sake of having a little money

[1] As an example of this see the story of the Molecatcher in Miss Mitford's tales, *Our Village*.

coming in, though, in fact, the profit can be but very small; but they feel that they get something when the money comes, and do not feel exactly what they expend for the children because they are fed out of the common stock. At 10 years of age they are removed from their boarding houses, and generally put out as parish apprentices, at best a slavish condition; but sometimes they are hardly used, and sometimes all moral and religious instruction is utterly neglected. I speak from observation; for (I am sorry to say it) we have daily before our eyes an example of such neglect in the apprentice of one of our near neighbours. From the age of seven or eight till he was 11 or 12 years old the poor boy was employed in nursing his mistress's numerous children, and following them up and down the lanes. Sunday was no holiday for him; he was not, like others, dressed clean on that day, and he never went to Church. I recollect, when I first came to live in this country, a little more than eight years ago, observing his vacant way of roaming about. I observed that there was an appearance of natural quickness with much good temper in his countenance; but he looked wild and untutored. It was the face of a child who had none to love him, and knew not in his heart what love was. He is now 16 years old and a strong handsome-featured boy; but, though still the same traces of natural sense and good temper appear, his countenance expresses almost savage ignorance with bold vice. To this day he does not know a letter in a book; nor can he say his prayers; (as Peggy Ashburner expressed it strongly in speaking of him to Sara, "That poor lad, if aught were to happen to him, cannot bid God bless him!"). His master has a couple of crazy horses and he now employs him in carrying slates to the next market-town, and, young as he is, he has often come home intoxicated. Sometimes no doubt the liquor is given to him, but he has more than once been detected in dishonest practices, probably having been tempted to them by his desire of obtaining liquor. I hope and believe that it does not often happen in this neighbourhood that parish apprentices are so grossly neglected as this boy has been; and I need not give you my reasons for thinking that there is not another family in Grasmere who would have done the like; nor could it have been so bad even in this instance if the boy had not come from a distant place, and consequently the parish officers are not in the way of seeing how he goes on, and I am afraid that in such cases they seldom take the trouble of making inquiries.'

It was experiences such as these which moved the Wordsworths to try to do something to help the Green children to have a better start in life.

'You will not wonder, after what I have said, that we have been anxious to preserve these orphans, whom we saw so uncorrupted, from the possibility of being brought up in such a manner, especially as there is no likelihood that they would all have been quartered in their native Vale. From the moment we heard that their parents were lost we anxiously framed plans for raising a sum of money for the purpose of assisting the parish in placing them with respectable families; and to give them a little school-learning; and I am happy to tell you that others at the same time were employing their thoughts in like manner; and our united efforts have been even more successful than we had dared to hope.'[1]

The parish had agreed to allow 2s. a week for each of the five children until they were fit to go to service or be apprenticed.[2] The Wordsworths hoped to raise enough money to be able to ensure that they could have some say in the choice of foster-parents, pay a more liberal allowance and clothe the children well, and ensure a decent education and apprenticeship for them.[3] One of the first subscribers was Bishop Watson of Llandaff, perhaps busier in the Lakes than in his diocese; he gave 10 guineas, as did Lord Muncaster, and the names of many other prominent people appear in the subscription book, Princess Sophia of Gloucester, the Dukes of Bedford and Devonshire, Lord and Lady Lonsdale, Lord and Lady Holland, Lord Spenser, Lord Kinnaird and Lord Lauderdale, Lady Carrington, Lady Dougall and Lady Beaumont; help also came from the writers Scott, Southey, Landor, Rogers, W. L.

---

[1] Dorothy Wordsworth, op. cit.

[2] See preface to the Subscription book, in the handwriting of Sara Hutchinson. MS. in Dove Cottage library. Jane received nothing from the parish as she was over 10 and the five children eligible were George, John, William, Thomas and Hannah. George, however, went to his half-brother, James.

[3] See letters of Dorothy to Catherine Clarkson, dated 28th March, 1808, and 10th May, 1808, and letter of William to Richard Sharp dated 25th April, 1808. See also the preface to the Subscription book.

Bowles, Charles Lloyd, Joanna Baillie, John Wilson (Christopher North) and de Quincey. But there are many subscriptions from humble people ranging from 3d. to 2s. 6d., and the sum raised is a fine example of voluntary help from all classes of the community. An account of the tragedy appeared in the *Gentlemen's Magazine* in April and among the manuscripts in Dove Cottage Library is an anonymous letter addressed to the Minister of the Parish of Grasmere, Kendal, Westmorland, dated 9th April and postmarked from Southampton, 11th April, 1808.

'Sir, I take the liberty of troubling you with the enclosed two notes, not knowing any person at Grasmere to whom I could send it, for the relief of the poor children of the name of Green, whose misfortune in losing their parents in the snow I read in the newspaper the other day, and, as a trifle, may be acceptable, will be obliged to you to lay out the little I have it in my power to send as you think will be the most useful to them. I know not whether they are in distress or not, but conclude that eight children of a labouring man cannot be in very affluent circumstances when they have lost the support of their parents—should it, however, be otherwise and they should not be in want of any assistance, you will have the goodness to distribute the sum among the poor of Grasmere, who must have been a good deal distressed by this hard winter—with every apology for giving you so much trouble, I remain, Sir, your obliged servant, "Amicus".'

By the end of April more than £200 has been lodged in the Kendal Bank and when the list closed a total of £500 4s. 3d. had been subscribed by 277 people. the Wordsworths being responsible for collecting about a third of it.[1] All this was undertaken at a time when they were themselves undergoing

[1] In her letters to Mrs. Clarkson, dated 10th May, 1808, and to Jane Marshall, dated the following day, Dorothy says that the Wordsworth family 'have subscribed nothing ourselves, the providing for Sally being as much as we can afford.' Before the tragedy they had not intended to keep Sally on, as she was so unsatisfactory with the children, and had already hired another nursemaid. They now agreed to keep her, not as a servant, but in order to send her to Grasmere School and to teach her to sew, to try to fit her for a good place later. In the same letter Dorothy says how important it is that their name cut a great figure in the list of subscribers as it has given William's wife a place on the Committee, where she can withstand the busy, meddling management of another Committee member, Mrs. North, who was not a countrywoman, but the wife of a merchant who came from Liverpool.

great personal anxiety. They were nursing both William's little son John, who was feverish and sick with continual headache, and Sara Hutchinson, Mrs. Wordsworth's sister, who had alarmed them all by a dreadful attack of pain in the chest and coughing blood.

A Committee was set up to regulate the expenditure of the money which had been raised ('a charitable fund for the relief, maintenance, bringing up and putting out into the world of the children of the said George Green and Sarah his wife'), and to superintend the children. The Committee, consisting of Mrs. Watson, the wife of the Bishop of Llandaff, Mrs. Lloyd, Mrs. North, Mrs. King, Mrs. Wordsworth and Miss Susannah Knott, met on 7th April, 1808, and Miss Knott was invited to become Secretary. It was decided that, in addition to the 2s. weekly allowance which the parish had agreed to make until the younger children reached the age of 10, that 1s. a week should be paid from the funds for each child, and 1s. 6d. extra a week for Hannah, the baby.[1] The Committee was concerned that the trust should primarily benefit these five younger children, Jane and Hannah, and the three boys, John, William and Thomas, for Mary and Sally, and now apparently George, had entered on their working life, and had less at stake, though the Committee stood by them. They, therefore, set about finding foster-homes for the children. Dorothy said that it had been declared with one voice by the people of the parish, men and women alike, that the baby and Jane should not be parted from each other. They consequently decided to place Jane and Hannah together with Mr. and Mrs. Watson on the hillside at Winterseeds. Mr. Watson was described as a clever, ingenious man, a skilled blacksmith whose forge was by Tongue Ghyll on the Keswick Road (his name may be found stamped on one of the hinges of the Grasmere Church door) and Mrs. Watson was 'a fine scholar' who would teach Jane both sewing and reading. The Watsons never had any children of their own. They took Jane and Hannah, they said, because George Green's first wife and Mr. Watson's mother were sisters, and, though the relationship with the children was not a blood one, it provided a kinship and made them feel a real obligation to

---

[1] Actually the foster-mother (Mrs. Watson) took both Jane and the baby together for 2s. per week.

help. The unpopular Mrs. North (who knew the Watsons) was asked occasionally to visit, to pay the boarding-out allowance to Mrs. Watson, and superintend any necessary expenditure.

The two little boys, William and Thomas ('in petticoats') were placed not far away, with Mr. and Mrs. Dawson, who lived at Ben Place on the other side of the Swan Inn. The Dawsons were very respected people in the village, had brought up a now grown-up family, but had lost a 20-year-old son the previous year. By taking the two little boys they hoped to have something other to think about than their own private trouble. John, aged seven, was placed with a Mr. Fleming, who appears to have been a sheep-farmer, either an elderly bachelor or widower, with a housekeeper; he was the godfather of Jane. John had been very frightened when there had first been talk of his being boarded-out because, he said, the master of the house where it was suggested he should go had once had a quarrel with his father. When Mr. Fleming's name was mentioned John was glad and said he would like to go there because he knew Mr. Fleming had been kind to his mother and father and had given them two sheep. Mrs. Wordsworth and Mrs. King supervised these placings and paid the boarding-out allowances.

There was evidently some committee trouble at the very beginning. Dorothy tells us that before the first committee had ever met, Mrs. North, who wanted to be in charge of the boarding-out, had arranged by herself that all the children should board with an old woman who was, in fact, quite unfit to look after them. However, the ladies appear to have handled Mrs. North very tactfully and eventually Miss Knott (who had been temporarily looking after the boys), Mrs. North and Dorothy (deputizing for her sister-in-law who was nursing little John Wordsworth) took the children round to their new homes and saw them 'settled in'. 'Jane and her sister took possession of their new abode with the most perfect composure; Jane went directly to the fireside, and seated herself with the Babe on her knee; it continues to call out 'Mam!' and 'Dad!' but seems not to fret for the loss of either; she has already transferred all her affections to her sister, and will not leave her for a moment to go to anyone else.' At Ben Place Mr. and Mrs. Dawson came down the lane to meet the ladies and the

boys, and were about to take the two small ones, William and
Thomas, by the hand 'but they clung to Miss Knott, the lady
who had fetched them from their father's cottage on the day of
the funeral, and had treated them tenderly ever since. The
younger sat upon her lap while we remained in the house, and
his brother leaned against me; they continued silent; but I
felt some minutes before our departure, by the workings of his
breast, that the elder boy was struggling with grief at the
thought of parting with his old friend. I looked at him and
perceived that his eyes were full of tears; the younger child,
with less foresight, continued calm till the last moment, when
both burst into an agony of grief.

We have since heard that a slice of bread and butter quieted
their distress; no doubt the good woman's kind looks, though
she gave to the bread and butter the merit of consoling them,
had far more effect. She is by nature loving to children, mild
and tender. . . .[1]

Lastly, the committee ladies took the seven-year-old John
along to Mr. Fleming. The lad could not say a word, he was
crying his heart out, and old Mr. Fleming, who has been used
to seeing him at his sheep-dippings, tried to make him feel
at home. 'He took hold of him and patted his head as lovingly
as if he had been his grandfather, saying "Never fear, mun!
Thou shalt go upon the hills after the sheep; thou *kens my*
sheep!" '

The accounts connected with the boarding-out of the
children were kept by Miss Knott with scrupulous neatness,
and entered in an exquisite copperplate hand in an exercise
book still extant in the Dove Cottage library. For the first two
years the annual expense of maintaining the five boarded-out
children came to £20, but as they grew older expenses mounted
for clothing and school fees so that the annual expenses on the
fund came to between £43 and £46 until the children began to
be self-supporting.[2] The receipted bills from tradesmen,
apothecary and schoolmaster, all carefully handwritten and
headed 'for the orphans of Green', 'for Green's children' have

[1] They were some time later overheard saying one to the other, 'My Daddy
and Mammy's dead, but we will never go away frae this house'.

[2] Sally left the Wordsworths in 1812 and there was additional expenditure for
a time for her board and washing, but in the same year Mr. Fleming appears to
have 'adopted' John as no payments were made for him from date.

been neatly docketed by Miss Knott and are still preserved; school fees amounted to 5s. or 7s. a quarter according to the age of the child, with, in winter, an extra 1s. or 1s. 6d. a week for the cost of heating, and there were often extras like 6d. per week for 'writing quills and copies', 5d. per week for reading, 8d. for a spelling book and 6s. 5d. for a *History of England*. The clothing bills include amounts for greatcoats, stockings, shoes and clogs, frocks and shirts, calico and yards of linen for shirts, lining and buttons and fustian for jackets, materials for suits, boys' and girls' hats, cotton gowns, gloves, mits and pattens, checked aprons and shifts, and New Testaments were brought for 1s. 9d. each.[1] The children seem to have kept very well on the whole, there are only two bills from Mr. Scambler, the apothecary, and these are dated 7th January, 1812, and 7th February, 1813; they do not refer to any child by name. They are for lotion, powders, bleeding, blister, mixture, and the expense of journeys from Ambleside.

In 1813 Miss Knott gave up the secretaryship and Mrs. Wordsworth took it on, and nothing is orderly in the account book again. She once wrote 'nothing in the course of my life ever bothers me like accounts' and looking at these papers one can understand this. Some of the records are in a small green book used by William and containing at one end, in the poet's hand, the introductory lines to the exordium of 'The Excursion'. Mrs. Wordsworth's accounts, blotched, crossed out (even with a page cut out!) begin on the following page and continue till 1828 when the youngest child, Hannah, came of age, and the funds could be portioned out. The auditor, however, found everything very satisfactory. Subscriptions had totalled £500 4s. 3d. The expenses over the 20 years had been £397 11s. 10d. The poet's confidential clerk, John Carter, prepared the accounts and final statement. Prudent investing of the money had resulted, after all the expenses of bringing up and educating and apprenticing the children had been met, in a balance of £536 19s. 6d. in hand, some £36 more than the total amount of the original subscriptions. This was distributed among the eight children, Mary, Sally and George coming in for their share. They all received a lump sum of £60 each and

[1] The Wordsworths evidently went to town on Sally's Bible when she left them. It cost 5s. 6d.

£20 was given to their half-brother James Green, who had maintained and brought up George quite independently of the fund's help. All the children were living, and all of them, except George, who was working in Hendon, came to Rydal Mount to receive their share. All, except the eldest, Mary, signed their names in their own handwriting. Mary made her mark.

The story is a fine example of an involved community coming together to fulfil their duty towards their neighbour and fulfilling it with prudence and with charity. The community tried to meet the needs of the children by placing them in homes where the family ties would not be weakened and where they still could share in familiar scenes and associations. It is a pity that the records tell us little about the dynamics of the fostering, but the local traditions indicate that all turned out well. Experience teaches us that there must have been many ups and downs, but there is only one record of a problem, that of the adolescent William, who, at the age of 17, was provided with a suit of clothes and a box, and found a place with a Mr. Gee, a friend of the Wordsworths in Rydal. Among the papers in Dove Cottage library is a note from William, addressed to Geo. Gee, Rydal, and dated Thursday, 9th March, 1821. 'I take this opportunity of writing to you to let you know that I can get a place as soon as ever I please and one a good deal better than ever you will have. So, therefore, I am determined not to stay any longer about such a filthy place.' The letter is signed with an enormous and quite indecipherable flourish for a name. Alas, three months later, in Mrs. Wordsworth's account book there is an item £1 10s. 'advanced for Willy, he being out of a place'.

But perhaps the best indication about the success of the fostering is found in the story told by Mr. Fleming's housekeeper, who one day went with John and her master to a mountain enclosure near Blind Tarn Ghyll, where they had some sheep. They passed by the child's old home and as they did so John, who had been looking about the fields, turned to her with confidence and said 'My mother's ewe has got a fine lamb'. Let us hope that the other children were equally satisfied with their new lives.

APPENDIX VIII

CHILD CARE AND THE SOCIAL WORK SERVICES
A Chronology

	CHILD CARE	SOCIAL WORK SERVICES
1945	Curtis Committee set up to inquire into the death of a foster child.	
1946	Curtis Committee reported, revealing the inadequate standard of local authority child care.	
1947	Training Council in Child Care set up to train social workers in Child Care.	Carnegie U.K. Trust Report (First Younghusband Report) on employment and training of social workers in Britain recommending a Carnegie School of Social Work on American lines should be set up in England for graduates.
1948	Children Act (establishing a children's department with trained children's officer in each local authority).	
1951		Second Younghusband Report —supplementary survey on social work in Britain, suggesting broader and more generic social work education.
1952	Children and Young Persons (Amendment) Act imposing a duty on children's departments to investigate situations reported of children at risk.	
1954		Carnegie Course set up at L.S.E. to train graduates as social workers in child care, medical social work, psychiatric social work and probation on a 'generic' social work basis.

CHILD CARE	SOCIAL WORK SERVICES
1956 Ingleby Committee set up to consider ways in which delinquency might be treated and child neglect and suffering be prevented.	
1959	Mental Health Act enabling local authorities to give support to the mentally disabled in their own families and community.
1960	Third Younghusband Report on social workers in local authority health and welfare services, emphasizing need for training at different levels and inaugurating additional social work training outside universities.
1961 Ingleby Report recommends more efficient detection and help for families at risk (Cmd. 1191). Kilbrandon Committee set up in Scotland to consider treatment of juvenile delinquents and children in need of care or protection or beyond parental control.	
1962	Health Visiting and Social Workers (Training) Act which set up a Council for Social Work Training able to award the National Certificate in Social Work for non-graduate training.
1963 Children and Young Persons Act covering jurisdiction of juvenile courts, extending power to promote welfare of children and protecting families at risk.	
1964 Kilbrandon Report on Children and Young Persons in Scotland recommending flexible and discriminating measures for dealing with young offenders and recommending the reorganization of services for	

246

CHILD CARE	SOCIAL WORK SERVICES

children's problems into a new
local department concerned with
'social education' of children
(Cmnd 2306).
Labour Party pamphlet, *Crime:
A Challenge to us All*, correlating
delinquency with social
deprivation, parental neglect
and lack of social services.

1965 Government White Paper, *Child,
Family and Young Offender*,
proposing the abolition of
juvenile courts and the setting up
of family courts (Cmnd 2742).

Seebohm Committee set up to
inquire into the organization of
the local authority personal
social services and to consider
the changes necessary to secure
an effective family service.

1966 Government Joint Circular on
Homeless Families, calling for
co-ordination of the work for
these families undertaken by
housing and welfare and
children's departments in the
local authority.

Government White Paper,
Social Work and Community.
Proposals for reorganization of
local authority social services in
Scotland (Cmnd 3065).

1968 Government White Paper,
Children in Trouble, moving away
from the concept of delinquency
in childhood and suggesting new
methods within the community
for dealing with children in
trouble, centred upon family
help and social work skills in
assessing what is required
(Cmnd 3601).

Seebohm Report on
reorganization of social services
in the local authority
(Cmnd 3703).
Health Service Green Paper for
discussion on reorganization of
hospital, local authority health
and general practitioner
services.
Social Work (Scotland Act)
concerned with the
amalgamation and
reorganization of the personal
social services, including the
probation service, and
instituting children's panels in
place of juvenile courts.
Gulbenkian Report,
*Community Work and Social
Change*, an inquiry into the
nature and extent of
community work and proposals
for training in it.

CHILD CARE	SOCIAL WORK SERVICES
1969 Children and Young Persons Act concerned with the treatment of children in need of care, or delinquent, within their own regional community.	
1970	Chronically Sick and Disabled Persons Act, extending local authority provisions for the welfare, educational and residential services for deprived groups in the community.

1970
LOCAL AUTHORITY SOCIAL SERVICES ACT
concerned with the amalgamation and reorganization of the personal social services.

LEGISLATION REFERRED TO
IN THE TEXT

1887   Probation of First Offenders Act, 50 and 51 Vict., c. 25, *p. 107*n.

1889   Prevention of Cruelty to and Protection of Children Act, 52 and 53 Vict., c. 44, *pp. 63*n, *65*n, *101, 104.*

1889   Poor Law Amendment Act, 52 and 53 Vict., c. 56, *pp. 63, 65, 93, 116.*

1891   Custody of Children Act, 54 and 55 Vict., c. 3, *p. 65.*

1894   Prevention of Cruelty to Children (Amendment) Act, 57 and 58 Vict., c, 27, *pp. 103, 104.*

1894   Prevention of Cruelty to Children Act, 57 and 58 Vict., c. 41, *p. 103.*

1897   Infant Life Protection Act, 60 and 61, Vict., c. 57, *p. 99.*

1899   Poor Law Act, 62 and 63 Vict., c. 37, *pp. 65, 93.*

1901   Youthful Offenders Act, 64 Vict., c. 20, *p. 107*n.

1906   Education (Provision of Meals) Act, 6 Edw. VII, c. 57, *pp. 107, 111.*

1907   Probation of Offenders Act, 7 Edw. VII, c. 17, *pp. 107*n, *129*n.

1907   Notification of Births Act, 7 Edw. VII, c. 40, *p. 107.*

1907   Education (Administrative Provisions) Act, 7 Edw. VII, c. 43, *p. 107.*

1908   Children Act, 8 Edw. VII c. 67, *pp. 102*n, *108, 109, 118, 124, 125, 127, 129*n.

1911   National Insurance Act, 1 and 2 Geo. V, c. 55, *p. 112*n.

1918   Maternity and Child Welfare Act, 8 and 9 Geo. V, c. 29, *p. 116*n.

1926   Adoption Act, 16 and 17 Geo. V. c. 29, *p. 116.*

1926   Legitimacy Act, 16 and 17 Geo. V., c. 60, *p. 117.*

1929   Local Government Act, 19 Geo. V., c. 17, *pp. 100, 125.*

1930   Poor Law Act, 20 Geo. V., c. 17, *pp. 126, 146.*

1933   Children and Young Persons Act, 23 and 24 Geo. V., c. 12, *pp, 103*n, *126, 130, 141*n, *146, 147, 152*

1936   Public Health Act, 26 Geo. V. and 1 Edw., VIII, c. 49, *pp. 146. 150, 152.*

1937   Children and Young Persons (Scotland) Act, 1 Edw. VIII and 1 Geo. VI., c. 37, *p. 152*n.

1939   Adoption of Children (Regulation) Act, 2 and 3 Geo. VI., c. 27, *pp. 146, 151, 152.*

1944   Education Act, 7 and 8 Geo. VI., c. 31, *p. 148.*

1945   Family Allowances Act, 8 and 9 Geo. VI., c. 41, *pp. 149*n, *152.*

1946   National Insurance (Industrial Injuries) Act, 9 and 10 Geo. VI., c. 62, *p. 149*n.

1946   National Insurance Act, 9 and 10 Geo. VI., c. 67, *pp. 149*n, *152.*

1946   National Health Service Act, 9 and 10 Geo. VI, c. 81, *p. 149*n.

1948   National Assistance Act, 11 and 12 Geo. VI., c. 29, *p. 149*n.

BIBLIOGRAPHY

The following have specific reference to the study of children in care:—

MARY D. AINSWORTH and JOHN BOWLBY, 'Research Strategy in the Study of Mother-child Separation'. Extrait du *Courier*, 1954, iv, 3. Centre International de l'Enfance.

LADY ALLEN OF HURTWOOD, *Whose Children?*, The Favil Press, 1945.

HANNAH ARCHER, *A Scheme for Befriending Orphan Pauper Girls*, Longman and Co., 1861.

BARBARA BAGWELL, 'Some Auxiliary Schemes of Dr. Barnardo's Homes', *Child Care*, Vol. 10, No. 3 (July, 1956).

JOSEPHINE BALLS, *Where Love Is. The Fostering of Young Children*, Gollancz Ltd., 1958.

HELEN BEST, *The War Baby. A discussion of the special problems raised by illegitimacy during the Great War*, Stanley Paul and Co., 1915.

A. F. G. BOURDILLON, *Voluntary Social Services. Their Place in the Modern State*, Methuen and Co., 1945.

JOHN BOWLBY, *Maternal Care and Mental Health*, World Health Organization, 1951.

A. H. BOWLEY, *Psychology of the Unwanted Child*, Livingstone, 1947. *Child Care. A handbook on the care of the child deprived of a normal home life*, Livingstone, 1951.

K. BRILL and H. R. IRVING, *Cruelty to Children*, Association of Children's Officers, 1953.

KENNETH BRILL, *Room for More*, National Association for Mental Health, 1959. *Children Not Cases*, National Children's Home, 1962.

CLARE BRITTON, 'Casework Techniques in the Child Care Services', *Case Conference*, Vol. I, No. 9, January, 1955.

BULLETINS OF THE CHILDREN'S OFFICERS' ASSOCIATION.

DOROTHY BURLINGHAM AND ANNA FREUD, *Young Children in War Time. A Year's Work in a Residential Nursery*, George Allen and Unwin Ltd., 1944. *Infants without Families. The Case for and against Residential Nurseries*, George Allen and Unwin Ltd., 1944.

GERALDINE CADBURY, *Young Offenders Yesterday and Today*, George Allen and Unwin, 1938.

J. ESTLIN CARPENTER, *The Life and Work of Mary Carpenter*, Macmillan, 1879.

MARY CARPENTER, *Reformatory Schools for the Children of the perishing and dangerous classes, and for juvenile offenders*, London, 1851. *Juvenile Delinquents, their condition and treatment*, London, 1853.

The Claims of Ragged Schools to Pecuniary Educational Aid, Partridge and Co., 1859.

W. E. CAVANAGH, *The Child and the Court*, Gollancz, 1959.

W. CHANCE, *Children under the Poor Law*, Swan, Sonnenschein and Co. Ltd., 1897.

G. CHESTERS, *The Mothering of Young Children*, Faber and Faber, 1956.

COUNCIL FOR CHILDREN'S WELFARE and the FISHER GROUP, *Families with Problems. A New Approach*, Council for Children's Welfare, 1958.

D. V. DONNISON, *The Neglected Child and the Social Services*, Manchester University Press, 1954.

D. V. DONNISON and MARY STEWART, *The Child and the Social Services*, Fabian Society, 1958.

O. J. DUNLOP, *English Apprenticeship and Child Labour*, T. Fisher Unwin, 1912.

D. M. DYSON, *No Two Alike*, Allen and Unwin, 1962.

SIR FREDERICK MORTON EDEN, *The State of the Poor*, London, 1797.

MARY ELLISON, *The Adopted Child*, Gollancz, 1958.

SHEILA FERGUSON and HILDE FITZGERALD, *Studies in the Social Services. History of the Second World War United Kingdom Civil Series*. Edited by W. K. Hancock and published by H.M.S.O. and Longmans, Green & Co., 1954.

SIR JOHN FIELDING, *A plan of the Asylum or House of Refuge for Orphans and other Deserted Girls of the Poor of the Metropolis*, London, 1758.

LETTICE FISHER, *Twenty-one Years and After. The Story of the National Council for the Unmarried Mother and her Child*, Published by the Council. 1937.

DONALD FORD, *The Deprived Child and the Community*, Constable, 1955.

P. G. GRAY and E. A. PARR, *Children in Care and the Recruitment of Foster Parents. Social Survey, London*. H.M.S.O., 1957.

W. CLARKE HALL, *The Queen's Reign for Children*, T. Fisher Unwin, 1897.

CLARKE HALL and MORRISON, *On Children*, Butterworth and Co., 1956.

M. PENELOPE HALL, *The Social Services of Modern England*, Routledge and Kegan Paul Ltd., 1958.

KATHLEEN HEASMAN, *The Evangelicals in Action*, Bles, 1962.

BASIL HENRIQUES, *The Home-Menders: the prevention of unhappiness in children*, Harrap, 1955.

FLORENCE DAVENPORT HILL, *Children of the State*, Macmillan and Co., 1889.

HOME OFFICE, *The Needs of Young Children in Care*, H.M.S.O., 1964.

G. V. HOLMES, *The Likes of Us*, Frederick Muller Ltd., 1948.

MARY HOPKIRK, *Nobody Wanted Sam*, John Murray, 1949.

I. R. HOSKINS, *Catholic Child Care in England*, Catholic Truth Society, London, 1956.

L. G. HOUSDEN, *The Prevention of Cruelty to Children*, Jonathan Cape,

1955.
DOROTHY HUTCHINSON, *In Quest of Foster Parents*, Columbia University Press, 1943.
LENA JEGER, *Illegitimate Children and Their Parents*, National Council for the Unmarried Mother, 1951.
D. JEHU, *Casework—Before admission to care*, Association of Child Care Officers, 1964.
BETI JONES, 'A Matter of Co-operation', *Child Care*, Vol. 9, No. 2 (April, 1955).
JEAN KASTELL, *Casework in Child Care*, Routledge and Kegan Paul, 1962.
DRAZA KLINE and HELEN MARY OVERSTREET, *Casework with Foster Parents*, Child Welfare League of America, Inc., Oct., 1956.
MARGARET KORNITZER, *Child Adoption in the Modern World*, Putnam, 1952.
Adoption, Putnam, 1959.
Mr. Fairweather and His Family, Bodley Head, 1960.
E. M. LEONARD, *The Early History of English Poor Relief*, C.U.P., 1900.
HILDA LEWIS, *Deprived Children. The Mersham Experiment. A Social and Clinical Study*, O.U.P., 1954.
JOHN H. LITTEN, 'I sat where they sat', *Child Care*, Vol. 8, No. 4 (October, 1954).
NER LITTNER, *Some Traumaitic Effects of Separation and Placement*, Child Welfare League of America, Inc., October, 1950.
R. LESLIE MELVILLE, *Life and Work of Sir John Fielding*, L. Williams, 1934.
ISOBEL MORDY, *The Child wants a Home. Foster-Homes: How and Why?* George G. Harrap and Co. Ltd., 1956.
CHERRY MORRIS (Ed.), *Social Casework in Great Britain*, Faber and Faber, 1955.
MARY MORRIS, *Voluntary Organisation and Social Progress*, Gollancz, 1955.
A. C. L. MORRISON, M. M. WELLS, E. ETON, L. G. BANWELL (Ed.), *The Children's Act, 1948 and the Nurseries and Child Minders Regulations Act, 1948*, Butterworth and Co. Ltd., 1948.
R. H. NICHOLS and F. A. WRAY, *The History of the Foundling Hospital*, Oxford University Press, 1935.
A. F. PHILP and NOEL TIMMS, *The Problem of the Problem Family*, Family Service Units, 1957.
A. T. PIERSON, *George Müller, of Bristol*, James Nisbet and Co. Ltd., 1899.
IVY PINCHBECK, 'The State and the Child in Sixteenth Century England', *British Journal of Sociology*, Vol. VII, No. 4 (December, 1956) and Vol. VIII, No. 1 (March, 1957).
HERBERT RATHBONE (Ed.), *Memoir of Kitty Wilkinson of Liverpool*, Henry Young and Sons, Liverpool, 1927.

255

GORDON ROSE, 'Co-ordinating Committees', *Case Conference*, Vol. IV, Nos. 2, 3 and 4 (June, July, Sept., 1957).

JANE ROWE, *Yours by Choice. A guide for adoptive parents*, Mills and Boon, 1960.

MILDRED DE M. RUDOLF, *Everybody's Children. The Story of the Church of England Children's Society*, Oxford University Press, 1950.

LUCY SINCLAIR, *The Bridgeburn Days*, Gollancz, 1956.

EMMA SMITH, *A Cornish Waif's Story*, Odhams Press Ltd., 1954.

D. H. STOTT, *Delinquency and Human Nature*, Carnegie United Kingdom Trust, 1950.
Saving Children from Delinquency, University of London Press, 1952.
Unsettled Children and their Families, University of London Press, 1956.

NOEL TIMMS, *Casework in the Child Care Service*, Butterworth, 1962.

GORDON TRASLER, *In place of parents*, Routledge and Kegan Paul, 1960.

CECIL F. WALPOLE, *The Silver Stream*, Epworth Press, 1947.
Golden Links, Epworth Press, 1950.

BENJAMIN WAUGH, *The Gaol Cradle. Who Rocks It?* Strahan and Co., 1873.

REV. N. WAUGH (Ed.), *These my Little Ones. The Origin, Progress and Development of the Incorporated Society of the Crusade of Rescue and Homes for Destitute Catholic Children*, Sands and Co., 1911.

ROSA WAUGH, *Life of Benjamin Waugh*, T. Fisher Unwin, 1913.

SIDNEY and BEATRICE WEBB, *English Poor Law Policy*, Longmans, Green and Co., 1910.

MARGARET WEDDELL, *Child Care Pioneers*, Epworth Press, 1958.

E. M. WIDDOWSON, 'Mental Contentment and Physical Growth', *The Lancet*, No. XXIV of Vol. I, 1951 (16th June, 1951).

A. E. WILLIAMS, *Barnardo of Stepney*, Guild Books, 1953.

E. C. WINES, *The State of the Prisons and of Child Saving Institutions in the Civilised World*, Cambridge University Press, 1880.

WOMEN'S GROUP ON PUBLIC WELFARE, *Our Towns. A Close-up*, O.U.P., 1943.
Children without Homes, O.U.P., 1945.
The Neglected Child and his Family, O.U.P., 1948.

WORLD HEALTH ORGANIZATION, *Deprivation of Maternal Care. A Re-assessment of its effects*. Public Health Papers, No. 14, Geneva, 1962.

NORMAN WYMER, *Father of Nobody's Children*, Hutchinson Authors Ltd.

A. F. YOUNG and E. T. ASHTON, *British Social Work in the Nineteenth Century*, Routledge and Kegan Paul, 1956.

Additional Bibliography

Since the second edition there has been a big development in literature relevant to the child care service. The following books will be found useful:—

GILVRAY ADAMSON, *The Caretakers*, Bookstall Publications, 1973.

R. BALBERNIE, *Residential Work with Children*, Pergamon, 1966.

PHILIP BARKER, *Care can Prevent: Child Care or Child Psychiatry*, Convocation Lecture, National Children's Home, 1973.

GORDON E. BARRITT, *The Edgworth Story*, National Children's Home, 1972.

C. BEEDELL, *Residential Life with Children*, Routledge & Kegan Paul, 1970.

M. BERLINS AND G. WANSELL, *Caught in the Act*, Penguin, 1974.

JULIET BERRY, *Social Work with Children*, Routledge & Kegan Paul, 1972.

BRUNO BETTELHEIM, *Truants from Life*, Free Press, New York, 1967.

PETER BOSS, *Social Policy and the Young Delinquent*, Routledge & Kegan Paul, 1967.

PETER BOSS, *Exploration into Child Care*, Routledge & Kegan Paul, 1971.

URIE BRONFENBRENNER, *Two Worlds of Childhood: U.S.A. and U.S.S.R.*, Allen & Unwin, 1971.

JULIUS CARLEBACH, *Caring for Children in Trouble*, Routledge & Kegan Paul, 1966.

E. CRELLIN, M. L. KELLMER PRINGLE AND P. WEST, *Born Illegitimate*, Longman (in association with National Children's Bureau), 1971.

BLEDWYN DAVIES, ANDREW BARTON AND IAN MCMILLAN, *Variations in Children's Services among British Urban Authorities*, Occasional Papers in Social Administration, No. 45, 1972.

R. DAVIS ET AL., *From Birth to Seven: A Report of the National Child Development Group*, Longman (in association with National Children's Bureau), 1972.

R. DINNAGE AND M. L. KELLMER PRINGLE, *Foster Home Care: Facts and Fallacies*, Longman (in association with National Children's Bureau), 1966.

B. DOCKER DRYSDALE, *Therapy in Child Care*, Longman, 1968.

B. DOCKER DRYSDALE, *Consultation in Child Care*, Longman, 1973.

VICTOR GEORGE, *Foster Care: Theory and Practice*, Routledge & Kegan Paul, 1973.

VICTOR GEORGE AND PAUL WILDING, *Motherless Families*, Routledge & Kegan Paul, 1972.

L. GOODMAN, *Notes on Juvenile Court Law*, Barry Rose Publishers, 1973.

D. GWYNNE AND JOHN BROWN, *Children under Supervision*, Social Services Department, Manchester, 1973.

Bibliography

M. P. HALL AND I. V. HOWES, *The Church in Social Work*, Routledge & Kegan Paul, 1965.

R. E. HELFER AND C. H. KEMPE, *The Battered Child*, University of Chicago Press, 1968.

J. S. HEYWOOD AND B. K. ALLEN, *Financial Help in Social Work*, Manchester University Press, 1971.

EILEEN HOLGATE (Ed.), *Communicating with Children*, Longman, 1972.

ROBERT HOLMAN, *Unsupported Mothers and the Care of their Children*, Mothers in Action, 1972.

ROBERT HOLMAN, *Trading in Children*, Routledge & Kegan Paul, 1973.

SHIRLEY JENKINS AND ELAINE NORMAN, *Filial Deprivation and Foster Care*, Columbia University Press, 1972.

R. D. KING, N. V. RAYNES AND JACK TIZARD, *Patterns of Residential Care: Sociological Studies in Institutions for Handicapped Children*, Routledge & Kegan Paul, 1971.

A. E. LEEDING, *Leeding's Child Care Manual*, Butterworth, 1971.

F. G. LENNHOFF, *Exceptional Children*, Allen & Unwin, 1967.

F. G. LENNHOFF WITH JOHN LAMPEN, *From Play to Work*, Shotton Hall, 1973.

H. MAAS AND R. ENGLES, *Children in Need of Parents*, Columbia University Press, 1959.

ALEXINE MCWHINNIE, *Adopted Child*, Routledge & Kegan Paul, 1968.

BETTY R. MANDELL, *Where are the Children? A Class Analysis of Foster Care and Adoption*, Lexington Books, 1973.

NIGEL MIDDLETON, *When Family Failed*, Gollancz, 1972.

JEAN PACKMAN, *Child Care Needs and Numbers*, Allen & Unwin, 1968.

JEAN PACKMAN, *Child's Generation*, Blackwell, 1975.

R. A. PARKER, *Planning for Deprived Children*, National Children's Home, 1970.

I. PINCHBECK AND M. HEWITT, *Children in English Society*, vols I and II, Routledge & Kegan Paul, 1969, 1973.

RICHARD POOLEY, *The Evacuee*, Anglo-American Publicity Service, 1973.

MIA KELLMER PRINGLE, *The Needs of Children*, Hutchinson, 1974.

MIA KELLMER PRINGLE, *Early Child Care*, Hutchinson, 1975.

ELIZABETH PUGH, *Social Work in Child Care* (Library of Social Work), Routledge & Kegan Paul, 1968.

B. N. RODGERS AND J. STEVENSON, *New Portrait of Social Work*, Heinemann, 1973.

JANE ROWE, *Parents, Children and Adoption*, Routledge & Kegan Paul, 1968.

JANE ROWE, *Yours by Choice*, Routledge & Kegan Paul, 1969.

J. ROWE AND L. LAMBERT, *Children Who Wait*, Association of British Adoption Services, 1973.

MICHAEL RUTTER, *Maternal Deprivation Re-assessed*, Penguin, 1972.

J. SEGLOW, M. L. KELLMER PRINGLE AND PETER WEDGE, *Growing Up Adopted*, National Children's Bureau, 1972.

OLIVE STEVENSON, *Someone Else's Child*, Routledge & Kegan Paul, 1965.

JOHN STROUD (Ed.), *Services for Children and their Families*, Pergamon Press, 1973.

NOEL TIMMS (Ed.), *The Receiving End: Consumer Account of Social Help for Children*, Routledge & Kegan Paul, 1973.

J. P. TRISELIOTIS, *In Search of Origins: The Experiences of Adopted People*, Routledge & Kegan Paul, 1973.

NORMA TUTT, *Care or Custody?*, Darton, Longman & Todd, 1974.

PETER WEDGE AND HILARY PROSSER, *Born to Fail?*, Arrow Books, 1973.

J. WHITTAKER AND A. E. TRIESCHMAN (Eds.), *Children away from Home; A Source Book of Residential Treatment*, Aldine Atherton, Chicago, 1972.

BARBARA WOOTTON, *Social Science and Social Pathology*, Allen & Unwin, 1959.

MARGARET WYNN, *Family Policy*, Penguin, 1972.

PARLIAMENTARY PAPERS

1833	(450)	xx	Employment of Children in Factories. R. Com. 1st Rep., mins. of ev., etc.
	(519)	xxi	—— 2nd Rep.
1834	(167)	xix, xx	—— Supplementary Reps.
1841	—	—	Training and Education of pauper children. Poor Law Commissioners. E. Chadwick, J. P. Kay, E. C. Tufnell, etc. Rep.
1842	[380]	xv	Children's Employment (Mines). R. Com. 1st Rep., etc.
1842	[381]	xvi	—— Apps. Pt. I. Sub-Commissioners. Rep., mins. of ev.
1842	[382]	xvii	—— Apps. Pt. II. Sub-Commissioners. Rep., mins. of ev.
1842	(H.L.——) xxvi		Sanitary condition of the Labouring Population. Poor Law Commissioners. (E. Chadwick). Rep.
1844	[572]	xvii	State of Large Towns and Populous Districts. R. Com. 1st Rep., mins. of ev., etc.
1847	(447)	vii	Criminal Law (Juvenile Offenders and Transportation) Sel. Cttee. H.L. 1st Rep.
1847	(534)	vii	—— 2nd Rep., mins. of ev., etc.
1852	(515)	vii	Criminal and Destitute Juveniles. Sel. Cttee. Rep., mins. of ev., etc.
1852–3	(674)	xxiii	Criminal and Destitute Chn. Sel. Cttee. Rep., mins. of ev., etc.
1852–3	(674–I)	xxiii	—— Index.
1870	(176)	lviii	The Boarding Out of Pauper Children in Scotland ; and in certain Unions in England. Reps.
1871	(372)	vii	Protection of Infant Life. Sel. Ctee. Rep., mins. of ev., etc.
1875	(9)	lxiii	Emigration of Pauper Children to Canada. A. Doyle. Local Government Inspector. Rep.
1875	(10)	lxiii	Pauper Schools. Observations on the report of Mrs. Senior to the Local Government Board as to the Effect

1875	(10)	lxiii—cont.	on Girls of the System of Education at Pauper Schools by E. Tufnell, late Inspector of Poor Law Schools in the Metropolitan District.
1875	(155)	lxiii	—— Letter by Mrs. Senior, reply to E. Tufnell.
1876	C.1585	xxxi	Education of pauper children. Reps. (5th Annual Rep. Local Government Bd.).
1878	(285)	lx	The Home and Cottage System of training and educating the Children of the Poor. F. J. Mouat, Local Government Bd. Inspector, Capt. J. D. Bowley, Rep. Education of Pauper Children. H. G. Bowyer, J. R. Mosley, Inspectors of Workhouse Schools. Reps.
1896	C.8027	xliii	Education and Maintenance of Pauper Children in the Metropolis. Dept. Cttee. Vol. I. Rep. (Mundella Report).
1897	C.8597	lxxvi Pt. II	Ophthalmic State of Poor Law Children in the Metropolis. S. Stephenson. Rep.
1903	Cd.1507	xxx	Physical Training (Scotland). Rep.
1904	Cd.2175	xxxii	Physical Deterioration. R. Comm. Rep.
1908	Cd.3899	xcii	Children under the Poor Law. T. J. Macnamara. Rep.
1909	Cd.4499	xxxvii	Poor Laws and Relief of Distress. R. Comm. Reps.
1918	Cd.8917	xviii	Transfer of functions of Poor Law Authorities in England and Wales. Rep. (Maclean Report).
1921	Cmd.1254	ix	Child Adoption. Cttee. Rep.
1924–5	Cmd.2401	ix	—— Second Report.
1926	Cmd.2711	viii	—— Third and Final Report.
1924–5	Cmd.2561	xv	Sexual offences against Young Persons. Departmental Cttee. Rep.
1926	Cmd.2592	xv	Sexual Offences against Children and Young Persons in Scotland. Departmental Cttee. Rep.
1927	Cmd.2831	xii	Treatment of Young Offenders. Departmental Cttee. Rep.
1936–7	Cmd.5499	ix	Adoption Societies and Agencies. Departmental Cttee. Rep.
1945–6	Cmd.6636	iv	The boarding out of Dennis and Terence O'Neill. Sir Walter Monckton. Rep.
1945–6	Cmd.6760	xx	Training in Child Care. Interdepartmental Cttee. Interim Report.
1945–6	Cmd.6911	x	Homeless Children. Interdepartmental Cttee. Rep. (Clyde Report).

1945–6	Cmd.6922	x	Care of Children. Interdepartment Cttee. Rep. (Curtis Report).
1951–2	(235)	v	Sixth Report with evidence taken before Sub-Committee D and appendices. Child Care.
1953–4	Cmd.9248	viii	Adoption of Children. Departmental Cttee. Rep. (Hurst Report).
1956–7	Cmd.9832		Child Migration to Australia. Fact-Finding Mission. Rep.
1960	Cmnd.1191		Report of the Committee on Children and Young Persons (Ingleby Report).
1964	Cmnd.2306		Children and Young Persons Scotland.
1965	Cmnd.2742		The Child, the Family and the Young Offender.
1966	Cmnd.3065		Social Work and the Community. Proposal for reorganizing local authority services in Scotland.
1968	Cmnd.3601		Children in Trouble.
1972	Cmnd.5107		Report of the Departmental Committee on the Adoption of Children.

A Guide to Adoption Practice, Advisory Council on Child Care, No. 2, H.M.S.O.

Intermediate Treatment Project, D.H.S.S. Development Group Report, H.M.S.O., 1973.

Children in Britain, Central Office of Information, Pamphlet No. 34, 1973.

Report of the Committee of Inquiry into the Care and Supervision provided in relation to Maria Colwell, D.H.S.S., H.M.S.O., 1974.

Statutes of England and Parliamentary Debates.
Annual Reports of the Poor Law Commissioners.
Annual Reports of the Local Government Board.
Annual Reports of the Ministry of Health.
Annual Reports of the Inspectors of Reformatory and Industrial Schools.
Reports of the Children's Branch of the Home Office.
Home Office Annual Statements of particulars of Children in Care in England and Wales.

INDEX

Routledge Social Science Series

Routledge & Kegan Paul   London, Henley and Boston

39 Store Street, London WC1E 7DD
Broadway House, Newtown Road, Henley-on-Thames,
Oxon RG9 1EN
9 Park Street, Boston, Mass. 02108

Contents

*Authors wishing to submit manuscripts for any series in
this catalogue should send them to the Social Science Editor,
Routledge & Kegan Paul Ltd, 39 Store Street,
London WC1E 7DD*

● *Books so marked are available in paperback*
All books are in Metric Demy 8vo format (216 × 138mm approx.)

International Library of Sociology

General Editor John Rex

GENERAL SOCIOLOGY

Barnsley, J. H. The Social Reality of Ethics. *464 pp.*
Belshaw, Cyril. The Conditions of Social Performance. *An Exploratory Theory. 144 pp.*
Brown, Robert. Explanation in Social Science. *208 pp.*
● Rules and Laws in Sociology. *192 pp.*
Bruford, W. H. Chekhov and His Russia. *A Sociological Study. 244 pp.*
Cain, Maureen E. Society and the Policeman's Role. *326 pp.*
●**Fletcher, Colin.** Beneath the Surface. *An Account of Three Styles of Sociological Research. 221 pp.*
Gibson, Quentin. The Logic of Social Enquiry. *240 pp.*
Glucksmann, M. Structuralist Analysis in Contemporary Social Thought. *212 pp.*
Gurvitch, Georges. Sociology of Law. *Preface by Roscoe Pound. 264 pp.*
Hodge, H. A. Wilhelm Dilthey. *An Introduction. 184 pp.*
Homans, George C. Sentiments and Activities. *336 pp.*
Johnson, Harry M. Sociology: *a Systematic Introduction. Foreword by Robert K. Merton. 710 pp.*
●**Keat, Russell,** and **Urry, John.** Social Theory as Science. *278 pp.*
Mannheim, Karl. Essays on Sociology and Social Psychology. *Edited by Paul Keckskemeti. With Editorial Note by Adolph Lowe. 344 pp.*
Systematic Sociology: *An Introduction to the Study of Society. Edited by J. S. Erös and Professor W. A. C. Stewart. 220 pp.*
Martindale, Don. The Nature and Types of Sociological Theory. *292 pp.*
●**Maus, Heinz.** A Short History of Sociology. *234 pp.*
Mey, Harald. Field-Theory. *A Study of its Application in the Social Sciences. 352 pp.*
Myrdal, Gunnar. Value in Social Theory: *A Collection of Essays on Methodology. Edited by Paul Streeten. 332 pp.*
Ogburn, William F., and **Nimkoff, Meyer F.** A Handbook of Sociology. *Preface by Karl Mannheim. 656 pp. 46 figures. 35 tables.*
Parsons, Talcott, and **Smelser, Neil J.** Economy and Society: *A Study in the Integration of Economic and Social Theory. 362 pp.*
Podgórecki, Adam. Practical Social Sciences. *About 200 pp.*
●**Rex, John.** Key Problems of Sociological Theory. *220 pp.*
Sociology and the Demystification of the Modern World. *282 pp.*
●**Rex, John** (Ed.) Approaches to Sociology. *Contributions by Peter Abell, Frank Bechhofer, Basil Bernstein, Ronald Fletcher, David Frisby, Miriam Glucksmann, Peter Lassman, Herminio Martins, John Rex, Roland Robertson, John Westergaard and Jock Young. 302 pp.*
Rigby, A. Alternative Realities. *352 pp.*
Roche, M. Phenomenology, Language and the Social Sciences. *374 pp.*

Sahay, A. Sociological Analysis. *220 pp.*
Simirenko, Alex (Ed.) Soviet Sociology. *Historical Antecedents and Current Appraisals. Introduction by Alex Simirenko. 376 pp.*
Strasser, Hermann. The Normative Structure of Sociology. *Conservative and Emancipatory Themes in Social Thought. About 340 pp.*
Urry, John. Reference Groups and the Theory of Revolution. *244 pp.*
Weinberg, E. Development of Sociology in the Soviet Union. *173 pp.*

FOREIGN CLASSICS OF SOCIOLOGY

● **Durkheim, Emile.** Suicide. *A Study in Sociology. Edited and with an Introduction by George Simpson. 404 pp.*
● **Gerth, H. H.,** and **Mills, C. Wright.** From Max Weber: *Essays in Sociology. 502 pp.*
● **Tönnies, Ferdinand.** Community and Association. (*Gemeinschaft und Gesellschaft.) Translated and Supplemented by Charles P. Loomis. Foreword by Pitirim A. Sorokin. 334 pp.*

SOCIAL STRUCTURE

Andreski, Stanislav. Military Organization and Society. *Foreword by Professor A. R. Radcliffe-Brown. 226 pp. 1 folder.*
Carlton, Eric. Ideology and Social Order. *Preface by Professor Philip Abrahams. About 320 pp.*
Coontz, Sydney H. Population Theories and the Economic Interpretation. *202 pp.*
Coser, Lewis. The Functions of Social Conflict. *204 pp.*
Dickie-Clark, H. F. Marginal Situation: *A Sociological Study of a Coloured Group. 240 pp. 11 tables.*
Glaser, Barney, and Strauss, Anselm L. Status Passage. *A Formal Theory. 208 pp.*
Glass, D. V. (Ed.) Social Mobility in Britain. *Contributions by J. Berent, T. Bottomore, R. C. Chambers, J. Floud, D. V. Glass, J. R. Hall, H. T. Himmelweit, R. K. Kelsall, F. M. Martin, C. A. Moser, R. Mukherjee, and W. Ziegel. 420 pp.*
Johnstone, Frederick A. Class, Race and Gold. *A Study of Class Relations and Racial Discrimination in South Africa. 312 pp.*
Jones, Garth N. Planned Organizational Change: *An Exploratory Study Using an Empirical Approach. 268 pp.*
Kelsall, R. K. Higher Civil Servants in Britain: *From 1870 to the Present Day. 268 pp. 31 tables.*
König, René. The Community. *232 pp. Illustrated.*
● **Lawton, Denis.** Social Class, Language and Education. *192 pp.*
McLeish, John. The Theory of Social Change: *Four Views Considered. 128 pp.*
Marsh, David C. The Changing Social Structure of England and Wales, *1871-1961. 288 pp.*
Menzies, Ken. Talcott Parsons and the Social Image of Man. *About 208 pp.*

Mouzelis, Nicos. Organization and Bureaucracy. *An Analysis of Modern Theories. 240 pp.*

Mulkay, M. J. Functionalism, Exchange and Theoretical Strategy. *272 pp.*

Ossowski, Stanislaw. Class Structure in the Social Consciousness. *210 pp.*

Podgórecki, Adam. Law and Society. *302 pp.*

Renner, Karl. Institutions of Private Law and Their Social Functions. *Edited, with an Introduction and Notes, by O. Kahn-Freud. Translated by Agnes Schwarzschild. 316 pp.*

SOCIOLOGY AND POLITICS

Acton, T. A. Gypsy Politics and Social Change. *316 pp.*

Clegg, Stuart. Power, Rule and Domination. *A Critical and Empirical Understanding of Power in Sociological Theory and Organisational Life. About 300 pp.*

Hechter, Michael. Internal Colonialism. *The Celtic Fringe in British National Development, 1536–1966. 361 pp.*

Hertz, Frederick. Nationality in History and Politics: *A Psychology and Sociology of National Sentiment and Nationalism. 432 pp.*

Kornhauser, William. The Politics of Mass Society. *272 pp. 20 tables.*

Kroes, R. Soldiers and Students. *A Study of Right- and Left-wing Students. 174 pp.*

Laidler, Harry W. History of Socialism. *Social-Economic Movements: An Historical and Comparative Survey of Socialism, Communism, Co-operation, Utopianism; and other Systems of Reform and Reconstruction. 992 pp.*

Lasswell, H. D. Analysis of Political Behaviour. *324 pp.*

Martin, David A. Pacifism: *an Historical and Sociological Study. 262 pp.*

Martin, Roderick. Sociology of Power. *About 272 pp.*

Myrdal, Gunnar. The Political Element in the Development of Economic Theory. *Translated from the German by Paul Streeten. 282 pp.*

Wilson, H. T. The American Ideology. *Science, Technology and Organization of Modes of Rationality. About 280 pp.*

Wootton, Graham. Workers, Unions and the State. *188 pp.*

CRIMINOLOGY

Ancel, Marc. Social Defence: *A Modern Approach to Criminal Problems. Foreword by Leon Radzinowicz. 240 pp.*

Cain, Maureen E. Society and the Policeman's Role. *326 pp.*

Cloward, Richard A., and **Ohlin, Lloyd E.** Delinquency and Opportunity: *A Theory of Delinquent Gangs. 248 pp.*

Downes, David M. The Delinquent Solution. *A Study in Subcultural Theory. 296 pp.*

Dunlop, A. B., and **McCabe, S.** Young Men in Detention Centres. *192 pp.*

Friedlander, Kate. The Psycho-Analytical Approach to Juvenile Delinquency: *Theory, Case Studies, Treatment. 320 pp.*

Glueck, Sheldon, and **Eleanor.** Family Environment and Delinquency. *With the statistical assistance of Rose W. Kneznek. 340 pp.*

5

Lopez-Rey, Manuel. Crime. *An Analytical Appraisal. 288 pp.*
Mannheim, Hermann. Comparative Criminology: *a Text Book. Two volumes. 442 pp. and 380 pp.*
Morris, Terence. The Criminal Area: *A Study in Social Ecology. Foreword by Hermann Mannheim. 232 pp. 25 tables. 4 maps.*
Rock, Paul. Making People Pay. *338 pp.*
●**Taylor, Ian, Walton, Paul,** and **Young, Jock.** The New Criminology. *For a Social Theory of Deviance. 325 pp.*
●**Taylor, Ian, Walton, Paul,** and **Young, Jock** (Eds). Critical Criminology. *268 pp.*

SOCIAL PSYCHOLOGY

Bagley, Christopher. The Social Psychology of the Epileptic Child. *320 pp.*
Barbu, Zevedei. Problems of Historical Psychology. *248 pp.*
Blackburn, Julian. Psychology and the Social Pattern. *184 pp.*
●**Brittan, Arthur.** Meanings and Situations. *224 pp.*
Carroll, J. Break-Out from the Crystal Palace. *200 pp.*
●**Fleming, C. M.** Adolescence: Its Social Psychology. *With an Introduction to recent findings from the fields of Anthropology, Physiology, Medicine, Psychometrics and Sociometry. 288 pp.*
● The Social Psychology of Education: *An Introduction and Guide to Its Study. 136 pp.*
●**Homans, George C.** The Human Group. *Foreword by Bernard DeVoto. Introduction by Robert K. Merton. 526 pp.*
● Social Behaviour: *its Elementary Forms. 416 pp.*
●**Klein, Josephine.** The Study of Groups. *226 pp. 31 figures. 5 tables.*
Linton, Ralph. The Cultural Background of Personality. *132 pp.*
●**Mayo, Elton.** The Social Problems of an Industrial Civilization. *With an appendix on the Political Problem. 180 pp.*
Ottaway, A. K. C. Learning Through Group Experience. *176 pp.*
Plummer, Ken. Sexual Stigma. *An Interactionist Account. 254 pp.*
●**Rose, Arnold M.** (Ed.) Human Behaviour and Social Processes: *an Interactionist Approach. Contributions by Arnold M. Rose, Ralph H. Turner, Anselm Strauss, Everett C. Hughes, E. Franklin Frazier, Howard S. Becker, et al. 696 pp.*
Smelser, Neil J. Theory of Collective Behaviour. *448 pp.*
Stephenson, Geoffrey M. The Development of Conscience. *128 pp.*
Young, Kimball. Handbook of Social Psychology. *658 pp. 16 figures. 10 tables.*

SOCIOLOGY OF THE FAMILY

Banks, J. A. Prosperity and Parenthood: *A Study of Family Planning among The Victorian Middle Classes. 262 pp.*
Bell, Colin R. Middle Class Families: *Social and Geographical Mobility. 224 pp.*

Burton, Lindy. Vulnerable Children. *272 pp.*

Gavron, Hannah. The Captive Wife: *Conflicts of Household Mothers.*
190 pp.

George, Victor, and **Wilding, Paul.** Motherless Families. *248 pp.*

Klein, Josephine. Samples from English Cultures.
1. Three Preliminary Studies and Aspects of Adult Life in England.
447 pp.
2. Child-Rearing Practices and Index. *247 pp.*

Klein, Viola. The Feminine Character. *History of an Ideology. 244 pp.*

McWhinnie, Alexina M. Adopted Children. *How They Grow Up. 304 pp.*

Morgan, D. H. J. Social Theory and the Family. *About 320 pp.*

Myrdal, Alva, and **Klein, Viola.** Women's Two Roles: *Home and Work.*
238 pp. 27 tables.

Parsons, Talcott, and **Bales, Robert F.** Family: Socialization and Interaction Process. *In collaboration with James Olds, Morris Zelditch and
Philip E. Slater. 456 pp. 50 figures and tables.*

SOCIAL SERVICES

Bastide, Roger. The Sociology of Mental Disorder. *Translated from the
French by Jean McNeil. 260 pp.*

Carlebach, Julius. Caring For Children in Trouble. *266 pp.*

George, Victor. Foster Care. *Theory and Practice. 234 pp.*
Social Security: *Beveridge and After. 258 pp.*

George, V., and **Wilding, P.** Motherless Families. *248 pp.*

● **Goetschius, George W.** Working with Community Groups. *256 pp.*

Goetschius, George W., and **Tash, Joan.** Working with Unattached Youth.
416 pp.

Hall, M. P., and **Howes, I. V.** The Church in Social Work. *A Study of
Moral Welfare Work undertaken by the Church of England. 320 pp.*

Heywood, Jean S. Children in Care: *the Development of the Service for the
Deprived Child. 264 pp.*

Hoenig, J., and **Hamilton, Marian W.** The De-Segregation of the Mentally
Ill. *284 pp.*

Jones, Kathleen. Mental Health and Social Policy, 1845-1959. *264 pp.*

King, Roy D., Raynes, Norma V., and **Tizard, Jack.** Patterns of Residential
Care. *356 pp.*

Leigh, John. Young People and Leisure. *256 pp.*

● **Mays, John.** (Ed.) Penelope Hall's Social Services of England and Wales.
About 324 pp.

Morris, Mary. Voluntary Work and the Welfare State. *300 pp.*

Nokes, P. L. The Professional Task in Welfare Practice. *152 pp.*

Timms, Noel. Psychiatric Social Work in Great Britain (1939-1962).
280 pp.

● Social Casework: *Principles and Practice. 256 pp.*

Young, A. F. Social Services in British Industry. *272 pp.*

SOCIOLOGY OF EDUCATION

Banks, Olive. Parity and Prestige in English Secondary Education: a Study in Educational Sociology. *272 pp.*

Bentwich, Joseph. Education in Israel. *224 pp. 8 pp. plates.*

●**Blyth, W. A. L.** English Primary Education. *A Sociological Description.*
    1. Schools. *232 pp.*
    2. Background. *168 pp.*

Collier, K. G. The Social Purposes of Education: *Personal and Social Values in Education. 268 pp.*

Dale, R. R., and **Griffith, S.** Down Stream: *Failure in the Grammar School. 108 pp.*

Evans, K. M. Sociometry and Education. *158 pp.*

●**Ford, Julienne.** Social Class and the Comprehensive School. *192 pp.*

Foster, P. J. Education and Social Change in Ghana. *336 pp. 3 maps.*

Fraser, W. R. Education and Society in Modern France. *150 pp.*

Grace, Gerald R. Role Conflict and the Teacher. *150 pp.*

Hans, Nicholas. New Trends in Education in the Eighteenth Century. *278 pp. 19 tables.*

●   Comparative Education: *A Study of Educational Factors and Traditions. 360 pp.*

●**Hargreaves, David.** Interpersonal Relations and Education. *432 pp.*

●   Social Relations in a Secondary School. *240 pp.*

Holmes, Brian. Problems in Education. *A Comparative Approach. 336 pp.*

King, Ronald. Values and Involvement in a Grammar School. *164 pp.*
    School Organization and Pupil Involvement. *A Study of Secondary Schools.*

●**Mannheim, Karl,** and **Stewart, W. A. C.** An Introduction to the Sociology of Education. *206 pp.*

Morris, Raymond N. The Sixth Form and College Entrance. *231 pp.*

●**Musgrove, F.** Youth and the Social Order. *176 pp.*

●**Ottaway, A. K. C.** Education and Society: An Introduction to the Sociology of Education. *With an Introduction by W. O. Lester Smith. 212 pp.*

Peers, Robert. Adult Education: *A Comparative Study. 398 pp.*

Pritchard, D. G. Education and the Handicapped: *1760 to 1960. 258 pp.*

Stratta, Erica. The Education of Borstal Boys. *A Study of their Educational Experiences prior to, and during, Borstal Training. 256 pp.*

Taylor, P. H., Reid, W. A., and **Holley, B. J.** The English Sixth Form. *A Case Study in Curriculum Research. 200 pp.*

SOCIOLOGY OF CULTURE

Eppel, E. M., and **M.** Adolescents and Morality: *A Study of some Moral Values and Dilemmas of Working Adolescents in the Context of a changing Climate of Opinion. Foreword by W. J. H. Sprott. 268 pp. 39 tables.*

●**Fromm, Erich.** The Fear of Freedom. *286 pp.*

●   The Sane Society. *400 pp.*

Mannheim, Karl. Essays on the Sociology of Culture. *Edited by Ernst Mannheim in co-operation with Paul Kecskemeti. Editorial Note by Adolph Lowe. 280 pp.*

Weber, Alfred. Farewell to European History: *or The Conquest of Nihilism. Translated from the German by R. F. C. Hull. 224 pp.*

SOCIOLOGY OF RELIGION

Argyle, Michael and **Beit-Hallahmi, Benjamin.** The Social Psychology of Religion. *About 256 pp.*

Glasner, Peter E. The Sociology of Secularisation. *A Critique of a Concept. About 180 pp.*

Nelson, G. K. Spiritualism and Society. *313 pp.*

Stark, Werner. The Sociology of Religion. *A Study of Christendom.*
  Volume I. *Established Religion. 248 pp.*
  Volume II. *Sectarian Religion. 368 pp.*
  Volume III. *The Universal Church. 464 pp.*
  Volume IV. *Types of Religious Man. 352 pp.*
  Volume V. *Types of Religious Culture. 464 pp.*

Turner, B. S. Weber and Islam. *216 pp.*

Watt, W. Montgomery. Islam and the Integration of Society. *320 pp.*

SOCIOLOGY OF ART AND LITERATURE

Jarvie, Ian C. Towards a Sociology of the Cinema. *A Comparative Essay on the Structure and Functioning of a Major Entertainment Industry. 405 pp.*

Rust, Frances S. Dance in Society. *An Analysis of the Relationships between the Social Dance and Society in England from the Middle Ages to the Present Day. 256 pp. 8 pp. of plates.*

Schücking, L. L. The Sociology of Literary Taste. *112 pp.*

Wolff, Janet. Hermeneutic Philosophy and the Sociology of Art. *150 pp.*

SOCIOLOGY OF KNOWLEDGE

Diesing, P. Patterns of Discovery in the Social Sciences. *262 pp.*

●**Douglas, J. D.** (Ed.) Understanding Everyday Life. *370 pp.*

●**Hamilton, P.** Knowledge and Social Structure. *174 pp.*

Jarvie, I. C. Concepts and Society. *232 pp.*

Mannheim, Karl. Essays on the Sociology of Knowledge. *Edited by Paul Kecskemeti. Editorial Note by Adolph Lowe. 353 pp.*

Remmling, Gunter W. The Sociology of Karl Mannheim. *With a Bibliographical Guide to the Sociology of Knowledge, Ideological Analysis, and Social Planning. 255 pp.*

Remmling, Gunter W. (Ed.) Towards the Sociology of Knowledge. *Origin and Development of a Sociological Thought Style. 463 pp.*

Stark, Werner. The Sociology of Knowledge: *An Essay in Aid of a Deeper Understanding of the History of Ideas. 384 pp.*

URBAN SOCIOLOGY

Ashworth, William. The Genesis of Modern British Town Planning: *A Study in Economic and Social History of the Nineteenth and Twentieth Centuries. 288 pp.*

Cullingworth, J. B. Housing Needs and Planning Policy: *A Restatement of the Problems of Housing Need and 'Overspill' in England and Wales. 232 pp. 44 tables. 8 maps.*

Dickinson, Robert E. City and Region: *A Geographical Interpretation 608 pp. 125 figures.*

The West European City: *A Geographical Interpretation. 600 pp. 129 maps. 29 plates.*

● The City Region in Western Europe. *320 pp. Maps.*

Humphreys, Alexander J. New Dubliners: *Urbanization and the Irish Family. Foreword by George C. Homans. 304 pp.*

Jackson, Brian. Working Class Community: *Some General Notions raised by a Series of Studies in Northern England. 192 pp.*

Jennings, Hilda. Societies in the Making: *a Study of Development and Redevelopment within a County Borough. Foreword by D. A. Clark. 286 pp.*

●**Mann, P. H.** An Approach to Urban Sociology. *240 pp.*

Morris, R. N., and **Mogey, J.** The Sociology of Housing. *Studies at Berinsfield. 232 pp. 4 pp. plates.*

Rosser, C., and **Harris, C.** The Family and Social Change. *A Study of Family and Kinship in a South Wales Town. 352 pp. 8 maps.*

●**Stacey, Margaret, Batsone, Eric, Bell, Colin,** and **Thurcott, Anne.** Power, Persistence and Change. *A Second Study of Banbury. 196 pp.*

RURAL SOCIOLOGY

Haswell, M. R. The Economics of Development in Village India. *120 pp.*

Littlejohn, James. Westrigg: *the Sociology of a Cheviot Parish. 172 pp. 5 figures.*

Mayer, Adrian C. Peasants in the Pacific. *A Study of Fiji Indian Rural Society. 248 pp. 20 plates.*

Williams, W. M. The Sociology of an English Village: *Gosforth. 272 pp. 12 figures. 13 tables.*

SOCIOLOGY OF INDUSTRY AND DISTRIBUTION

Anderson, Nels. Work and Leisure. *280 pp.*

● Blau, Peter M., and Scott, W. Richard. Formal Organizations: *a Comparative approach. Introduction and Additional Bibliography by J. H. Smith.* 326 pp.

Dunkerley, David. The Foreman. *Aspects of Task and Structure. 192 pp.*

Eldridge, J. E. T. Industrial Disputes. *Essays in the Sociology of Industrial Relations. 288 pp.*

Hetzler, Stanley. Applied Measures for Promoting Technological Growth. *352 pp.*

Technological Growth and Social Change. *Achieving Modernization.* 269 pp.

Hollowell, Peter G. The Lorry Driver. *272 pp.*

● Oxaal, I., Barnett, T., and Booth, D. (Eds). Beyond the Sociology of Development. *Economy and Society in Latin America and Africa.* 295 pp.

Smelser, Neil J. Social Change in the Industrial Revolution: *An Application of Theory to the Lancashire Cotton Industry, 1770–1840. 468 pp. 12 figures. 14 tables.*

ANTHROPOLOGY

Ammar, Hamed. Growing up in an Egyptian Village: *Silwa, Province of Aswan. 336 pp.*

Brandel-Syrier, Mia. Reeftown Elite. *A Study of Social Mobility in a Modern African Community on the Reef. 376 pp.*

Dickie-Clark, H. F. The Marginal Situation. *A Sociological Study of a Coloured Group. 236 pp.*

Dube, S. C. Indian Village. *Foreword by Morris Edward Opler. 276 pp.* 4 plates.

India's Changing Villages: *Human Factors in Community Development.* 260 pp. 8 plates. 1 map.

Firth, Raymond. Malay Fishermen. *Their Peasant Economy. 420 pp. 17 pp. plates.*

Gulliver, P. H. Social Control in an African Society: a Study of the Arusha, Agricultural Masai of Northern Tanganyika. *320 pp. 8 plates. 10 figures.*

Family Herds. *288 pp.*

Ishwaran, K. Tradition and Economy in Village India: *An Interactionist Approach.*

Foreword by Conrad Arensburg. 176 pp.

Jarvie, Ian C. The Revolution in Anthropology. *268 pp.*

Little, Kenneth L. Mende of Sierra Leone. *308 pp. and folder.*

Negroes in Britain. *With a New Introduction and Contemporary Study by Leonard Bloom. 320 pp.*

Lowie, Robert H. Social Organization. *494 pp.*

Mayer, A. C. Peasants in the Pacific. *A Study of Fiji Indian Rural Society.* 248 pp.

Meer, Fatima. Race and Suicide in South Africa. *325 pp.*

Smith, Raymond T. The Negro Family in British Guiana: *Family Structure and Social Status in the Villages. With a Foreword by Meyer Fortes. 314 pp. 8 plates. 1 figure. 4 maps.*

Smooha, Sammy. Israel: Pluralism and Conflict. *About 320 pp.*

SOCIOLOGY AND PHILOSOPHY

Barnsley, John H. The Social Reality of Ethics. *A Comparative Analysis of Moral Codes. 448 pp.*

Diesing, Paul. Patterns of Discovery in the Social Sciences. *362 pp.*

●**Douglas, Jack D.** (Ed.) Understanding Everyday Life. *Toward the Reconstruction of Sociological Knowledge. Contributions by Alan F. Blum. Aaron W. Cicourel, Norman K. Denzin, Jack D. Douglas, John Heeren, Peter McHugh, Peter K. Manning, Melvin Power, Matthew Speier, Roy Turner, D. Lawrence Wieder, Thomas P. Wilson and Don H. Zimmerman. 370 pp.*

Gorman, Robert A. The Dual Vision. *Alfred Schutz and the Myth of Phenomenological Social Science. About 300 pp.*

Jarvie, Ian C. Concepts and Society. *216 pp.*

●**Pelz, Werner.** The Scope of Understanding in Sociology. *Towards a more radical reorientation in the social humanistic sciences. 283 pp.*

Roche, Maurice. Phenomenology, Language and the Social Sciences. *371 pp.*

Sahay, Arun. Sociological Analysis. *212 pp.*

Sklair, Leslie. The Sociology of Progress. *320 pp.*

Slater, P. Origin and Significance of the Frankfurt School. *A Marxist Perspective. About 192 pp.*

Smart, Barry. Sociology, Phenomenology and Marxian Analysis. *A Critical Discussion of the Theory and Practice of a Science of Society. 220 pp.*

International Library of Anthropology

General Editor Adam Kuper

Ahmed, A. S. Millenium and Charisma Among Pathans. *A Critical Essay in Social Anthropology. 192 pp.*

Brown, Paula. The Chimbu. *A Study of Change in the New Guinea Highlands. 151 pp.*

Gudeman, Stephen. Relationships, Residence and the Individual. *A Rural Panamanian Community. 288 pp. 11 Plates, 5 Figures, 2 Maps, 10 Tables.*

Hamnett, Ian. Chieftainship and Legitimacy. *An Anthropological Study of Executive Law in Lesotho. 163 pp.*

Hanson, F. Allan. Meaning in Culture. *127 pp.*

Lloyd, P. C. Power and Independence. *Urban Africans' Perception of Social Inequality. 264 pp.*

Pettigrew, Joyce. Robber Noblemen. *A Study of the Political System of the Sikh Jats. 284 pp.*

Street, Brian V. The Savage in Literature. *Representations of 'Primitive' Society in English Fiction, 1858–1920. 207 pp.*

Van Den Berghe, Pierre L. Power and Privilege at an African University. *278 pp.*

International Library of Social Policy

General Editor Kathleen Jones

Bayley, M. Mental Handicap and Community Care. *426 pp.*

Bottoms, A. E., and **McClean, J. D.** Defendants in the Criminal Process. *284 pp.*

Butler, J. R. Family Doctors and Public Policy. *208 pp.*

Davies, Martin. Prisoners of Society. *Attitudes and Aftercare. 204 pp.*

Gittus, Elizabeth. Flats, Families and the Under-Fives. *285 pp.*

Holman, Robert. Trading in Children. *A Study of Private Fostering. 355 pp.*

Jones, Howard, and **Cornes, Paul.** Open Prisons. *About 248 pp.*

Jones, Kathleen. History of the Mental Health Service. *428 pp.*

Jones, Kathleen, with **Brown, John, Cunningham, W. J., Roberts, Julian,** and **Williams, Peter.** Opening the Door. *A Study of New Policies for the Mentally Handicapped. 278 pp.*

Karn, Valerie. Retiring to the Seaside. *About 280 pp. 2 maps. Numerous tables.*

Thomas, J. E. The English Prison Officer since 1850: *A Study in Conflict. 258 pp.*

Walton, R. G. Women in Social Work. *303 pp.*

Woodward, J. To Do the Sick No Harm. *A Study of the British Voluntary Hospital System to 1875. 221 pp.*

International Library of Welfare and Philosophy

General Editors Noel Timms and David Watson

● **Plant, Raymond.** Community and Ideology. *104 pp.*

● **McDermott, F. E.** (Ed.) Self-Determination in Social Work. *A Collection of Essays on Self-determination and Related Concepts by Philosophers and Social Work Theorists. Contributors: F. P. Biestek, S. Bernstein, A. Keith-Lucas, D. Sayer, H. H. Perelman, C. Whittington, R. F. Stalley, F. E. McDermott, I. Berlin, H. J. McCloskey, H. L. A. Hart, J. Wilson, A. I. Melden, S. I. Benn. 254 pp.*

Ragg, Nicholas M. People Not Cases. *A Philosophical Approach to Social Work. About 250 pp.*

● **Timms, Noel,** and **Watson, David** (Eds). Talking About Welfare. *Readings in Philosophy and Social Policy. Contributors: T. H. Marshall, R. B. Brandt, G. H. von Wright, K. Nielsen, M. Cranston, R. M. Titmuss, R. S. Downie, E. Telfer, D. Donnison, J. Benson, P. Leonard, A. Keith-Lucas, D. Walsh, I. T. Ramsey. 320 pp.*

Primary Socialization, Language and Education

General Editor   Basil Bernstein

Adlam, Diana S., *with the assistance of Geoffrey Turner and Lesley Lineker.* Code in Context. *About 272 pp.*

Bernstein, Basil. Class, Codes and Control. *3 volumes.*
   1. *Theoretical Studies Towards a Sociology of Language. 254 pp.*
   2. *Applied Studies Towards a Sociology of Language. 377 pp.*
● 3. *Towards a Theory of Educatiomal Transmission. 167 pp.*
Brandis, W., and **Bernstein, B.** Selection and Control. *176 pp.*
Brandis, Walter, and **Henderson, Dorothy.** Social Class, Language and Communication. *288 pp.*

Cook-Gumperz, Jenny. Social Control and Socialization. *A Study of Class Differences in the Language of Maternal Control. 290 pp.*
●**Gahagan, D. M.,** and **G. A.** Talk Reform. *Exploration in Language for Infant School Children. 160 pp.*

Hawkins, P. R. Social Class, the Nominal Group and Verbal Strategies. *About 220 pp.*

Robinson, W. P., and **Rackstraw, Susan D. A.** A Question of Answers. *2 volumes. 192 pp. and 180 pp.*

Turner, Geoffrey J., and **Mohan, Bernard A.** A Linguistic Description and Computer Programme for Children's Speech. *208 pp.*

Reports of the Institute of Community Studies

●**Cartwright, Ann.** Parents and Family Planning Services. *306 pp.*
   Patients and their Doctors. *A Study of General Practice. 304 pp.*
Dench, Geoff. Maltese in London. *A Case-study in the Erosion of Ethnic Consciousness. 302 pp.*
●**Jackson, Brian.** Streaming: *an Education System in Miniature. 168 pp.*
Jackson, Brian, and **Marsden, Dennis.** Education and the Working Class: *Some General Themes raised by a Study of 88 Working-class Children in a Northern Industrial City. 268 pp. 2 folders.*
Marris, Peter. The Experience of Higher Education. *232 pp. 27 tables.*
   Loss and Change. *192 pp.*
Marris, Peter, and **Rein, Martin.** Dilemmas of Social Reform. *Poverty and Community Action in the United States. 256 pp.*

Marris, Peter, and Somerset, Anthony. African Businessmen. *A Study of Entrepreneurship and Development in Kenya. 256 pp.*

Mills, Richard. Young Outsiders: *a Study in Alternative Communities. 216 pp.*

Runciman, W. G. Relative Deprivation and Social Justice. *A Study of Attitudes to Social Inequality in Twentieth-Century England. 352 pp.*

Willmott, Peter. Adolescent Boys in East London. *230 pp.*

Willmott, Peter, and Young, Michael. Family and Class in a London Suburb. *202 pp. 47 tables.*

Young, Michael. Innovation and Research in Education. *192 pp.*

● Young, Michael, and McGeeney, Patrick. Learning Begins at Home. *A Study of a Junior School and its Parents. 128 pp.*

Young, Michael, and Willmott, Peter. Family and Kinship in East London. *Foreword by Richard M. Titmuss. 252 pp. 39 tables.*

The Symmetrical Family. *410 pp.*

Reports of the Institute for Social Studies in Medical Care

Cartwright, Ann, Hockey, Lisbeth, and Anderson, John L. Life Before Death. *310 pp.*

Dunnell, Karen, and Cartwright, Ann. Medicine Takers, Prescribers and Hoarders. *190 pp.*

Medicine, Illness and Society

General Editor W. M. Williams

Robinson, David. The Process of Becoming Ill. *142 pp.*

Stacey, Margaret, *et al.* Hospitals, Children and Their Families. *The Report of a Pilot Study. 202 pp.*

Stimson, G. V., and Webb, B. Going to See the Doctor. *The Consultation Process in General Practice. 155 pp.*

Monographs in Social Theory

General Editor Arthur Brittan

● Barnes, B. Scientific Knowledge and Sociological Theory. *192 pp.*

Bauman, Zygmunt. Culture as Praxis. *204 pp.*

● Dixon, Keith. Sociological Theory. *Pretence and Possibility. 142 pp.*

Meltzer, B. N., Petras, J. W., and Reynolds, L. T. Symbolic Interactionism. *Genesis, Varieties and Criticisms. 144 pp.*

● Smith, Anthony D. The Concept of Social Change. *A Critique of the Functionalist Theory of Social Change. 208 pp.*

Routledge Social Science Journals

The British Journal of Sociology. *Editor – Angus Stewart; Associate Editor – Leslie Sklair. Vol. 1, No. 1 – March 1950 and Quarterly. Roy. 8vo. All back issues available. An international journal publishing original papers in the field of sociology and related areas.*

Community Work. *Edited by David Jones and Marjorie Mayo. 1973. Published annually.*

Economy and Society. *Vol. 1, No. 1. February 1972 and Quarterly. Metric Roy. 8vo. A journal for all social scientists covering sociology, philosophy, anthropology, economics and history. All back numbers available.*

Religion. Journal of Religion and Religions. *Chairman of Editorial Board, Ninian Smart. Vol. 1, No. 1, Spring 1971. A journal with an interdisciplinary approach to the study of the phenomena of religion. All back numbers available.*

Year Book of Social Policy in Britain, The. *Edited by Kathleen Jones. 1971. Published annually.*

Social and Psychological Aspects of Medical Practice

Editor Trevor Silverstone

Lader, Malcolm. Psychophysiology of Mental Illness. *280 pp.*

● **Silverstone, Trevor,** and **Turner, Paul.** Drug Treatment in Psychiatry. *232 pp.*

Printed in Great Britain by
Lowe & Brydone Printers Limited, Thetford, Norfolk